# Looking Back into the Future

by Robert S. Kreider

Bethel College
North Newton, Kansas
1998

Wedel Series logo by Angela Goering Miller

ISBN 1-889239-00-3

Printed by Mennonite Press, Newton, Kansas.
Copyright 1998 by Bethel College.

# Cornelius H. Wedel Historical Series

Series editor:  vols. 1-4, David A. Haury
                vols. 5-11, John D. Thiesen

# Contents

# Series Preface

Cornelius H. Wedel, the first president of Bethel College from the beginning of classes in 1893 until his death in 1910, was an early scholar of Anabaptist-Mennonite studies. His four volume survey of Mennonite history, published from 1900 to 1904, helped to rescue Anabaptism and Mennonitism from their marginal and denigrated portrayal in standard works of church history. Wedel saw Anabaptism and Mennonitism as part of a tradition of biblical faithfulness going back to the early church. He saw his people not in isolation but as a part of God's wider plan in world history.

The founders of Bethel College had a vision to promote the liberal arts through the cultivation of the intellect in all fields of knowledge and to serve the church through the preservation of Mennonite values and preparation for service. The 1994 college mission statement continues the commitment to "intellectual, cultural, and spiritual leadership for the church." The Cornelius H. Wedel Historical Series, initiated by the Mennonite Library and Archives at Bethel College as part of the college centennial celebration in 1987, hopes to further these goals by publishing research in Anabaptist and Mennonite history with a special emphasis on works with a connection to Bethel College, such as campus lecture series and projects based on the holdings of the Mennonite Library and Archives.

John D. Thiesen
Series Editor

# Introduction

This volume was prepared as a part of a symposium held on the Bethel College campus in the fall of 1998. The symposium, "Walls and Windows: Building and Nurturing Viable Community," grew out of an extended community's desire to honor an influential and loved elder in our midst, Robert S. Kreider. For decades, Robert Kreider has himself built and nurtured community–local and global–through his work as CPS camp worker, MCC worker, church leader, college dean and president, writer, speaker, mediator, family member, friend, and for me and many others, mentor. The works in this volume serve as illustration of the symposium theme and of a guiding orientation in Kreider's life and work.

It is typical of Robert Kreider's style and substance that the articles that follow are, more often than not, story, narrative, thoughtful reflection rather than abstract discourse. Once, in a Sunday School class at the Bethel College Mennonite Church, I recall someone asking Robert to share his interpretations of the Biblical notion of grace. He gracefully declined the invitation to theologize and intellectualize, choosing, instead, to share experiences of grace–his own and the stories of people he had encountered in his journey. It is clear from both his life and his writing that Kreider is drawn to the particular expressions, the incarnations of important dimensions of human experience, of God's hand in that experience, rather than to their abstractions, "theological cleverness." In the stories of particular people, Kreider finds parables, filled with meanings that point to truth. The articles in this volume are testimony to his own engagement, throughout his life, in the particular, and in those engagements, his encounters with the profound, universal and sacred.

From the first article, an oration on abuses of children in the workplace written in 1934 by fifteen-year-old Kreider, through those written in each of the decades that followed, the reader will share in the personal history of one man, but also in the history of a particular faith tradition engaged with the world. From the time of his early role as a leader in a CPS camp for conscientious objectors in Colorado, Kreider has been at the forefront of the Mennonite engagement of the world, giving voice to a witness of peace, justice, and service based on the words and acts of Christ. His personal history serves to illuminate the realities of that engagement, in Ohio, Colorado and Kansas, in Europe, Africa, Asia and Latin America.

In this volume, the reader will experience dimensions of Robert Kreider that are familiar to those who know him personally.

We encounter a man of endless curiosity who approaches his world with expectancy and openness. We need "eyes to see, ears to hear, senses to receive," he tells us, only hinting at the receptive, curious, absorbing, probing style that has framed his activity, chronicled in these writings, through the decades.

He is a seeker and gatherer of wisdom. Again and again, we find the words, "I asked," as he probes for what sustains, inspires and restores others. He expects to find, finds, and records wisdom and insight wherever he goes–in Washington, D.C., Guatemala, Ethiopia, and in whomever he meets–a president in Washington, a *campesino* in El Salvador, an aging pastor in China, a child in Kansas.

His writing shows a man filled with an awareness of grace. "What gives you hope," he asks those who have faced life's most discouraging circumstances, knowing that those who have suffered most often have the keenest sense of gratitude and awareness of God's presence. "Carried on wings of eagles" is a metaphor that appears in these articles, expressing his personal identification with the Old Testament confidence in the sustaining, elevating goodness of God.

We learn something of Kreider's approach to life in the repeated occurrences of certain self-descriptive verbs: "I love," "I am fascinated with," "I am captivated by," "I like," "I am intrigued by," "I am drawn to." They show Kreider's appreciation of and gift for expressing the simple joys of living–Kansas prairies, a creek bank in Ohio, the healing presence of wife Lois, a child's enchantment, words and names, newspapers and books.

We feel Kreider's personal courage motivated by a sense of calling: a young man's exploration of pre-World War II Germany; a visit to an off-limits ICBM silo in Kansas; a patient but firm insistence on the honoring of negotiated arrangements in a CPS camp; graceful, persuasive confrontations with newspaper editors and readers on issues of racism, violence, war and peace in atmospheres not particularly friendly to counsel or critique.

The building and nurturing of communities, while a pursuit shared by all, often turns on the leadership of a few. In the circle of Mennonite-related institutions, churches, church agencies and colleges, and communities, a handful of key persons have played that role. Few have been as quietly and unobtrusively influential as has Robert S. Kreider, via his words, but more via his deeds. It is a gift of immeasurable value that these institutions and communities have an opportunity to visit and explore that leadership, the understandings, the faith and the commitments that have been its source, via the collected writings that appear in this volume. We share it with others in gratitude to Robert Kreider and in the hope of inspiring others to follow his model in their own journeys in their own communities.

Douglas A. Penner
President, Bethel College

# Chronology

| | |
|---|---|
| January 2, 1919 | Birth, Sterling, Illinois, parents Amos E. and Stella Kreider. Father: co-pastor of Science Ridge Mennonite Church and farmer. |
| 1921 | Family moves to Goshen, Indiana, where father is professor of Bible at Goshen College. |
| 1923 | Robert enters kindergarten at Fifth Street School. |
| 1926 | Family moves to Bluffton, Ohio, where father is professor at Witmarsum Theological Seminary. Robert enters third grade. |
| 1931 | Father becomes pastor of First Mennonite Church, Bluffton, Ohio. |
| 1935 | Robert graduates from Bluffton-Richland High School. Family moves to Newton, Kansas, where father is professor of Bible at Bethel College. |
| 1937 | Robert serves as volunteer in Quaker summer work camp at Sharp's Chapel, Tennessee. |
| 1938 | Summer cycling and hitch-hiking trip to Europe. |
| 1939 | Graduates from Bethel College. Enters Chicago Theological Seminary and Divinity School of the University of Chicago. |
| 1941 | Receives master's degree in social ethics from the Divinity School of the University of Chicago. |
| August 14, 1941 | Conscripted as a conscientious objector; assigned to Civilian Public Service Camp (CPS), No. 5, at Colorado Springs, Colorado. |
| 1942-43 | Educational Secretary for Mennonite Central Committee-CPS, Akron, Pennsylvania. |
| 1943 | Six month trip to South Africa enroute to serve in West China; return after program cancelled. |
| 1944-45 | Director and co-director of the Hospital Section of MCC-CPS. |
| Dec. 12, 1945 | Discharged from CPS. |

| | |
|---|---|
| Dec. 30, 1945 | Married to Lois Sommer, Pekin, Illinois. |
| 1946-1948 | MCC member of the Council of Relief Agencies Licensed for Operation in Germany (CRALOG), director of MCC relief work in Germany. |
| 1949 | Director of MCC relief work in Europe. Enters doctoral program in history at the University of Chicago. |
| 1951-1952 | Lay pastor of the Woodlawn Mennonite Church, Chicago, Illinois |
| 1952 | Family moves to Bluffton, Ohio; assistant professor of history at Bluffton College. |
| 1952-1969 | Member of the Board of Christian Service of the General Conference of Mennonites. |
| 1953 | Receives doctorate in history from the University of Chicago. |
| 1954-1965 | Academic Dean of Bluffton College. |
| 1959-1974 | Member of the Executive Committee of the Mennonite Central Committee. |
| 1960-1961 | Leave from Bluffton College for an assignment with the Mennonite Central Committee to establish the Teachers Abroad Program. |
| 1965-1972 | President of Bluffton College. |
| 1969-1971 | Member of the Commission on Overseas Mission of the General Conference. |
| 1970-1971 | Six-month sabbatical leave to the Mediterranean area, including consultative services for MCC; accompanied by family–wife Lois, and children: Esther, Joan, Karen, David, and Ruth. |
| 1972-1974 | Director of self-study for the Mennonite Central Committee and secretary for the Department of Higher Education of the General Conference; three month trip to Africa and Asia for MCC. |
| 1975-1984 | Moved to North Newton, Kansas, to take position of Director of the Mennonite Library and Archives and professor of Peace Studies. |
| 1975-1998 | Chair of the Editorial Committee of the Mennonite Experience in America book series. |

| | |
|---|---|
| 1978-1984 | Recording Secretary of the Mennonite World Conference. |
| 1978-1979 | Interim Academic Dean of Bethel College. |
| 1984-1986 | Administrative Vice President of Bethel College. |
| 1985-1986 | Director of the Kansas Institute for Peace and Conflict Resolution. |
| 1987-1988 | Consultant to the Bluffton College Study Center (part-time). |
| 1989- | Establishment of the Martyrs Mirror Trust; co-director. |
| 1990 | Curated the exhibit "Mirror of the Martyrs," Kauffman Museum. |
| 1990-1996 | Series of overseas trips with each of the five children and spouses. |
| 1992 | Center Fellow at the Young Center for the Study of Anabaptist and Pietist Groups, Elizabethtown College |
| 1995 | Curated the exhibit "MCC–The Gift of Hope," Kauffman Museum. |

# Selected Bibliography

## Books

*The Anabaptist-Mennonite Time Line.* Newton, KS: Faith and Life Press, 1986.

*Anatolian Carpets: A Family Connection.* North Newton, KS: Kauffman Museum, 1986.

*Christians True in China,* editor. Newton, KS: Faith and Life Press, 1988.

*An Ebersole Story–The Ancestry and Descendants of Abraham D. Ebersole and Anna Rutt,* co-author with David J. Rempel Smucker and Roy Umble. Goshen, Indiana: Ebersole Family Association, 1996.

*Hungry, Thirsty, a Stranger,* co-author with Rachel Goossen. Scottdale, PA: Herald Press, 1988.

*Joseph and Elizabeth,* co-author with Jakob Miller and Eileen Roth, North Newton, KS: Shoemaker Family Association, 1998.

*Map / Guide to the Mennonite Communities of South Central Kansas,* Newton, KS: Faith and Life Press, 1995.

*The Mirror of the Martyrs,* co-author with John S. Oyer. Intercourse, PA: Good Books, 1990.

*Singing in the West, We Strike Up for a New World.* North Newton, KS: Bethel College, 1987.

*Unity Amidst Diversity,* co-editor with Ronald Mathies. Akron, PA: Mennonite Central Committee, 1995.

*When Good People Quarrel,* co-author with Rachel Goossen. Scottdale, PA: Herald Press. 1989.

*Where are we Going?* The Schowalter Memorial Lecture Series, Newton, KS: Faith and Life Press, 1971.

## Articles (a very partial list)

"The Anabaptist Conception of the Church in the Russian Mennonite Environment, 1789-1870," *Mennonite Quarterly Review,* January 1951.

"CPS: A 'Year of Service with Like-Minded Christian Young Men'–Camp No. 5, Colorado Springs, Colorado, 1941-42," *Mennonite Quarterly Review,* October 1992.

"Environmental Influences Affecting the Decisions of Mennonite Boys of Draft Age," *Mennonite Quarterly Review,* October 1942.

"The Good Boys of CPS," *Mennonite Life,* September 1991.

"The Impact of MCC Service on American Mennonites," *Mennonite Quarterly Review,* July 1970.

**Museum Exhibits Curated**

"The Mirror of the Martyrs," 1990-1998. Exhibited in 49 venues.
"MCC: The Gift of Hope," 1995-1996. Exhibited in two venues.

*Robert, one year old, Sterling, Illinois, 1920.*

*Amos E. and Stella Kreider and sons, Gerald (left) and Robert (right), Goshen, Indiana, 1925.*

# 1934: Do You Hear the Children Weeping?

*Robert Kreider was fifteen years old and a Bluffton, Ohio, high school junior when he wrote and presented this oration in the annual Ohio high school forensic contest, a competition in which he reached the state semifinals. This was in the Spring of 1934, the time of the Great Depression, the second year of the administration of Franklin Delano Roosevelt.*

In 1776 the fathers of our country drew up that memorable document in human history, the Declaration of Independence. It was established on the principle that all men are created equal and are endowed by their maker with certain inalienable rights. Our nation was dedicated to the proposition that all men are entitled to life, liberty and the pursuit of happiness. In 1863 President Lincoln issued the famous Emancipation Proclamation. Three and one-half million slaves were liberated from the ravages of selfish lords. Human slavery was ended in the United States. In 1933 is another landmark in the course of human progress. Almost a year has passed since Congress enacted and the President signed the bill known as the National Recovery Act. One million five hundred thousand children were released from toil in the industries of our country.

In ancient times fanatical worshipers threw themselves down before the grim, cruel idol Moloch. Small babies were plucked from their mothers' arms and cast upon the red hot palms of the monster. They were a merciful people, however, when compared with the American exploiter who fattened upon the toil of little children. In America innocent, helpless children have been tossed upon the altar of unscrupulous capitalistic greed.

President Roosevelt pointed his accusing finger at child labor because of its harmful effects upon children, society and adult labor. The depression brought back the sweat shop with all its suffering and misery. While more than a million children were laboring in the industries of our country, adults were forced to remain idle. Our president saw that our economic and social setup was radically wrong when the support of the nation depended upon the back breaking toil of children.

In squalid tenement homes that are poorly heated, badly ventilated, boys and girls started their toil early in the morning and continued late into the night. For their work of finishing garments they received distressingly low wages. Children, with little power of resistance, bent over dusty streams of coal picking out the slate with their lacerated fingers. Small girls stood barefooted in pools of water twisting coils of wet hemp. Children rose at four in the morning to go to the textile mills where they labored all day long in the deafening din and dust laden air of the factory. Thousands of little children in the Middle Atlantic states were employed hour after hour crawling in the furrows of truck gardens, pulling and weeding. Such was the bare existence of one and a half million children in our country before the days of the National Recovery Act.

Since the children of today are the citizens of tomorrow, they are entitled to a balanced development of body, mind and soul. A child employed in industry does not receive such a necessary development. He is debarred from completing a much needed education. He is employed under conditions that seriously impair his physical growth. He is surrounded by an unwholesome environment that tears down his moral life. He is engaged in work that dulls his mind and crushes his spirit.

We agree that education is indispensable to the development of the mind. Through our system of public schools such development is made available to all. But when our nation permitted a million children to leave school every year and enter upon an industrial career, these children lost a splendid opportunity for preparation. Child labor deprives a child of his rights to an education. It robs him of that which rightly belongs to him and makes him less fit to fill his place as a citizen. Education is the eternal debt which society owes to childhood.

To develop physically, children need relaxation, good food, sleep, play, freedom from care. But child laborers are denied these necessities. Their nervous energy is burned up. Their taxing, monotonous tasks teach them nothing. The hours of play which are the right of childhood are taken from them. Disease, over-strain, accidents, which are the result of child labor, weaken their bodies. Certain muscles suffer from excessive fatigue, which often bring about permanent deformities.

Equally harmful are the moral and spiritual effects of child labor. Long hours, excessive exertion and permanent fatigue weaken the power of resistance so that the child easily yields to the many temptations about him. Tired and discouraged, working children often fall into association with the morally unfit. Their moral senses become stunted. Child labor is a menace to virtue and the highest type of morals.

In this period of development youth is susceptible to all the evils of child labor. These seriously injure and handicap boys and girls for later life. The evils affect not only the individual but also society. Child labor gives to society wrecked human beings, broken homes, ignorant citizens and an enfeebled race. Working children are found to contribute more than their proportionate share toward crime. Becoming wearied, dull, deformed and old, these child labor individuals pass on their weakened condition to the next generation. The result is a weakened race.

Child labor has been helpless and easily exploited. As a class of workers they were unorganized. They had no power of collective wage bargaining. Over a million were hired for a very low wage. They performed the same mechanical tasks as adults. As a result adult wages fell to the child labor level. The group of unemployed adults increased or the entire family worked in order to gain a livelihood. Under favorable wage conditions the father alone should be able to support the family. Organized labor has finally lifted its voice in protest.

Friends, these are the results when children are permitted to be exploited. The lives of little children are ruined, society is weakened. This human suffering caused by unscrupulous employers whose eyes are blinded by avarice and greed must not continue! No longer dare our future be sacrificed in the arms of Moloch.

Over these wretched scenes of moral and social injustice came the protecting wings of the Blue Eagle. These protecting wings are now outspread—safeguarding the lives of the little children from the unprincipled exploiter. This legislative act, the N.R.A., has offered to the unfortunate child laborer a new bill of rights and a new promise for happiness and liberty.

Of the 288 codes put into effect by the National Recovery Administration all have consented not to employ any person under 16. Those persons, however, between the ages of 14 and 16 may be employed outside of manufacturing industries for not more than three hours a day, providing these hours will not interfere with school work.

The abolition of child labor is of course temporarily limited to the life of the N.R.A. If we desire our children not to return to those intolerable conditions, the American public during the coming year must awaken to its responsibility for the support of this constructive labor program. These great gains for the children of our land must be made permanent. Upon us rests the obligation of protecting the lives of our future citizens. This phase of the N.R.A. program should receive the hearty support of every parent and of every public-minded citizen of America.

Do you hear the children weeping, O my brothers,
    Ere the sorrow comes with years?
They are leaning their young heads against their mothers,
    And that can not stop their tears.
Our blood splashes upward, O gold-heaper,

    And your purple shows your path!
   But the child sob in the silence curses deeper
    Than the strong man in his wrath.

 Child labor is a mighty challenge to the American public. The issue is now sharply drawn. The lives of millions of our children are in our hands. The question must be answered by us. Which way will we take? Return to the grim cruel altar of the modern Moloch or will we protect our children by making this phase of the N.R.A. a permanent legislative act?

# 1938: Pi Kappa Delta and the 'Jim Crow' Clause

*An editorial printed in* The Bethel Collegian, *May 12, 1938. Kreider and Aldous Mercomes, black student, were the only Bethel College students in forensics who were not installed as charter members of Pi Kappa Delta. The national organization did not remove its racial discrimination clause for ten years, not until after World War II.*

Saturday evening a group of Bethel forensic stars will be installed as charter members in the Pi Kappa Delta. But a shadow creeps across this scene. A small minority refuses to join the organization because the constitution contains a "Jim Crow" clause prohibiting from its membership any member of the African race. To increase the gravity of the situation is the fact that an otherwise eligible Bethel candidate for membership in the Pi Kappa Delta is barred because he is of the Negro race.

A majority of the charter members are joining the Pi Kappa Delta with the verbal intention of fighting the "Jim Crow" clause, seeking to eliminate any trace of racial discrimination in the organization. If this position is more than a pious rationalization, it is a stand which is sound from the viewpoint of successful social change. To those who ascribe to this viewpoint we owe our support in their task at reform; and we urge that they keep faith with that trust.

There are then a few who refuse to join the Pi Kappa Delta. They feel that their action represents to the local chapter in a symbolic way that the Pi Kappa Delta is a "Jim Crow" organization and that one cannot rest until that onerous African clause is stricken from the constitution.

Our plea is that the Bethel chapter of the Pi Kappa Delta will never cease their efforts to blot out this unchristian and ethically damnable clause, even if it should mean a resignation of the entire Bethel chapter–R. K.

*Rollin Moser and Robert Kreider, right, at Oakengates, Shropshire, England, in an International Voluntary Service for Peace work camp, July 1938.*

# 1938: Hitch-Hiking and Cycling in Europe on the Eve of World War II

*Published in the* Bluffton News, *October 1998.*

In the spring of 1938, now more than sixty years ago, Rollin Moser and I had the same idea: a trip to Europe, a couple of weeks in an International Voluntary Service for Peace (IVSP) work camp in Oakengates, England, followed by hitch-hiking to Scotland, and then cycling through Western Europe. We did not know each other: Rollin, to be a senior at Bluffton College, and I, also to be a senior at Bethel College, Newton, Kansas. A mutual Bluffton College friend, Karl Schultz, alerted us to each other's plans.

In 1937 the idea was separately conceived when Pierre Cerresole, Swiss founder of IVSP, visited Quaker summer work camps we were attending: Rollin's in Mississippi and mine in Tennessee.

That summer of 1938 we blithely ignored the risk of being caught in a war brewing. Early that year Hitler had seized Austria in what he called the *Anschluss* and immediately began to demand that Czechoslovakia surrender the Sudetenland. Prime Minister Chamberlain flew twice to Germany to confer with Hitler, this followed by the capitulation at Munich. Franco's forces were winning the war in Spain. Soon Hitler would be threatening to seize the Polish Corridor.

En route to New York I stopped off in Bluffton to meet Rollin ("Red"), who was in his last week before exams. In my journal I recorded that he was "a good conversationalist," an "intensely likable fellow." I found his room littered with all kinds of travel information. He urged me to join the American Hostel Association for inexpensive travel in European youth hostels. We immediately plunged into outlining joint plans.

I then headed for four days in New York City, while Red had another week of college. This my first visit, I packed the days full, crisscrossing Manhattan on foot, busses and subways. I saw two Broadway plays: 23-year old Orson Welles in Shaw's "Heartbreak House" and British actor Sir Cedric Hardwick in "Shadow and Substance." At a grubby off-Broadway theater I saw a Soviet film, "Country Bride," a propagandistic story of idealistic workers bringing in the harvest on a collective farm. At Radio City I saw Betty Grable in "Vivacious Lady," plus the Rockettes. Expenses listed in my journal were: plays, $1.20 and $1.70; films, 25¢ and 40¢; hotel, $2.25; newspaper, 3¢....

Saturday midnight, June 11, I sailed for Europe on the S. S. *St. Louis* of the Hamburg-America Line. I did not then know that the following spring the *St. Louis* would sail for North America with

907 Jewish refugees, stopping at U. S., Cuban and South American ports–every country refusing to accept them. After many months the *St. Louis* returned to Antwerp to deposit its human cargo, many of whom later died in Nazi death camps.

Following are entries adapted from my travel journal–a mixture of present and past tense:

*June 12*. The one in the lower bunk in this tiny windowless cabin is 40-year old Frank Doruska, a Chicago taxicab driver who is returning to his native Czechoslovakia to marry. He tells of entering the Austrian army at 18, captured by the Russians, held two years as a prisoner of war in South Russia, released, transferred to the Italian front.... The ship is teeming with families returning to the Fatherland, most pro-Hitler.... Pictures of Adolf Hitler are everywhere.

*June 20-21, Southampton, England*. Thrilled to see on arrival an English Bobbie on the dock. I stayed in my first youth hostel, one shilling (24 cents) a night. Bought a new, 3-speed Royal Enfield bicycle for seven pounds. Headed north down the left side of the road to Winchester, Runnymede, Windsor, and Eton.

*June 22-23, Henley on the Thames*. Hosted by Nigel Bicknell, whom I had met the summer before at the Quaker work camp in Tennessee. Dinner and breakfast with Nigel and his rowing crew from Corpus Christi College, Cambridge, who are competing in the four-day Henley Regatta. It's like old grad's week with elderly men in their college blazers lining the river banks. Corpus Christi came in fourth in a field of 24.

*June 24-25*. I cycled north to Oxford, where I roamed the streets and dreamed of studying there someday; on to Shakespeare's Stratford, where I saw the "Comedy of Errors" (balcony seat, 34 cents). I continued north through Kidderminster where I stopped to watch my first cricket match. With stops to poke into crumbling castles and ancient baths, I proceeded on into Shropshire, first known to me through Housman's "The Shropshire Lad."

*June 25-July 1, Oakengates*. My first day at the IVSP camp with 20 volunteers from eight countries. Oakengates is a grimy industrial and mining town in what is designated as a "depressed area"–honeycombed underground with 400 abandoned mines and above ground scarred with mounds of tailings. Many people are on the dole. Eleven pubs within two blocks of the railroad station. Our job is to attack with pick and shovel Charlton Mound, one of the mine heaps, to level it for a playground. We pitch the debris into horse-drawn carts. Monotonous work punctuated by morning and afternoon tea and fascinating conversations....

*July 5-15, Oakengates.* Red and I, the "two Yanks," drew public attention. A reporter and cameraman from the *Shrewsbury Chronicle* did a story on this "adventurous pair." The Anglican vicar invited us for dinner and on an afternoon-evening took us on a tour of ancient historical sites, including a 3,000 year old Celtic castle and the ruins of a Roman outpost, Uriconium. The director of the co-op, a member of the Labor Party, invited us for dinner and conducted us on a walking tour of Oakengate historical sites. On our last day two aristocratic ladies invited us to their mansion for dinner and drove us into Wales for a head start on our hitch-hiking. In those days young Americans were rare and special.

On the walking tour of Oakengates we saw a 20-year old sign scrawled on a deteriorating factory wall: "To Hell with the Kaiser!" In the summer of 1938 we sensed that another war was creeping closer. Three of our IVSP brothers were refugees from Nazi Germany, one who had been in and out of concentration camps. Local Air Raid Prevention units were urging everyone to purchase a gas mask.

*July 16-25, hitchhiking through Wales, England, Scotland to Harwich on the North Sea.* We were on the move from Aberystwyth in Wales on the Cardigan Sea to Ashton Keynes in the Cotswold Hills, north to Wordsworth's Lake Country, to Edinburgh and the Loch Country of Scotland, south to Harwich on the North Sea. Invariably those who gave us rides spoke admiringly of Americans, often insisting on providing us with free meals. A few years later England would be overrun with Americans.

Highlight of this period was our visit to the Society of Brothers community at Ashton Keynes in the Cotswolds. This was a pacifist communal group which in the 20s had been gathered together by Eberhard Arnold at Rhoenbruderhof near Fulda, Germany. Expelled from Germany by Nazi authorities, the group, aided by Quakers and Dutch Mennonites found a refuge in the Cotswolds. This Bruderhof of 250–each member in simple peasant dress, housed in an old farmstead of stone buildings–was to us like stepping into a medieval village. Hearing of our friendship with Dr. C. Henry Smith of Bluffton and Dr. Cornelius Krahn of Bethel College, the leaders called on Rollin and me to talk about American Quaker work camps and the American Hutterites. They presumed Red and I to be authorities!

*July 26-August 3, Belgium and the Netherlands.* We made a night crossing from Harwich, England, to Antwerp, Belgium, and "at last we had the feeling that we were in a foreign country." In Antwerp we began cycling again: Antwerp, Brussels, Rotterdam, The Hague, Amsterdam and Friesland in northern Holland. Keeping account of every penny spent, I was impressed how inexpensive everything was: 13¢ for bed in a hostel, 11¢ for breakfast, 13¢ for a haircut. I also recorded, "Red and I have been particularly impressed with the beauty of Belgian women and the best of all are those in Brussels." That observation amidst comments about Rubens, Steen and the Flemish masters.

Dr. Smith and Dr. Krahn gave us lists of Mennonite notables in the Netherlands to whom we should introduce ourselves. All of the pastors we stopped to see were off on holidays. However, in the Hague at the Mennonite (*Doopsgezinde*) Church we were pleased to meet Jacob ter Meulen, librarian of the Hague Peace Palace Library, who invited us to his home for lunch with finger bowls and maids. Then a tour of the Peace Palace. In Amsterdam we met Jan Gleysteen, a book dealer, who was the only Mennonite conscientious objector in the Netherlands in World War I.

Heading north to Friesland, we cycled through a beautiful countryside. Our destination was the well-scrubbed village of Witmarsum, birthplace in 1496 of Menno Simons, who was once a Catholic priest and became leader of a group of persecuted Anabaptists. Having made our pilgrimage to the Mecca of our faith, we turned toward Germany.

*August 4-11, Germany.* At Nordhorn, just inside the German border, "we were initiated into Nazi Germany with 'Heil Hitlers,' swastika flags everywhere, propaganda posters, army men in uniforms, military trucks, Hitler youth cycling and hiking." Cycling south through the industrial *Ruhr Gebiet* "it was 100 kilometers of black, dirty cities, rough cobblestone streets, detours, smoke-laden air, roaring diesel trucks. Finally we arrived in Cologne at seven in the evening after a weary day.... To compensate for all the difficulty, we saw as the sun was setting, the grandest architectural [sight] I have ever seen: Cologne Cathedral." The following day we cycled up the enchanting Rhine Valley with vineyards on the hillsides and castles on the crests of mountains–Snow White and Seven Dwarfs country. At Koblenz we caught a Rhine boat on to Bacharach.

At Castle Stahleck, converted into a youth hostel (*Jugendherbergen*), we stayed in our last hostel. Increasingly annoyed with noisy Hitler Youth overrunning these hostels, we had our fill. Thenceforth, we chose inexpensive country inns (*Gasthaeuser*).

At Bingen we left the beauty of the Rhine and pointed south into the rural Palatinate (*Pfalz*), the home for a few generations of my ancestors. On that Sunday we saw everywhere Hitler Youth–marching, cycling, hiking. Also, truckloads of soldiers on weekend training maneuvers, plus marching men in work corps carrying polished shovels. On the sides of some buildings we saw signs saying, "Jews not wanted." As a balance to such negative images, we enjoyed a superb meal in a village *Gasthaus*.

A few hours later came a highlight of the summer: a visit at Weierhof in the home of Dr. Christian Neff, an elderly, beloved leader of German Mennonites, editor of a three-volume encyclopedia, *Mennonitisches Lexikon*. He insisted we stay for supper. We talked about his American friends–C. Henry Smith, Cornelius Krahn, Harold Bender–and our travels. I recorded, "I have heard he is none too sympathetic with National Socialism–Bravo! He is such a venerable old gentleman that no one will [dare] harm him.… When we left, the whole family gathered to say *Auf Wiedersehen* but not the customary *Heil Hitler*."

The following evening in the university town of Heidelberg we were invited to stay in the home of a sister of a Mennonite pastor. "Today we decided it was time we began talking politics–a subject which everyone said was taboo in Germany.… At breakfast in the kitchen we talked about National Socialism.… She worships Hitler, hates Jews, hates Moscow worse, states Moscow is behind the Czechoslovakian difficulty, hopes there will be no war, but expects war any moment. Everyone boasts of Germany's present strength. She likes Hitler's program of making Germany self-sufficient."

That Monday afternoon and evening, another highlight of the summer for Red and me. In a suburb of Karlsruhe Professor Benjamin Unruh received us into his home and held us spellbound with his passionate advocacy of National Socialism. Back in 1920 he had fled the Soviet Union. I recorded how he dominated the conversation, these among his assertions I recorded: "He spoke at length of the disreputable financial activities of Jews. The only alternative he felt was that which Hitler did: suppress them. He believes that all nations must cooperate in finding a home for the Jews.… He is for a 'positive Christianity' which speaks not at all of politics but only about God and love, etc.… Unruh hopes a national church will be established. He respects Pastor Niemoeller but thinks he is a royalist, who mixes politics and religion.… Only when every nation develops a strong racial and geographical (*Blut und Boden*) nationalism can we have a lasting internationalism. He used the analogy of an orchestra with many different instruments."

Unruh, a big man with flowing white hair, went on and on: "Oh, and Hitler is a good man. He is more generous than anyone Germany has known. And he is a simple peasant boy, who hates no one. He loves Germany and he loves the whole world. Hitler doesn't want war. Hitler is like your George Washington." At this point he leaped up and saluted and declared, "Heil George Washington. Heil Hitler."

After supper in a dimly lighted room he showed us where they would hide in the next war in case of attack. He spoke ominously of the newly established strength of the Siegfried Line positioned on the east side of the Rhine facing the Maginot Line on the French west side of the Rhine.

It was a dazzling performance. I recorded, "My total impression is still that National Socialism is a mild form of insanity, that I will continue to oppose dictatorship, but I felt more tolerant toward Germany. The Germans are good people seeking security as we all are. They fear other nations as all nations do.... But poor Unruh, I believe it is difficult for such a man or any thinking man to attempt to integrate the philosophy of National Socialism with a previously established philosophy of life."

We managed to stop at meal times at the homes of Germans whose addresses Red had been given. The story was always the same: warm hospitality, adulation of Hitler, delight in meeting two young Americans, anxiety over the threat of war. Leaving one home, a beautiful young girl gave each of us a red carnation.

At the German-Swiss border Red and I had our smiling pictures taken with Nazi border guards. Undetected by the guards, under our shirts we had stuffed Nazi posters and propaganda sheets.

*August 11-21, Switzerland.* Here Red was in his element. He could speak *Bernerdietsch*, the language of his home and ancestors. And he had lots of addresses of distant relatives. Before arrival we had purchased an 8-day, third-class ticket on the Swiss Railways. With it, we poked into every town in Switzerland that had a rail connection. Glorious scenery and delicious Swiss chocolate....

Another summer highlight came in Geneva where we met O. B. Gerig of the League of Nations Secretariat. A Wayne County, Ohio, native, he was a classmate at Goshen with my father. When we arrived in his office we found Gerig in gloomy talk with a reporter from the *London Daily Express*. I recorded in my journal: "Gerig and all Geneva feels very depressed about the international situation. Many expect war before the month is over. Of course, Germany is the problem child. They view the feverish efforts of the German peasantry to get in the harvest, the war maneuvers, the Czech-Sudeten friction–all with alarm. Gerig does not feel that much of German policy is bluff. Nevertheless, the situation is charged with danger and plenty of it. For these and other reasons he wishes to have his children in U. S. schools.... We talked for more than an hour about this and as to how the nations would line up in case of war. He is still a devout pacifist, but favors the use of international police power as the less harmful of alternatives."

Reporting that he was responsible for a League exhibit at the 1939 New York World's Fair, he inquired whether we would be interested in working there next summer as attendants. I noted, "That would be a marvelous summer, but my expectations must not soar too high." Before leaving for a diplomatic reception, he took us to an international hostel, on the banks of Lake Geneva (*Lac Leman*) and paid for our room and meals.

That evening as we walked along the garden pathway by the lake, we had a strange mixture of feelings: exhilaration over that possibility of next summer in New York City and a brooding fear that a great war was about to erupt in Europe.

*August 21-26, France.* Back in Basel, I took leave of Red, who would be spending another week in Switzerland. Having sold my bicycle in Basel, I took a streetcar to the French border and began hitch-hiking. It was one of the worst days of the summer: a couple short rides and then hours of walking in a drenching rain and no rides. Near Belfort, I found myself somewhere in the area of the French Maginot line. Soldiers stopped me and demanded identification. My passport did not satisfy. I could not explain myself in French. I was held for a time and then, with a shrug of bewilderment, they released me. Soon I caught a good ride in a truck headed toward Paris. Five days later in Cherbourg I boarded the S. S. *Deutschland* for my return voyage, arriving in Newton, Kansas, the day before classes began at Bethel College.

What a summer for a 19-year-old! I kept a record of every penny spent on that three-month trip to Europe in 1938. The total cost, including ocean fare and domestic costs to and from New York, added up to less than $350. An incredible bargain, even then. In those days no college credit was given for such an experience. Today as I reflect back on that summer, I marvel that my parents granted me permission to venture off to Europe with the mounting rumblings of war. As a once-upon-a-time college dean, I would now grant Rollin and Robert a full semester of academic credit for that summer, providing I could read and correct the spelling in their journals.

# 1938: There Is No Difference

*An editorial in* The Bethel Collegian, *September 29, 1938, prompted by an editorial in* The Mennonite, *September 27, 1938, entitled, "Is There No Difference." J. R. Thierstein, editor of* The Mennonite, *sought to make a case that Stalin's Soviet Russia was far worse than Hitler's Nazi Germany. R. R. is Robert Regier, managing editor.*

A defense of Naziism against the horrors perpetually being committed by the Soviet government is presented by the editor of a religious paper in its current issue. The position is taken that there is a great difference between the German and Russian governments and that Hitler's government is a bit on the virtuous side.

We must confess that this article was shocking to youth who trusted that religious publications defended nobler loyalties than devotion to National Socialism.

A Christian periodical, we feel, is treading on very dangerous ground when it seeks to justify National Socialism. We deplore even more the intimation in a second article that God is using Adolf Hitler to rectify the injustices in Europe. We do not propose to defend Russian communism to the slightest degree in these columns. We loathe Stalinism as an arch-enemy of democracy and Christianity. But we would like to protest against the favorable treatment which the Nazi totalitarian regime is receiving. We sincerely believe that the Nazi dictatorship is evil, even as the Stalinist state, because both political systems are devoid of any respect for human personality.

It is argued in the above-mentioned article that while perhaps a few unfortunate Jews *may* have lost their lives in Germany, millions of innocents were slaughtered in Russia. From all we have heard and read, the treatment of the German Jews is about as cruel and malicious as any race could receive. It is true that millions of people have been killed or forced into exile in Russia. It is also true that at this very moment Hitler stands ready to plunge tens of millions of people into a war which can produce only one thing–a stigma to civilization in all of Europe, and deeper depression than the world has ever before seen.

It is difficult to understand why Semitic hatreds are so prevalent among religious peoples. When a Christian publication makes the statement that "for the persecution of the Jews there is at least some reason..." one wonders how such a judgment embodies the spirit of love.—R. K. and R. R.

# 1941: The "Good Boys of CPS"

*This article, a companion piece to* "CPS: A Year of Service with Like-minded Christian Young Men," *appeared in* Mennonite Life, *September 1991. For footnoting of sources, see the original article.*

"Mennonites were truly the 'good boys' of the CPS system.... Mennonite CPS'ers engaged in no walkouts, work slowdowns, strikes, or acts of noncooperation to protest the nature of CPS as a Selective Service program." Thus does Perry Bush describe Mennonite men who constituted 38 percent of the 11,996 men in Civilian Public Service (CPS) camps during World War II. Mennonites were the largest denominational block in CPS, outnumbering the Brethren (12 percent) and Friends (8 percent).

The "good boy" label is apt but, perhaps, a bit too facile. Mennonite CPS men, a majority of farm background, were accustomed to arduous hand labor. Their productivity on the project drew more praise than wrath from their work supervisors. Mennonite men, nurtured in more communitarian environments, could accept vexatious government regulations and posturings with less discomfort than COs of more individualistic temperament. Mennonites might be chided for their docility or lauded for their endurance. Our experience at CPS Camp No. 5, Colorado Springs, Colorado, suggests that Mennonite CPS men did resist the authorities. In their encounters with the powers, they probably were less vocal than some of their CPS comrades in publicizing their frustrations and acts of resistance. This may have helped to create the image of the "truly good boys of CPS." An examination of the records of work projects in each MCC-administered CPS camp and unit would probably reveal confrontations similar to the ones experienced at Colorado Springs. Certainly in the 26 MCC-administered hospital and training school units, MCC staff members were occasionally compelled to refuse and to resist the authorities.

This article reviews the relation between the COs of the Colorado Springs CPS camp and the "powers and principalities," that is, Selective Service and the Soil Conservation Service. The study is confined to the first fifteen months of Camp No. 5 that opened June 5, 1941, one of fourteen CPS camps launched in May and June 1941. During the first year of CPS, drafted COs were confined almost exclusively to base camps where they were engaged in pick and shovel work in soil conservation, forestry, and land reclamation. Not until late 1942 did substantial numbers of men have opportunity to transfer out of base camps into mental hospitals, dairy projects, public health and other programs.

This study is extracted from a paper presented at the Conference on Mennonites and Alternative Service in World War II, May 30-June 1, 1991, held at Goshen College, Goshen, Indiana. That paper described the emergence of the CO community at CPS Camp No. 5 where I was assigned as a CO from August 15, 1941 to September 20, 1942. Beginning in mid-September 1941, I was appointed Educational and Assistant Director, one of the first drafted men to be selected for a staff position. Albert Gaeddert, a 34-year-old pastor and former high school teacher and coach, served as Director. As the year progressed and the program expanded, Gaeddert was called by Henry A. Fast, General Director of MCC-CPS, to go on special assignments, leaving the assignee Assistant Director responsible for liaison with the project authorities.

The Colorado Springs camp, built in September 1934 for the Civilian Conservation Corps (CCC), was located two and a half miles northeast of the city limits of Colorado Springs at Templeton Gap, a broad pass along State Route 189. The drab, sun-drenched camp consisted of ten wooden barracks: a long combination structure combining MCC office, three apartments, library, and infirmary; a kitchen-dining hall; five 120-foot dormitories–one combined with offices for the Soil Conservation Service, another combined with classroom and lounge; a chapel and woodworking shop; a storeroom and laundry; and a bathhouse. All buildings were 20 feet wide, most 120 feet long. The thinly insulated board-and-batten barracks were heated with furnaces fired with coal purchased at a nearby mine. To the south of the central area were clustered assorted garages, a blacksmith shop, and warehouses for the Soil Conservation Service.

In early 1941 a company of 118 CCC men evacuated the camp at Templeton Gap. Albert Gaeddert and John Gaeddert, the latter on temporary assignment as business manager, with some volunteers from Colorado Springs churches, launched into repairing, painting, and outfitting the facilities. Albert Gaeddert, reflecting a depression-nurtured frugality, accounted for each purchase, including four sheets of wallboard, two pounds of nails, and a toilet stool costing $9.50. He corresponded with Selective Service, Washington, D. C., and a variety of Army Quartermaster Corps headquarters to obtain needed equipment: 595 blankets and 175 steel cots from Chicago; 175 pillows from Atlanta; 600 items from the Presidio of San Francisco; 175 mattresses from Omaha; kitchen equipment from Fort Sam Houston and much more. Gaeddert pursued an elusive task of seeking a permit of occupancy for the buildings owned by the Colorado Springs Company, a firm that had disagreed on lease understandings with the departing Civilian

Conservation Corp (CCC). In the flurry of final arrangements, the MCC staff found itself funding start-up costs that should have been borne by Selective Service or Soil Conservation Service.

The first drafted COs who arrived on the morning of June 6, 1941, yielded to a closely scheduled life prescribed for the recently evacuated CCC company. A daily routine was established: 5:30 rising bell; 6:00 breakfast, followed by group devotions; 7:00 leave for project work; 30 minute break in the field for lunch; 4:30 to 5:00 return to camp; 6:00 supper, followed by sports and evening meetings and classes; 9:30 lights out. On Sundays, the rising bell was a half hour later with worship at 8:45, a truck leaving for worship services in town at 9:45 and camp Sunday School at 10:00; Christian Endeavor or worship service at 7:30 p.m. On Saturdays work ended at noon unless makeup time was required for bad weather earlier in the week. On Saturdays one-third of the crews remained in camp for maintenance duties.

Eighty-five percent of the men were to be engaged in project work, fifteen percent permitted for camp administration services. Camp jobs came to be allocated as follows: eleven in the kitchen including three cooks; five in the laundry; and a dozen on "special detail"–night watchman, infirmary assistant, janitors, gardeners, carpenters and office clerks. Men could apply for positions in camp based on interests, skills (typing, cooking, carpentry), and health factors. The camp director, in consultation with others, assigned jobs in camp. The MCC salaried staff consisted of the director, matron and dietitian, and, for the first six months, a business manager.

All absences from camp required written permission. A *liberty* was granted for absence from camp during non-working hours on one day, to be terminated by 10:30 p.m. A *leave* covered an absence on holidays or a weekend, beginning at the end of work on Saturday noon (unless there was Saturday afternoon makeup work) and ending at midnight Sunday. A *furlough* was accumulated at the rate of two and a half days a month for a total of 30 days per year. No more than 15 percent of the men could be on furlough at one time. In emergencies declared by the Soil Conservation Service or Selective Service, all furloughs could be banned.

Once a month, the MCC camp office submitted to the National Service Board for Religious Objectors (NSBRO) triplicate copies giving daily account of the activity of each man in the conscripted society. A copy of these reports was transmitted to Selective Service.

Every day some men remained in camp, excused by the camp physician and confined to the infirmary or recuperating in the dormitories or assigned light work about camp. The percentage of men listed as sick leaped from three percent in November 1941 and six percent in December 1941 to almost 17 percent in January 1942 and almost 21 percent in February 1942. Those on sick leave dropped off to 10 percent in June, 6.5 percent in July and 4 percent in August. Those on sick leave often had to endure the taunts of "goldbricking" from the men who went to the field in disagreeable weather.

The most precious bit of freedom enjoyed by the men was furlough time– saved and counted with care, applied for months in advance, particularly sought after for holidays and harvest time. The percentage on furlough rose from seven percent in May 1942 to 15 percent in June and 12 percent in July–the harvest months in Oklahoma, Kansas, and Nebraska.

Regulations prohibited the men from living with their wives in town. Other Selective Service restrictions were more advisory than mandatory. For example the possession of personal automobiles was discouraged and the deposit of car keys with the camp director required.

Although the men as conscripts were expected to account for each day, the editor of the camp paper affirmed that this cooperation was voluntary, not forced:

> We have recognized the government's right to expect sacrificial service from its citizens.... We will give the cooperation needed to operate a camp. Even though we are not forced to abide by any regulations, are we not obligated to put forth our best efforts to fulfill the requests of our leaders?

Walter L. Makens headed an eight-member Soil Conservation Service staff with offices at the end of Dormitory 1. The camp SCS staff was responsible to SCS officials in Colorado Springs, which had a research section. Selba Young, District Soil Conservationist and local rancher, actively engaged in all camp project decisions. During 1941 on every workday morning at seven, approximately 50 men left on open trucks to go to SCS projects on ranches within 50 miles in El Paso County: Fountain Valley to the south and Monument Valley to the north. The men were divided into four crews, each with an assignee crew foreman and truck driver. An SCS technical foreman supervised the four crews. In addition, six men served on a research crew gathering rainfall and drainage data, three surveyors, a team of mechanics in the maintenance shops, others in the SCS office. Periodically the SCS staff conducted mandatory safety meetings, "the driest meetings I've ever attended" commented one crew foreman.

Some of the men, many who had managed farm enterprises, winced at the patronizing commands of SCS staff accustomed to talking down to 18-year-old CCC boys from the city. The men remember tongue lashings, such as an occasion when a SCS supervisor assembled a group of men and berated them in sergeant style. One recalled how a CO failed to show proper interest and was startled to hear the SCS supervisor bark at him, "And yes sir, Mr. Idiot, I'm talking to you." Beginning on June 1, 1942, the men endured the ordeal of "breaking in" a new SCS director who was transferred from a CCC camp.

Despite the lingering image that CPS men were naive CCC boys, the SCS staff often spoke to visitors praising the cooperativeness and productivity of the COs. In February 1942 on an inspection visit, Victor Olsen of Selective Service congratulated the men as having a "production record second to none" in CPS. On several occasions SCS staff entertained their CO assistants, once at a picnic for twenty in Cheyenne Canyon.

During the summer and fall of 1941, the work consisted of "constructing diversion ditches, check dams, terraces, reservoirs and stock ponds, fences and irrigation systems... sometimes the development of wells and springs, the planting of perennial grasses and trees, the treatment of eroded gullies, the protection of stream banks."

In 1941 the men worked with pick and shovel; no power equipment was available. On one 680-acre ranch in the Monument Valley, they constructed 1,230 linear feet of diversion ditches, devoted 100 man-hours to building fences, 700 hours to developing three springs, and 176 hours to digging water-spreading ditches in a 10-acre field.

During those first months, the men grumbled but accepted with no serious complaint the primitive hand work. After all, their "one year of service" would soon pass. With Pearl Harbor, the declaration of war, and conscription stretching out into an uncertain future, pick and shovel work seemed to some a less adequate alternative to military service. In January crews went to the field even when temperatures dropped to ten and twenty degrees below zero. The men remember picking away at the frozen ground and moving little more than "a bushel of icy clods a day." This menial labor yielded varieties of dark humor: "Is this really 'work of national importance'?"

In a summary of all Soil Conservation Service work completed from June 12, 1941 to December 1, 1942, in 40 types of projects, the men had contributed a total of 31,061 man-days of service. Added to this were 3,210 man days of work for the U. S. Forest Service. The value of the labor was estimated at $2.50 per man-day (26 cents an hour) for a total 18-month contribution of $85,677.50.

CPS men were of that last generation to know American agriculture before the pick and shovel was replaced by the bulldozer and backhoe. In April 1942 SCS acquired four caterpillar tractors, a bulldozer, and a carry-all. This acquisition liberated nine men from handwork to the operation of power equipment–for the nine a morale boost.

In February 1942, the U. S. Forest Service opened work for a crew of fifteen on the scenic Gold Camp Road to Cripple Creek. Two months later two crews–one led by an Old Order Amishman and the other by a Hutterite–began planting trees in the Pike National Forest. The Forest Service planned to plant several million trees in the area.

In July, four men were assigned to a forest research project. In September the camp paper reported "the most lofty CPS work project in the nation:" an eight-man crew living at an elevation of 11,000 feet and, among other projects, shingling the roof of the Summit House of Pikes Peak at an elevation of 14,100 feet.

The early 1940s was a generation before the upsurge of national concern for the environment. The Soil Conservation Service and the Forest Service made little or no effort to link this "work of national importance" with national environmental policy. The lectures by the SCS staff are not remembered for their ecological sensitivity and vision. As a matter of fact, pacifists then had much to learn about the bonding between war, peace, and environment.

In August 1942 Paul Comly French asked Kreider and Gaeddert for their evaluation of the work program at Camp No. 5, posing for them a dozen questions. "Was it made work?" he asked. He explained that this request was prompted by concerns from CPS men and conversations with Col. Kosch of Selective Service. Kreider responded with a report incorporating comments from the CPS crew foremen. He listed a number of good projects: reclaiming a tract of fertile swamp land, the repairing of the Mountain Mutual Irrigation System (well-planned, properly supervised, materials always at hand), tree planting–although tedious and hard work, crews using power-equipment feel "they are getting things accomplished," even pick and shovel work building diversion ditches "when crews are sufficiently large that daily progress is apparent."

Kreider identified a number of criticisms: crews out of work by mid-day for lack of planning; SCS lacking tools and equipment for the job, leading, for example, to the continuous use of camp carpentry tools; failure to give the men adequate training for fighting forest fires; summer work for the Forest Service largely consisting of road repair in recreational areas; lack of adequate staff supervision–leaving management of fencing crews to the ranchers. The most severe criticism was the favoritism shown to the big ranchers. One of the equipment operators observed that his work was done almost exclusively on the "tremendously large ranches." Only once did he work for a man "who really needed help and was poor. Work on the big ranches was largely fencing, "a far cry from soil conservation." The men were asked to help with ranch work: "dehorn, brand and castrate cattle." Kreider reported that, "The SCS men seem to wish to do everything they can to please these big ranchers." He observed that camp morale "hit its lowest level" when the men were assigned to thinning and blocking sugar beets and were asked to transport scrap rubber and scrap iron and engage in "semi-defense" projects. He wrote to French, "As a result of these requests, the campers lose all the more confidence in the technical agency."

"We sense," continued Kreider, "that the members of the technical agency lack interest in their jobs." One of the foremen commented that the CPS men "have more of the spirit of soil conservation than the technical men." A series of classes on soil conservation the previous winter "fell flat," deteriorating into a "repetition of the safety rules." Kreider stated that the men had been longing for an SCS staff who could "explain interestingly the fundamentals of soil conservation and the social and economic philosophy behind it." He added, "Some of us believe that the genius of the SCS is educational... to demonstrate model soil conservation practices on representative farms of the community." He concluded his grim assessment, "The SCS staff is not very inspiring. As a result men on the field crews do not have much of a feeling of accomplishment nor a love for their work. That which keeps them going is their conscience that any decent man must do at least a full day's work."

The camp suffered repeatedly from confusing, conflicting lines of command from the local Soil Conservation Service and from Selective Service in Washington–on the one hand, but not always in agreement–and NSBRO and MCC on the other. Selective Service commands were expected to be communicated via NSBRO to the camps. Camp No. 5 received conflicting signals, for example, on the length of the work day. Before the first camp had opened, Henry

Fast had asked Paul Comly French for clarification. He declared, "I do not object to the eight hour work program... but I think the government needs to be reasonable on the transportation time. I am concerned that this does not degenerate into slave labor." In a visit in February 1942, Victor Olsen of the Washington headquarters staff of Selective Service ordered men at Camp No. 5 "to work 44 hours a week and no transportation time was to be counted on government time." Gaeddert had received no communication from Selective Service or the NSBRO confirming this order, tantamount to a 60 hour week.

In late May SCS Project Superintendent Makens declared an emergency in the sugar beet fields and canceled all furloughs—just on the eve of many long-awaited furloughs to return home to help in the Kansas and Oklahoma wheat harvest. This action came without verification from Selective Service. Such issues—and there were many—invariably led the camp director to wire or write the NSBRO, always with a copy to MCC, asking for confirmation. Ambiguity in lines of command meant conflict.

Critical issues persistently arose: "What was 'civilian work of national importance'?" And "Who determines it?" The Soil Conservation Service staff, accustomed to work with CCC boys, saw these as their decisions. The camp director, backed by the NSBRO and MCC and propelled by the sensitivities of the men, saw these as joint decisions laced with concerns of conscience. COs, who had never thought much about what was appropriate work for a pacifist, were stimulated by dorm discussions to think about these issues.

In the winter of 1941-1942, a conflict occurred that could have been explosive. Sam Yoder, an Amishman, describes being sent out with a crew led by LeRoy Miller, another Amishman, to work on a ranch south of Colorado Springs. They were told to drain an earthen dam. Ranchers were present to catch the trapped fish. All around CPS crew members saw surveyor's stakes. The COs asked the purpose of the stakes. The ranchers replied, "Oh, they are planning to build an army camp here." At lunch Miller's crew discussed their misgivings: "We've taken a stand against the military. We could just as well be working in a defense factory making things for the military." They all walked off the job, got in the truck, and drove back to camp. On the way back to camp, they met two SCS men and were asked to explain their departure. The crew volunteered to make up time with other work on Saturday. Sam Yoder recalls that General Lewis B. Hershey, Director of Selective Service, visited the camp to reprimand the CPS men, but also to assure them that such an incident would not happen again.

No camp records have been found to document such a visit. Stories of 50 years ago have a way of drifting. This incident on the site of what soon became Camp Carson gives evidence that there may have been more spontaneous civil disobedience in MCC camps than was publically reported and heralded.

Stresses on the project came to a head during the summer of 1942, the camp work force then at full strength. Few special service units had yet opened to relieve the feeling of entrapment in base camps. Issues over "work of national importance" erupted in late May and early June 1942 when the SCS took the crews off soil conservation and forestry work and assigned them to thinning sugar beets as a part of a war emergency. Men saw billboard advertisements praising beet raising as war work, beet sugar being used for making explosives. The crisis was intensified by the arrival on June 1 of a new SCS Project Superintendent, Tom Titman, who was schooled in giving orders to CCC boys and was new to COs. Vernon Karber, a CPS man working then in the SCS office, remembers an outburst from Titman soon after his arrival: "I wish this place would be bombed to hell." Karber responded. "Well, Mr. Titman, you are in this with us."

Meanwhile, local rancher and district SCS official Selba Young had promised county war manpower officials and ranchers that inexpensive CPS labor would be available in the beet fields. Selective Service shifted the men from soil conservation and forestry work without authorization from Selective Service in Washington. Particularly critical was the fact that during this period, Camp Director Gaeddert was absent from camp traveling for MCC in the interests of a rapidly expanding program. Camp management was left in the hands of Assistant Director Kreider, a 23-year-old assignee. SCS Director Titman and Young were loath to be admonished by a CO conscript, even though he be the officially appointed Assistant Director.

A conflict soon burst forth that persisted for more than four months. Intimations of the conflict came as early as May 14, 1942, when Gaeddert reported to Fast that Selba Young had sought approval from Col. Lewis F. Kosch, Chief of the Camp Operations Division of Selective Service, for permission to shift crews into work in the beet fields. Gaeddert was open to the possibility but raised questions. The beginnings of the conflict are summarized in a two-page letter the Assistant Director wrote on June 15, 1942, to Fast, which opened as follows:

> I feel that our relations with the technical agency, the SCS, have grown more serious.... First, the SCS has given

evidence of ignorance of our CPS convictions in their demands.... They interpret our stand as being solely that of opposition to the bearing of arms.... Second, the SCS, I believe, has been assuming more than its rightful prerogatives... telling us what to do rather than planning on a mutual basis....

First, the emergency farm program of beet thinning and blocking. Neither Albert nor I was here when the SCS said that our manpower was to be diverted into the beet fields, that furloughs were to be canceled, etc.... Selba Young of SCS made commitments of our labor to the County War Board... in advance of our full authorization.... He proceeded with such speed that we found a *fait accompli* in our laps. Much of the blame for such a situation is ours, we must confess.

Second, Mr. Titman, the Project Superintendent, came into the office last week and asked whether some governmental construction group could use a crew of our truck drivers out at the army airport. I said no to that. Yesterday Selba Young called up and asked for a written statement on the reasons for our decision.

Third, yesterday again Mr. Titman came to me and inquired whether we would authorize men and trucks to be used for the collection of scrap rubber. Again I said no. He asked for a statement, which I prepared and which I enclose.

[A] further proof of their ignorance of our essential convictions is that they demand written statements from us on these matters.... I learn these written statements have irritated the SCS no end. What surprises me is that the SCS has lost faith in the importance of soil conservation and forestry work.... If our work simply becomes that of collecting scrap rubber, driving army trucks, thinning sugar beets, we then will have become little more than an auxiliary to the War Board and the Office of Civilian Defense.

The statements were brief, deferential but firm in their refusal. In his letter of June 15, Kreider continued with report of intensified misunderstanding and conflict:

Fourth, an unfortunate incident arose this morning between Selba Young and me. When I stepped out of the dormitory this morning I noticed a movie cameraman and a photographer with Graflex camera taking pictures of the men leaving for the fields. I approached both men and asked them what they were doing, where they received authorization.... One man said he was a Paramount Newsreel man. The other... with *Life Magazine*.... Authorization, they said, came from Selba Young. I then went to the SCS office to speak to Mr. Young. I asked the purpose of these photographers and stated that we preferred to have no publicity of our beet work. Mr. Young snapped back that this was government property and government work and that pictures would be taken here if they chose to do so. The newsreel cameraman approached us and listened in on the conversation.... Mr. Young concluded with a "Well, Kreider, this side of your program better be publicized if you want it to be continued." With that he strode off with the photographers.... Immediately after the brief talk I wrote a letter to Mr. Young. I feel that the SCS has been taking some advantage of us during Albert's absence.... They find the protests of this "youngster" more irritating than would they find Albert's refusals.

Kreider ended his letter to Fast with the comment, "We are not in a panic about these events." He sent a copy of the Fast letter to his parents explaining, "Perhaps this is a subject which should be kept inside the Kreider household and the letter destroyed. There is no need to fear that I am in a den of lions.... At any rate administering a CPS camp is a real educational experience, even though it be nerve-wracking at times."

The situation grew worse. Word came back with the crews on the day of confrontation, that the photographers had pursued to the end of a field Amishmen in their distinctive dress and bearded Holdeman men who in their reluctance to have their pictures taken had fled from the cameramen. Men returned from the fields incensed but feeling captive to the need to maintain good community relations. Kreider wrote Young a letter explaining the MCC position. Young responded with a blistering letter. Several days later Gaeddert returned, reviewed the situation, and wrote Fast supporting Kreider in his decisions, explaining that the Assistant Director was regarded by the SCS staff as "just another assignee" and reviewing the complications caused by unauthorized SCS commitments.

The MCC staff negotiated an accommodation with the SCS staff. The order to cancel furloughs was lifted. Hours of work were lengthened. French granted permission for crews to work for several days in the beet fields to complete the thinning operation. Only volunteers were to be sent to the beet fields. The money earned thinning beets, $39.50 an acre, was to be set aside for a "relief and reconstruction fund to be used after the war." An uneasy peace prevailed.

In early July peace in camp was broken by the arrival of Victor A. Olsen of Selective Service, Washington, who immediately heard from SCS staff their version of recent events. Olsen delivered Kreider a "sustained, vicious tongue-lashing." Kreider wrote his parents, "Olsen believed everything he heard from the SCS. What we said was only 'god damn lies....' He shouted at me that it could be heard outside the buildings.... If this symbolizes the current thinking of Selective Service, some of us will be choosing jail to camp one of these days."

On Friday evening Olsen, who six months before had lauded the men for their "production record second to none," spoke to the assembled CPS men:

> He barked at us; growled at us; snarled at us.... Olsen wants to see in our camps an A- 1 work program characterized by maximum quality and quantity of work, accompanied by a dictatorial disciplinary system (no camp councils, no community contacts, no this or that), and above all a complacency about all controversial issues. We disagree with him on all points except his desires concerning the work program.

On the following morning before the Saturday cleanup, Olsen took the Assistant Director on a tour of inspection of the camp and dictated to him a long list of detailed comments on irregularities in camp maintenance. This report apparently soon came to the attention of Colonel Kosch who wrote Paul Comly French reprimanding the church agencies for leaving camps in the hands of assignee assistant directors. Within a year, however, most CPS camp directors and assistant directors were drawn from the ranks of CO assignees.

Several days after the Olsen flare-up, Gaeddert returned for a brief visit. He wrote to French protesting the unfairness and inaccuracy of Olsen's inspection report. Relations with SCS appeared to improve, but other conflicts over issues of work continued, even when a non-assignee, Emmanuel Hertzler, was loaned from the Fort Collins camp as an interim director. Meanwhile, NSBRO and MCC officials quietly commended the men and camp leadership and acknowledged that it was urgent to fill the vacant directorship of Camp No. 5. None of this was reported in the *Pike View Peace News*, which Kreider helped edit. Despite these altercations with the Soil Conservation Service and Selective Service, the public image of the Colorado Springs camp continued to be tranquil, positive, and upbeat. Men in distant CPS camps might well have thought of the Mennonites of Colorado Springs as "good boys of the system."

"Good boys" though they might have been, the COs of Camp No. 5 unquestionably lost some institutional innocence as they were caught in the complexities and arbitrary machinations of government operations. The men who later transferred to huge custodial mental hospitals found reenforcement for their sense of entrapment and engagement in the struggles of "moral man in an immoral society."

# 1941: CPS: A "Year of Service with Like-minded Christian Young Men"

*Appeared in the* Mennonite Quarterly Review, *October 1992. Five sections excerpted from a much longer article. The following begins on page ten of the article. Footnotes on sources may be found in the original article.*

*An Emerging Community*

Camp No. 5 opened in June 1941 with a burst of idealism and expectancy. On May 19, 1941, on the eve of the opening of the first three MCC camps, Henry Fast wrote to the directors encouraging them to visualize each camp as a "family relationship," and saying further: "It should lead [the men] to a desire to transform the whole camp life so that even its outward appearance of cleanliness, order, and beauty would reflect with credit the depth of their Christian conviction and concern." He advocated an orientation course–similar to one for freshmen in college–to help the men to a "quicker and happier adjustment" to camp life. Fast noted that such a course

> should help them to discover what an opportunity their camp life offers to experiment in the Christian democratic, cooperative way of life and to demonstrate the validity of their basic faith in Jesus' way of love and understanding. They should learn to see the application of all this to their life and relationships in camp, the work program and life in the residence halls, in the dining hall, to the use of their leisure time and to their relationships with the community.

Albert Gaeddert received no detailed instructions on how to build an instant community among the conscripted COs. A community identity emerged, nurtured by folk improvisation and tinkering. Reports spoke of good camp spirit. The men formed a softball league of seven dormitory teams. They staged volleyball and horseshoe tournaments, laid out tennis and croquet courts, built ping-pong tables. They organized classes in typing, public speaking, Bible, music, accounting, first aid, crafts, manual training and soil conservation. A choir held its first practice, with J. Hobart Goering chosen as director. The men elected a committee to plan Christian Endeavor meetings for Sunday evenings. They organized a Sunday school and elected teachers for five classes. A staff gathered to publish a camp paper and–from sixty-eight nominations–chose the name *Pike View Peace News.* Carpenters built a closet for each pair of cots. One evening "everyone chipped in a nickel for some ice cream."

The camp opened its door to visitors—eight hundred during the first three months, from twenty-two states. On Sunday noons in the summer of 1941 at least 40 to 50 guests joined the campers for dinner; one Sunday, 75. Friends and relatives were curious about this experimental community—a camp set on a hill. The country was not yet at war; automobile travel was not yet restricted by the rationing of gasoline.

Recreation and religious life programming developed in predictable patterns, but much in the life of this largely male community was unique and less predictable. A flow of news items in the camp paper during the first fifteen months offers glimpses of an emerging community: Camp No.5 established perhaps the only CPS radio station, W9HOM. A crew went into Pike National Forest and cut two 70-foot spruce trees to install as masts for the antenna of the shortwave radio station, with two wave lengths, a daytime range of one hundred miles and a nighttime range of two thousand miles. The radio station was a short-lived operation; several days after Pearl Harbor, federal authorities ordered it shut down.... On the first anniversary of registration day (October 16, 1940), men met in the assembly hall to observe an hour of quiet meditation.... In October 1941 the business manager, Ray Schlichting, and volunteers established a camp store, with toiletries, candy, stamps and other merchandise offered at wholesale prices. A Service Club was added, providing a community checking service for members who deposited five or more dollars.... On Armistice Day many campers fasted out of "a sense of fellowship with the people of Europe who [were] forced to suffer the effects of starvation due to the food blockade." A $25 check was sent to MCC for European relief.... Sixty visitors were guests at a Thanksgiving dinner.... On December 1, in an economy move, MCC gave the men their last monthly allowance of $1.50. Six assignee comments were reported, all accepting the MCC action.... In January the camp began taking Sunday morning offerings for MCC overseas relief.... The camp met for breakfast fifteen minutes early to allow for an extended devotional period when two men left for training for the China unit.... Three Palmer brothers, COs paroled from prison to Camp No. 5, introduced campers to rug weaving.... Instrumentalists organized a camp orchestra.... On Saturday evenings a group gathered to listen to recorded classical music.... In February the men helped Mrs. Riesen, the matron's mother, celebrate her eighty-fifth birthday.... In April the men staged an amateur night, with the eight dormitories competing for prizes.... On April 24 an auction of unclaimed laundry yielded receipts totaling $7.95, to be used for the purchase of a sock-mending machine.... At first the camp had five barbers, then nine, with the bathhouse serving as the "local barber college...." The men contributed funds to pay the expenses for three campers to represent them at a regional CPS conference at Newton, Kansas.

The most discussed social event of the year occurred on June 6, 1942–a picnic on the bluff above the camp, followed by a "Graduation Day" ceremony complete with "class song," "class will," "class prophecy, commencement address" and the awarding of "degrees" to the fifteen men who had completed one year of service.... One man emerged as the camp jeweler and watch repairman.... On June 20, 1942, the camp held a dinner honoring Albert Gaeddert and his family on the eve of his departure to become assistant general director of MCC-CPS. A multi act skit was presented portraying the "life of a great man"–Gaeddert, that is.... On September 4 crews returning from the field were shocked to learn of the sudden death, from a brain tumor, of 30-year-old Curt Dyck–this news coming just as his parents arrived for a weekend visit. The camp gathered for a memorial service. Because Dyck was not a church member, his death triggered much discussion as to whether the unbaptized can be saved.

Step by step the COs conscripted and assigned to work at Templeton Gap merged into a community. Without a formal confession of faith or a rite of baptism, without the ceremony of holy communion, this community drifted toward becoming a congregation.

*A Quasi-Congregation*

Recognizing that Mennonites adhered to differing church polities, no one made a case that Camp No. 5 was really a Mennonite congregation. However, Albert Gaeddert, as all of the first MCC camp directors, was a pastor. From Henry Fast's letter welcoming the assignees to a fellowship of "like-minded Christian young men," to the dedicatory prayer on the June 5 arrival at the camp, to the daily devotional period after breakfast, the camp became a congregation. The morning meditations–with hymn singing, prayer and announcements–helped to set the tone for the camp community. Gaeddert was worship leader and preacher on Sundays. In addition, the men were encouraged to attend Sunday school and Sunday evening Christian Endeavor meetings. Bible study was held on Wednesday nights. No ball games were scheduled on Sundays. The six-pamphlet Core Course series,

*Mennonites and Their Heritage*, was prepared to heighten Mennonite consciousness and identity in the camps. On his visits Fast delivered traditional Mennonite admonitory messages, in the following vein: "gird up your loins and fight the good fight." In his gentle devotional style Gaeddert spoke to the concrete issues of camp life: concern for fellow COs, the gift of caring, working conscientiously, witness to the community, stewardship of time, the dubious habit of smoking.

Some church constituents criticized camp leadership for failure to curb attendance at movies and bowling in town. One camper complained that the men "smoke and chew and swear like they do here [at home]." Some home pastors urged Gaeddert to report to them the deviant behavior of their members. Gaeddert once wrote to a Church of God in Christ, Mennonite (Holdeman) pastor that one of his men had shaved off his beard–for this group a signal that the man was slipping into the ways of the world. Four months later this man transferred to the army. On one occasion Orie Miller and a Mennonite pastor urged Gaeddert to report to home ministers the questionable behavior of their men in the camp. Kreider wrote, "Albert shuddered at such a thought. I tried to help him by pointing out that making a watchdog out of Albert might jeopardize his role.... Well, Orie Miller didn't press his point too far." Kreider explained that Gaeddert could lose his credibility with the men if he were to serve as an informant. A man who had been released from CPS wrote to Gaeddert a six-page letter telling how he had given up smoking in his new-birth experience. He requested that the letter be read to the men for their edification.

CPS raised puzzling, disturbing, stimulating questions of church and faith. Many–both in home congregations and among the men–expected the CPS camps to be Mennonite congregations. After all, the men had taken CO vows that were thought to hold them to higher moral and spiritual standards: church attendance, Bible reading, no smoking, no complaining, a readiness to volunteer and obey, and a consistent peace witness. To many a CO's disappointment, even this "city set on a hill" was flawed.

On the other hand, a CO coming to Camp No. 5 from a separate and pridefully correct background encountered the presence of Mennonites from ten other groups who were reasonably decent, and non-Mennonites from twenty other denominations who were reasonably decent. The men discovered that COs from other groups could pray, read the Bible and act kindly. In addition, there was the new experience of hearing sermons by preachers of other groups who were sound, biblical and interesting–above all, interesting. Despite its imperfections, this not-quite-a-congregation seemed to some better than the one remembered from home. Years later a CO who at Camp No. 5 had been conservative and judgmental confided to a fellow CPS alumnus that he had not been able to find a congregation that met his standards. However, he said, if Albert Gaeddert were to pastor a nearby church, he and his wife would join. Camp No. 5 was a new kind of congregation, with a rearranged set of "good guys" and "not so good guys." It became apparent that the essential ingredient for the good community–for the CPS congregation–was not so much doctrinal correctness and certitude as the feel of fraternity and shared values.

*Camp Discipline*

In a conscripted society backed by the gray eminence of Selective Service in Washington, one would expect to find resistance to rules and authority. Albert Gaeddert and others have difficulty recalling many discipline problems during that first year. To be sure, an incident of theft was addressed in a morning devotions period, followed by dormitory sessions to discuss a proper response. And a camper who was caught by state police without proper leave papers had to be bailed out of jail. Most of the problems were routine: tardiness in returning from leaves and furloughs, unmade beds in the dormitories, the use of private cars, noise after lights-out, smoking outside of designated areas. No incidents of drunkenness are remembered. A fight between two men out on project came to the attention of Gaeddert only years later. Some laxness in camp discipline led Gaeddert to admonish the men forcefully in one of his morning devotions. "We needed it," reported one of the men.

The editor of the camp paper, Roland Bartel, commented on January 24, 1942, regarding disciplinary style at Colorado Springs:

> We are fortunate that the policy in our camp has been that standards of conduct are adopted after a group discussion or with the general consent of the group. This policy is essential to our way of life and is fundamentally different from the policy of authoritative commands essential to the military way of life. One of the underlying assumptions of the CPS program is that a high standard of discipline can be arrived at democratically.... The policy has been to trust each individual's ability to self-discipline himself to fulfill the wishes of the group.... Obviously, most objections to rules are in reality leveled against the method of obtaining and enforcing them.

The men of Camp No. 5 were not unlike those in other camps as they imposed a discipline on each other in a multitude of subtle and not always kind ways–teasing, ridiculing, taunting, mimicking, challenging, questioning–and sometimes in praising and thanking. The men sanded the rough edges of one another's behavior but still had to accept varieties of personality and idiosyncrasies. In the dormitories the men developed their own unwritten prohibitions. A Holdeman Mennonite's protest against card playing in his dormitory was silenced by another CO's declaration, "I am a conscientious objector to war, not to card playing."

*Scavenging for Leadership*

Within the first year MCC struggled to find capable Mennonite pastors to direct the camps, which grew in number from four in June 1941 to sixteen a year later. The correspondence of Fast, Miller, Bender and Gaeddert through 1942 reveals a discouraging scavenger hunt for leadership from the Mennonite constituency. Beginning in May 1942, Fast sought a qualified replacement at Colorado Springs for Gaeddert, who was being drawn into work as Fast's assistant west of the Mississippi. It became increasingly clear that there was a need for camp directors who had broader qualifications than ordained status and a willingness to serve. Beginning with two 22-year-old assignees at Colorado Springs—Ray Schlichting as business manager and Kreider as assistant and educational director—Miller and Fast turned to recruiting camp leadership from the pool of drafted COs. The CPS men called to staff responsibilities were college-educated and had "worldly" experience in teaching, business and similar vocations.

However, at first and lingering through the CPS era there would be problems with youthful draftees as directors. An SCS project director who tended to think of CPS men as CCC boys could hardly accept, as his equal counterpart in administration, an assignee serving as acting camp director.

Nevertheless, in 1941 youthful, non-ordained men were thrust into positions of leadership in what came to be the largest church-related institution in Mennonite history, MCC-administered CPS. At war's end, from this reservoir of young men tested in CPS administration came leaders to staff missions, colleges, pastorates and church bureaucracies, as well as the mushrooming para-institutions of the church—Mennonite Disaster Service, relief sales, church camping associations, etc. Mennonite leadership patterns would be challenged by this influx of young non-ordained men and would be forever altered.

*A Community College*

Not only was Camp No. 5 a quasi-congregation; it was also a school. The government conscripted the men into a program of compulsory education, much of it formal and even more of it informal. Within the first six weeks the men started 10 classes (some short-lived)–3 taught by assignees, 2 by staff and 5 by teachers from the community. Four courses were added in October and November: photography, Spanish, spelling and grammar, and drama. Thirty percent of the men had attended college. In response to an educational questionnaire in October 1941, twenty campers expressed interest in courses for college credit, and several in courses for high school credit–these tuition-free by arrangement with Kansas Mennonite colleges. The men identified their interest in thirty-four courses and club activities. Fifteen campers enrolled for evening courses offered by the Colorado Springs Labor College, a twelve-week adult education program of the local board of education. In January 1942 thirty men enrolled in a farm course, planned by a committee, with eight agriculturalists scheduled as speakers. In February ten enrolled in a course in welding, and in May twenty-two enrolled in a course in farm accounting. The camp paper announced in July 1942 that forty-one men had completed a standard course in first aid, for a total of sixty-seven certified by that date. By July 25, 1942, the camp had accumulated a library of six hundred books.

Two features distinguished the Colorado Springs educational program: the abundance of speakers drawn to Camp No. 5 and the Core Course. In November 1941 the education committee launched "The Core Course, an all-camp study group," an experiment in CPS general education. The course, designed by Gaeddert and Kreider, projected four units of study, each six weeks in length: Pacifism and Nonresistance, Historical Rootage of Our Way of Life (church history), The Rural Community and Christian Citizenship (church-state issues). The course, which met twice a week, made use of more than 20 special speakers–4 from Bethel College, 3 from Tabor College, 2 from Goshen College, at least 8 from among Colorado Springs area pastors and professors, and camp staff, etc. Speakers from a distance spent a few days in the camp, giving several lectures, living with the men and sometimes going out on project with crews. This helped to demythologize the ivory tower professor. The men heard lectures on Anabaptism, hymnology, the biblical basis of peace, Gandhi, Mennonites in Paraguay, the history of the Church of the Brethren and the Friends, MCC relief work in Europe after World War I, missions in Argentina, race relations, postwar reconstruction, etc. With a quarter of the men from non-Mennonite groups, attention was given to multiple streams in Protestant history.

Envisioning the opportunity in CPS to inculcate Mennonite understanding and appreciation, September 1941 the MCC Executive Committee appointed Harold Bender of Goshen College as dean of MCC educational programming. He convened a meeting of camp educational directors in Chicago in October 1941. Bender focused his energies on editing a series of six 48-page booklets for use in a Mennonite Heritage Course (or Core Course), which each MCC-CPS camp was urged to offer. Realizing that the MCC Core Course booklets would not be available until a year later, and eager to get started, Kreider sent to Fast on November 11, 1941, an outline of the locally designed Core Course. He reported that the men responded favorably to the first sessions. Kreider wrote:

> We felt it inadvisable to limit the study to the "Mennonite Heritage".... We thought this method of approaching our denominational history would serve to bridge the cleavage between Mennonites and non-Mennonites. The feeling in camp against the non-Mennonites is too marked to be healthy.

Fast passed on to Harold Bender a copy of Kreider's November 11 letter and a tentative outline of the course, adding these comments:

> I am sending you an outline of what Kreider thought might serve as a good core course for their particular camp, which sometime ago had about 35 non-Mennonite boys out of a total number of 125 campees. It is obvious that a camp like that and another one like Marietta would have some difficulty making proper arrangements for a core course such as we had outlined for Mennonite boys. I am wondering whether... his suggested core course would not have considerable merit.

Immediately Bender voiced his displeasure to Fast and Miller:

> I am not altogether happy.... If an assignee like Robert Kreider cannot teach the [Mennonite] core course, and if his thinking is so much along the line of what he has worked out in this plan, my own frank conviction is that

we should drop the policy of having assignees serving as educational directors.

Bender proposed replacing Kreider with a nonassignee education director and sending him off to England.

On November 24 Orie Miller wrote to Bender that he had suggested that Fast have a "leisurely discussion with Kreider." Miller continued:

> In case you get into problems on the educational program [this should] be referred to our Executive Committee.... I feel that you have approached correspondence referred to in the right attitude and would encourage you to keep on in patience and with persistence, and feel sure that if we keep on working along these lines, we will get our problems worked out.

Several days later Fast came to Colorado Springs and sat down to counsel with Kreider, opening with Bender's appreciation for a "carefully prepared outline," but followed by blunt criticism of his "'watered down syncretism,' an FOR [Fellowship of Reconciliation] emphasis, neglect of the Mennonite Heritage." Kreider reported to his parents:

> His letter was pretty biting in spots. I fear that Bender has gathered the impression that Albert and I are young, liberal General Conference activists bent on setting the world aright... [and] out to beat the MCC in planning a course.... We intend to expand the section on religious heritage with a corresponding reduction in the... section on the rural community. We do not intend to yield to Bender's suggestion that we organize a Mennonite core course and follow strictly the MCC outline. With thirty non-Mennonites in camp we must guard against widening the gulf in our fellowship.... Although not all of our... topics include "Mennonite" in the title, nevertheless the treatment of the material will be rooted basically in a Mennonite interpretation... we intend to draw heavily from the Mennonite heritage and our Mennonite community experiences.... [Bender's] is a problem of knowing Albert and [me] and of understanding our camp.... I do not want Old Mennonite leaders to gain the impression that the young men of our group are wishy-

washy liberals with no keen appreciation of our Mennonite heritage.

Kreider followed with a letter to Fast, reviewing the above, inviting Bender to visit Colorado Springs, and identifying twenty-one Mennonite leaders being sought as Core Course speakers. Six months later Bender convened a meeting of camp education directors at Colorado Springs. He spoke in the Core Course. At this May meeting he held up the Colorado Springs program and Core Course as a model in the system.

Young assignee leaders in CPS were pressed into a crash course in discernment of acceptable Mennonite values and the maintenance of appropriate boundaries–the right words and the wrong words, the good persons and the suspect persons. Some COs yielded to these sensitivities and restrictions, and some fought them. Thus, CPS men in leadership positions struggled with issues of confrontation with authority and the art of survival.

Camp No. 5, as one of the first camps, enjoyed high visibility and drawing power for visitors and officials. The stimulation of visits and lectures of scores of leaders was a marked feature of camp life during the first year: from MCC, Henry Fast visited at least six times, Harold Bender twice, P. C. Hiebert twice, Orie Miller once; from the American Friends Service Committee, there were three visitors, including E. Raymond Wilson and Tom Jones; from the Fellowship of Reconciliation, A. J. Muste, James Farmer, Don Smucker and Carl Landes made visits; from the NSBRO came Paul Comly French and George Reeves, the latter three times; from Selective Service, Colonel Kosch, Major McLean and Victor Olson made two visits; there were week-long visits by two Lisle Fellowship voluntary service teams. Other distinguished persons, such as Robert Calhoun of Yale Divinity School and an executive of the Cooperative League of America, paid brief visits and were invariably drawn into impromptu meetings. A few days after Pearl Harbor, C. N. Hostetter, Jr., president of Grantham College and later chairman of the Mennonite Central Committee, led in a highly appreciated week of devotional messages. All of this was much richer intellectual fare than most campers had enjoyed in their home communities. After the novelty of the first year, and with the multiplication of CPS camps and units, Colorado Springs drew fewer visitors.

Camp No. 5 offered formal education: a Core Course, a variety of other courses–credit and noncredit–and a stream of visiting speakers. Undoubtedly more important was the informal education. In the winter months Kreider occasionally joined crews for pick-and-shovel work in the field. He wrote:

"I have a number of stiff joints and muscles scattered over my frame.... Especially does it get one in the hands to swing a pick. Ours was a very good crew–all hard working, serious fellows.... Yesterday I talked for hours with several from Iowa about their churches, the dress question, the possibilities for greater cooperation among Mennonites, farming practices... the Iowa Mennonites and high school and college education. Such conversations while one is working are really instructive. I wonder whether the educational director couldn't do more by getting out on the project and encouraging the project conversation along certain lines than by the more formal evening education program.

No MCC-CPS registrar in Akron kept a central record of each man's course attendance and completions. Even less was recorded of those indefinable layers of informal learning that have come to be known as "nontraditional education." CPS was an experiment in open-door and ungraded adult education, an experiment in a community college.

# 1944: An Ill Fated Mission

*Following are excerpts of an address given at a Sunday afternoon vesper service at Bluffton College in the early spring of 1944, soon after returning from a trip to South Africa. Lois Sommer, whom Robert met for the first time that evening, was a member of the women's choir that sang at the service.*

I come to you this afternoon not with a tale of success but with a report on an ill-fated mission. The late Neville Henderson, British ambassador to Berlin, wrote after the capitulation to Hitler at Munich in 1938, *The Failure of a Mission.* Ours was the failure of a mission.

In the summer of 1941 I was drafted. For reasons of conscience I chose to go to a Civilian Public Service camp. These past three years I, along with hundreds of other men in CO camps, have yearned for the opportunity to go to war ravaged lands to render relief service to stricken peoples.

In February of 1943 that opportunity knocked on the door of CPS. The Chinese National Government requested the services of 70 CPS men to do ambulance and relief work in West China. President Roosevelt gave his approval. Secretary of War Stimson gave his enthusiastic backing. Selective Service approved. And finally the State Department added its benediction. The work in West China was to be a cooperative project of the Quakers, Brethren and Mennonites, the American Friends Service Committee taking the lead. In China we were to be associated with the British Friends Ambulance Unit, already in the field, in its medical, relief and rehabilitation programs in Szechwan, Honan and Yunnan provinces. To the men in CPS this was headline news: foreign relief was opening for COs. Here was the "moral equivalent to war" which we had been seeking.

To serve as an advance guard for this 70-man unit, a smaller unit of eight was selected to proceed immediately to China to open the program. A year ago in April [1943] these selections were made and mine was the good fortune to be one of the eight. On May 1 our unit assembled at the Quaker center, Pendle Hill, near Philadelphia. Composing our unit of eight were sons of China missionaries, an engineer, school teachers, an agriculturalist, a male nurse, an office manager, students. We worked feverishly–purchasing equipment for three years abroad (this limited to 55 pounds per person for a flight into China); being measured for Quaker-grey uniforms; securing government permits for film, cameras, books, medical supplies; arranging with War Shipping Administration for transportation; securing passports from the State Department (my passport approved just four days before sailing). And there were orientation sessions with a string of "weighty" Quakers–Rufus Jones, Clarence Pickett, Howard Brinton, and others.

With high enthusiasm we set sail from Brooklyn Navy Yard on June 19, on a fast freighter, the S. S. *Peter Finney Dunne,* bound for the Persian Gulf and the Russian front with a cargo of tanks, trucks, munitions. The Mediterranean was closed to travel. Because of the war, ours of necessity was a circuitous route: to the South Atlantic, around the southern tip of Africa, thence to Bombay, across India by train, from Assam flight over the Himalayas to China.

Enroute to South Africa our ship, because of its speed, traveled without navy escorts. We were completely cut off from the outside world. Night and day the ship pursued a zig-zag course. A 20-man navy gun crew was on duty to man anti-aircraft guns and detonate anti-sub explosives. We had daily boat and fire drills. At night our ship was completely blacked out. We were warned that out there in the vast ocean Nazi submarines were lurking, ready to destroy Allied shipping.

A week after our departure, unknown to us, men in CPS received the staggering news that Congress had canceled overseas service for COs. To a 71-billion dollar appropriation bill for the army, Rep. Starnes of Alabama attached an amendment which effectively prohibited foreign service that fiscal year for COs. We knew nothing about this blow to our program. We were blithely sailing in the Atlantic out of range of mail or telephone. Those were pleasant days at sea–the five week voyage to Capetown, South Africa. We sweated over Chinese lessons and read dozens of books on China.

Late in July, early one Saturday morning, we sighted Table Mountain and the Lion's Head of Capetown, looming out of the sea, golden in the early morning sunlight. It was a magnificent sight–a sight which thrilled Bartholomew Diaz in 1489. Welling up in us was what seamen call, "channel fever"–an overwhelming urge to set foot on soil–this, African soil.

We disembarked and waited two weeks in Capetown for priority to get rail passage to travel 1,200 miles overland to Durban in Natal on the Indian Ocean. All the time we were pressing toward China, unaware of the Starnes Amendment. In Durban we arranged with the British Control Office for passage on a freighter bound for Bombay, India. On the very eve of our departure came the catastrophic news: the China program for CPS men had been canceled. That was six weeks after the action in Congress–six weeks for the news to catch up with us. Plans for three years were shattered. We recovered.

We remained three months in South Africa. For a time it appeared we might be granted draft board releases, thus permitting us to proceed to China. While waiting for such a green light, we worked in Durban hospitals. I served as Nurse Kreider on the emergency ward of Prince Edward VIII Hospital, a hospital for the Zulus. To perform my duties I learned a few words of Zulu such as *M'bushilo* (Have you had a bowel movement?).

Finally came a "No" from U.S. Selective Service. On October 15 we set sail from Durban on a Henry J. Kaiser-built Liberty Ship carrying coal to Rio de Janeiro. Again a zig-zag course and blackouts at night. Arriving in Rio, we learned that on our route a ship had been sunk six hours in advance of us and another 18 hours following. We were oblivious to the perils. After a week in Rio de Janeiro, where we left our hearts, we traveled in a convoy of 40 ships along the Brazilian coast, stopping in Dutch Guiana, Trinidad, Guantanamo Bay in Cuba, arriving in New Orleans a few days before Christmas. It is an eery feeling to stand on deck on a clear night and to recognize the dark forms of other ships silently pressing on all sides on a common course.

In wartime Cape Town and Durban we eight Americans were welcomed as old friends, invited into homes, asked lots of questions. They asked about movie stars Dorothy Lamour and Bing Crosby, orchestra leader Bennie Goodman and "Can you jitterbug?" A majority of us were six-footers. In the Durban hotel restaurant where we stayed, a woman asked the headwaiter, "Why are these Americans so tall?" "Oh, don't you know," he replied, "They don't smoke; they don't drink; and they have nothing to do with the women–that's why they are so tall." We discovered that America enjoyed a tremendous reservoir of goodwill. Some intimated that President Roosevelt and the U.S. would have answers to the baffling problems of a postwar world.

Many South Africans were pleased to compare the Union of South Africa with the United States–the two so much alike: both large countries, both with broad prairies (called *veld* in South Africa), desert, mountain ranges, thousands of miles of coastline, both young countries with a frontier spirit, both with memories of a terrible civil war (the Boer War in South Africa), both unresolved problems of race. The Prime Minister is General Jan Smuts, a commando leader during the Boer War, who remarked: "Look at the other British Dominions. No quarrels! No problems! Everything smooth and easy! How empty! How dull! Now the Union–there isn't a human problem under the sun we haven't in this one Union of ours: black, brown, yellow, white–we have them all." He added, "Can it be said we are a peaceful, amiable nation? Of course, it can't. But it cannot be said we are not an interesting nation. How exciting life is here!... I wouldn't be anything but a South African." Then he sighs, "What a nation we might be–with our qualities and opportunities, what a great powerful people, if only we could leave off quarreling, if only we had not so many hates."

I wish to speak briefly about three of South Africa's problems.

Problem one: the relation between the Dutch and the English. South Africa has a population of 10 million. Only two million of these are white–"Europeans" they call them. Of the two million, 40 percent are of English background and 60 percent of Dutch background. To this day tension exists between the Dutch and the English. It began in the 17th century when the Dutch established a colonial outpost at the southernmost tip of Africa on the trade route to India. There the Dutch lived peaceably until the Napoleonic wars when the British established control of the Cape Province. The Dutch resented the new government. In 1834 the British abolished slavery, angering the Dutch whose economic and social structures were based on slavery. Likening themselves to the children of Israel in the Exodus, Dutch farmers fled the Cape Province on what they called the Great Trek–one of the classic migrations of history: past the Orange River, the Vaal River, over the Drakensburg Mountains into the Transvaal and Natal. A measure of peace followed. But in 1867 diamonds were discovered at Kimberley and in 1886 gold on the Witwatersrand–both deep in Dutch territory of the Orange Free State and the Transvaal. Hordes of men of fortune poured into the interior to exploit these rich natural resources. Cecil Rhodes and other adventurers thought that where British subjects went the British flag should follow.

In 1899 a bitter war broke out, the Boer War. Arrayed against the British were Boer Kommandos, guerrilla fighters of Paul Kruger, Botha, Smuts. During that war a young British correspondent, Winston Churchill, emerged as a world figure. In 1902 the war ended, a British triumph. In 1910, in one of the magnanimous strokes of British statesmanship, South Africa was granted self government, uniting four provinces: Natal, the parliamentary capital in Cape Town in the Cape Province, the administrative capital in Pretoria in the Transvaal, and the judicial capital in Bloemfontein in the Orange Free State. The embers of animosity continued to smolder. To this day the Dutch "wave the bloody shirt." South Africa is not united. There is a lack of a sense of community in the dominant white group.

The English and the Dutch are a study in contrasts:

1. Language: English...Afrikaans

2. Religion: Anglican and Wesleyan...Dutch Reformed (Calvinists)

3. Urban...rural

4. British tea...Dutch coffee

5. Loyalty to the British crown...anti-British

6. Merchants, industrialists, professionals...Boer farmers

7. Pro-Allied in the war... lukewarm or hostile to the Allied side

8. Colonists whose dust is forever England... the Dutch: "this is our home, our native land."

9. Economy-minded... politics-minded

South Africa will never be a great nation until the Dutch and English blend their hearts and wills to the common task.

Second, South Africa has economic problems. South Africa aspires to become a great industrial nation. It is rich in minerals. South Africa's economy rests on gold. South Africans shudder to think what would happen if the United States and other nations would cease to purchase gold. It seems silly to mine gold in South Africa, ship it half way around the world and then bury it again in Kentucky. It has coal, iron and copper but lacks petroleum. It has cheap labor to be exploited, and exploitation is the word for it. But it lacks markets and domestic capital. South Africa is dependent on foreign products. You bathe in a Crane bathtub, ride down the left side of the road in a Ford or Chevrolet, listen to a Philco radio, brush your teeth with Colgate toothpaste.

Third, the problem of the white man and the black man. South Africa has eight million blacks and two million whites. General Smuts compares the Union to a ship with whites as officers and black as crew. Originally in South Africa there were three major native groups: Hottentots, Bushmen and Bantu. The first slaves of white men were Hottentots–many wiped out by measles and small pox, the remnant becoming a mixed race people, the Cape Coloured. The Bushmen are the unexcelled hunters of the Kalahari Desert. The largest group are the Bantu: Swazis, Zulus, Matabele, Basutoes and others. The other large non-European group in South Africa is Indian–a quarter of a million, mostly in Natal. They were imported in the 1860s as indentured laborers on sugar cane plantations. Among them one, Mahatma Gandhi, emerged as leader of the aggressive Indian nationalist movement. He came to South Africa as a young lawyer. In Durban one Sunday he went to St. Paul's Anglican Church to hear his good friend C. F. Andrews preach. That morning ushers barred him from admittance because of his color of skin. A few weeks later he was barred from a train going to Pietermaritzburg. From such experiences emerged the Indian Nationalist movement. In Durban we went to see and talk with Gandhi's son, editor of an Indian language newspaper and not so winsome as his father.

Indians and Kaffirs (the name often used for blacks–the heathen) do nearly all the unskilled labor–labor in the mines, pass the bricklayer his bricks, dig ditches, collect refuse. A European has to be very poor not to keep a black servant. The whole economy rests on the shoulders of the native. This fact–that manual labor is beneath the dignity of the white man–eats into the moral fiber of the white man. The eight million non-Europeans are at the bottom of the social ladder. They cannot vote. They are strictly segregated. They are hounded by hundreds of little restrictions and taxes. The two million white men are in mortal fear that the eight million black men will develop a race consciousness and challenge the white man's supremacy. That race consciousness is developing–slowly–perhaps thirty years behind that of India.

In South Africa I had my first opportunity to visit missions. We discovered missions to be in the forefront of the movement to educate native Africans. While for several days on the campus of Adams Mission College I learned that nine-tenths of education for natives beyond elementary school is mission supported.

In September when our group made an overnight rail trip to northern Zululand, a game reserve, two of us chose to travel third class–the lowest class for non-Europeans. When we appeared to buy tickets, the agent explained that no whites ever traveled third class, only natives. We were issued tickets finally and reluctantly. Boarding the train the conductor exclaimed, "Don't you know there is a color bar in this country? We don't mix the races in South Africa." In exasperation he muttered, "Oh, you Yanks!" That night we shared a squalid third-class compartment with five natives. In the morning we had opportunity to make friends with our traveling companions. We gave several of our sandwiches to an old, withered Zulu grandmother. She was appreciative, observed in the gesture of her people: cupping her hands and bowing her head. The most interesting personality in our compartment was the "preacher man," an itinerant minister for a Scandinavian mission. He, too, wished to know why we traveled third class. I explained that we wished to save money but more than that, we were eager to travel with the African people. Understanding, he smiled and responded, "Your people... my people... we are all the same." We felt we were forming friendships which crossed the barriers of nation, language and race. "Your people... my people... we are all the same."

In evaluating our six-months trip, I am most deeply impressed with the persons we met: Maurice Webb, the Quaker business man in Durban who introduced us to his Basuto friends; the Karl Wilker family, refugees from Nazi Germany; Simon, the Basuto nurse and my mentor in Prince Edward the Eighth Hospital; Mr. Mbatha, the keen young Zulu teacher who wishes to come to America to study; and the Zulu "preacher man."

Even more significant, essentially a spiritual experience, we learned how to take frustrations and failure. We were headed down a highway of three years of service in China. Suddenly the door slammed shut. Halfway around the earth, our plans were blocked. We had to turn around and go back. But out of it came an assurance that if we but be patient, if we but seek divine leading–someday soon the doors will open.

Along with hundreds of other young men in CPS I hope and pray for the time the way will open for us to go to war-ravaged lands to minister materially and spiritually to the needs of the victims of war.

Meeting of staff of Council of Relief Agencies Licensed for Operation in Germany (CRALOG), Germany, summer of 1946: left to right: Noel Field (Unitarian Service Committee), Carl Schaffnit (Lutheran World Relief), Eldon Burke (Brethren Service Committee), Robert Kreider (Mennonite Central Committee), Claude Shotts (American Friends Service Committee), Edmund Cummings (Catholic Relief Services).

# 1946: On Entering War Devastated Germany

*Serialized in* Mennonite Weekly Review, *May-June 1998, an article based on letters and notes from 1946.*

Never have I seen such destruction.... Acres and acres of pulverized stone and mortar.... Tiny little shop fronts dug out of hills of rubble. The neatness of the shop in strange contrast to the ugly piles of debris from which it emerges. I stepped into a shell of a department store where I saw almost no merchandise, only a few women looking through books of dress patterns. In the historic Roemer Platz one walks along winding paths among the rubble.... The opera house–a shell.... Somewhere in the devastation was the house of Goethe, but we could not locate it.... In the cathedral, of which only the spire still stands, archbishops once crowned the emperors of the Holy Roman Empire.... The Jewish quarter, the home of the Rothschild banking family, destroyed.... The central railway station, the gutted skeleton of a roof still standing, was filled with thousands of drably dressed people with sacks and battered luggage: refugees, returned prisoners of war, the homeless, people on the move.

Undamaged in all this destruction is the I. G. Farben building, headquarters of the great chemical cartel, now the central command post for the occupation. In all the obliteration bombing, why was this spared?

On the door of a dingy restaurant read the menu: potato soup, potato pancakes. That is all.... At noon we ate lunch at an American officer's club–a three course dinner with second servings. The tablecloth was of silk parachute cloth. A small orchestra played dinner music.

The above are notes from my first day in Germany, March 27, 1946, a stopover in Frankfurt am Main, enroute to Berlin. I was on assignment for the Mennonite Central Committee, representing the MCC in the Council of Relief Agencies Licensed for Operation in Germany (CRALOG), a new inter-agency relief program authorized by President Harry Truman a month before. I was headed for Berlin with two other CRALOG men: a representative of the International Red Cross and the American Friends Service Committee.

I was not the first MCC person to enter postwar Germany. C. F. Klassen, member of the MCC Executive Committee, had traveled extensively in Germany several months earlier visiting scattered Mennonite refugees from Russia and assessing ways to mobilize an MCC immigration effort. My job was not refugees, but relief. On February 9, only six weeks after Lois' and my wedding, I sailed from New York City for Le Havre on the S.S. *Argentina*, virtually a troop ship with eight passengers to a cabin. Then followed a month in France waiting for instructions, time spent in Paris and at Chalon sur Saone, center of MCC's relief operations in France.

On our arrival on March 28 in Berlin we reported to the Welfare Branch of the Office of Military Government–United States (OMGUS). We were billeted in an improvised transit hotel requisitioned from a German apartment owner. We were issued a currency exchange control book, an identification card, an OMGUS pass, a mess hall card, a PX (Post Exchange) card, a clothing and accessory ration card. We three in civilian dress in a sea of uniformed American personnel were given the assimilated officer's rankings of major to establish our pecking order in this military world. OMGUS headquarters, we learned, had been base for Herman Goering's Third German Air Force. Dahlem, this upper class area of southwest Berlin, was relatively undamaged. In this neighborhood had lived Foreign Minister Joachim von Ribbentrop and celebrities of stage and screen. Here also was the church once pastored by Martin Niemoeller.

Initially we faced some hostility from military officials vengeful toward the defeated Germans. An officer at the billeting desk reached into a drawer and flung on the table before us a couple dozen photographs of horrible scenes from a concentration camp he had liberated. He lashed out: "You are coming to help people who did that?" The Allies had set out to impose a hard peace by reducing Germany to a "pastoral state"–some calling it a "Goat Pasture Policy." At the Potsdam Conference in June 1945 the victors stripped Germany of its breadbaskets to the east: Pomerania, Silesia, and West and East Prussia. Germany was split into four zones, each occupied by one of the four victorious powers: the United States, Great Britain, Soviet Union, and France. Allies gave orders to strip factories of equipment for reparations pledged to the Soviet Union. The Allies also gave orders to expel German-speaking peoples from Eastern Europe and to ship them to this truncated Germany.

A starving Germany could embarrass the occupiers. Surveying the wasteland of defeated Germany, General Dwight D. Eisenhower, Supreme Commander of the Allied Forces, observed:

"Germany is destroyed.... They face a problem of real starvation." He then asked a haunting question: "What are we going to do just to prevent on our part having a Buchenwald of our own?" In that context of concern, CRALOG had been authorized.

In Berlin five more CRALOG representatives arrived to make ours a team of eight. In seeking to secure a working agreement with OMGUS, we soon were at odds with officials who wished to subordinate us to military authority, even to require us to wear uniforms. The head of the Welfare Branch insisted on such phrases as "representatives of" or "instruments of" or "on the staff of Military Government." Although the Catholics and Lutherans had no problems with OMGUS wording, the two Quakers, the Mennonite and the socialist from IRC balked. After three weeks of courteous but tenacious negotiating, a Major General from General Lucius Clay's staff appeared and yielded without qualification to our insistence of independent civilian status for the CRALOG team. I felt a bit sorry for the Welfare Branch colonel, who, like a good soldier, had thought he was defending correct military protocol. Really, however, we were completely dependent on the military for food, housing, gasoline, air and train travel, telephone and cable service. This was a military occupation.

During that month of negotiation in Berlin we traveled to Stuttgart to meet German relief agencies–Catholic *Caritas Verband*, Protestant *Evangelisches Hilfswerk*, German Red Cross, and labor's *Arbeiter Wohlfahrt*–to organize working relationships. In Bremerhaven we arranged for warehousing and port services–the first shipment expected in a few days. Dividing among us our responsibilities, I was assigned Land Greater Hesse that included the cities of Frankfurt, Wiesbaden and Kassel. Late in April the first CRALOG shipment arrived in Bremerhaven–the entire 424 tons of MCC origin, 4,745 cases of canned goods, 601 bales of clothing, 5,601 bags of flour. Among all the CRALOG partners, MCC came through first and with a big shipment. Immediately I sensed a rise in respect for MCC from German relief agencies and my CRALOG colleagues. In Germany food was power.

Back in Berlin we seized every opportunity to inspect the devastation in the center of the city. On street corners we saw stakes marking where Soviet soldiers had been killed in the street fighting a year before. We saw a once prosperous people reduced to hunters and gatherers: a *Tauschbaum* (exchange tree) where Germans offered heirlooms for food, sought lost family members; gaunt men pawing through the garbage cans at military residences; children following officers to snatch discarded cigarette butts; women trudging with sacks of firewood scavenged from woodland beyond the city limits; men in a city park grubbing out stumps for firewood; scarred, rusted streetcars packed with people.

*After my first trip into the center of Berlin I recorded the following:*

Ninety-five percent of downtown Berlin destroyed: government buildings, palaces, department stores, hotels, galleries. Walls still standing but no more than crumbling shells filled with rubble of bricks, plaster, plumbing, roofing. With a gust of wind, the air is filled with dust. A gray, brooding, overcast feeling pervades the scene. The rebuilding of Berlin will be a colossal, hopeless task. It will require a generation to rebuild. They say some German cities are more badly destroyed than Berlin. I wonder whether it would not be best to leave Berlin as it is–serving for later generations as a grim reminder of man's tragic stupidity, ruthlessness and inhumanity.

On the Potsdamer Platz, not far from Brandenburg Gate, I looked at a menu card posted on a door: potato bread and barley soup for 2 marks.... On the Potsdamer Platz we entered the strangest, most fantastic market in the world. Here and there were G.I.s selling cigarettes. Perhaps 20 Germans and Russians were gathered around a G.I. bidding on a pack of cigarettes. One pack sold for 180 marks. At the pegged rate of exchange of 10 cents a mark, that pack sold for $18.00. At the PX the G.I. paid five cents or a half mark for that pack. Cigarettes have almost displaced marks as legal tender. A man offered me a set of 15 beautiful postcard size pictures of prewar Berlin for one cigarette. The black market quotation on marks is a couple hundred to the dollar. The biggest buyers on Potsdamer Platz are Russian soldiers. They lug suitcases filled with stacks of marks. They especially like watches, particularly those with black faces. Several approached me to buy my camera.

*The following day we returned to the center of the city:*

The once wooded park, the Tiergarten, is a barren wasteland, here and there among the stumps patches of vegetable garden. On the side of the park near what was the headquarters of the Wehrmacht High Command is a gigantic concrete air-raid bunker that had a capacity for 20,000. A year ago on these very streets the disintegrating German army fought a fierce last ditch battle against invading Russian troops.

Beyond Brandenburg Gate extends the mile-long Unter den Linden, now denuded of trees. To the left is the burned out shell of the Reichstag and across the street the Air Ministry of Herman

Goering. To the right on Wilhelm Strasse is Hitler's residence, the Reichs Chancellery, now gutted. Facing a rubble-strewn plaza is the balcony where Hitler spoke to his admirers. Next door are the ruins of Paul Joseph Goebbels' Ministry of Public Enlightenment and Propaganda. In the garden of the Chancellery two Russian soldiers guarding the entrance to Hitler's bunker permitted us to enter when we told them we were Americans. We descended a flight of stairs and entered a maze of subterranean rooms, blackened walls, all chill and damp. Here Hitler and his mistress Eva Braun lived their last days and here he committed suicide. Scary, forbidding.

*We met Germans who told their stories*:

A son tells of how his father, an anti-Nazi, was beaten to death by the Nazis in 1942. His mother suffered nervous shock that left her partially paralyzed. He was imprisoned in 1943.

On the subway we met a woman of about 35 who held on her lap a boy of eight and at her feet a rusty buck saw and two sacks of twigs and branches she had gathered on the outskirts of the city. Asked how things were going, she said, "too much food to die and not enough to live."

At the opera in the Russian sector of the city where we heard Verdi's "Rigoletto," a girl of about 20 told us that with the approach of the Russian troops her mother had taken her out of the city to a village and there hid her from the pillaging, raping invaders. On the subway we encountered a drunken Russian soldier. It was evident that all in the subway car were mortally afraid of him.

We talked with a young mother of two who is a scrub woman in our office, her husband a prisoner of war in Holland. She works at OMGUS from five in the evening to three in the morning, her children left alone at home and hopefully sleeping from seven to three. The one meal she receives from OMGUS at midnight she takes home with her for her children. She spoke of the killing she has seen, adding that only now she is gradually becoming a human being again. We gave her two oranges to take home to her children. (In my notes I recorded my distress that as these persons tell their tales of cruelty–and my heart goes out to them–they seem not to be aware that in other lands are many peoples who also have suffered grievously, but at the hands of Nazi armies.)

I met a man who, to my surprise, acknowledged that he had worked in Goebbel's Ministry of Propaganda. The last time he saw Goebbels, he said, was April 19, 1945, about ten days before his suicide. He spoke of the cruelty of the Russians. I said, "Perhaps the

Russians are so cruel because they suffered so much from the Nazis." He responded with, "Perhaps."

Several times during that month of April 1946 I reflected in my notes on how Berlin offered the raw stuff for a great novel: memories of the recent street by street fighting, plundering, "Rape of Berlin;" jockeying for position of the four victorious powers–each with their sector of the city; the bleak wasteland; the bureaucratic confusion; a despairing, defeated people; the pervading fear of the Russians; spies and counter spies; refugees from the Soviet zone slipping into the city–an island of relative security; and the little glimpses of hope. In the background was the voice of Winston Churchill with his ominous warning of an Iron Curtain dividing Europe from Stettin on the Baltic to Trieste on the Adriatic–a line of hostility right through the heart of Berlin. Oh, for a Tolstoy to tell this story.

Early April 1946–MCC's biggest relief effort in history was about to begin.

I came to Germany to coordinate MCC relief work. Although C. F. Klassen had been in Berlin earlier, MCC had given me no Mennonite addresses, no leads to contact. Nonetheless, I felt an elemental need to find Mennonite refugees who must be out there in that war ravaged city. That is another story–the most intense two weeks in all my years of MCC service.

# 1946: Mennonite Refugees Hiding in Berlin

*Serialized in* Mennonite Weekly Review, *June 1996, an article based on letters and notes from Kreider's experience as Director of MCC's relief program in West Germany, 1946-48.*

I knew there were Mennonite refugees somewhere hiding in Berlin. After a series of efforts I was told that a group of refugees could be found in the apartment of J. J. Kroeker. He lived on Viktoria Luise Platz, a badly damaged area not far from the Tiergarten. I hastened there. Rubble lay in the streets. Windows of apartment buildings, shattered by the bombing, were boarded over. Stove pipes protruded from some windows. I did not have the precise address. I ventured into several buildings. I met a boy and asked for his help. He led me to one of the battered buildings, up a flight of stairs and down a dark hallway. Following is my description of that visit on the late afternoon of Wednesday, April 10, 1946:

> I heard voices. I could see light above the door. But when I knocked, the light was put out. Voices stopped. The boy whispered: *"Fluechtlinge"* (refugees). Repeated knocking but no response. He took me down to the *Hausfrau*, the woman caretaker, who accompanied me back to the apartment. She carried a tiny candle to light our way down the dingy, dark hall. The hall exuded gloom: creaky stairs, a damp chill, dark, a musty odor, a tattered elegance of the past. It felt ominous: an atmosphere of dread and lurking danger.
>
> The *Hausfrau* knocked loudly on the door and shouted that an American visitor had come. The door opened a crack and an elderly woman peeked out. She said that Mr. Kroeker was not there and closed the door. The *Hausfrau* knocked again. I added, *"Ich bin Mennonit."* The woman opened the door wide. I stepped into the darkness and saw about me a dozen people, mostly women and children. Before the *Hausfrau* excused herself, she asked whether I could get these people some food because they had no ration cards and they were hungry. Soon I was telling them who I was, where I came from, what I was doing in Germany. Their caution melted away. To them I was a cousin from across the seas. A profound experience–my baptism as an MCC worker.

C. F. Klassen of the Mennonite Central Committee Executive Committee, who visited Berlin briefly in December 1945, had found a group of Mennonite refugees from Russia in the city. MCC, however, had given me no addresses or leads to pursue in searching for the refugees. I had come to Berlin, March 28, 1946, but for a different MCC assignment. My job was relief work under the umbrella of the Council of Relief Agencies Licensed for Operation in Germany (CRALOG). In a few days I would be leaving Berlin to go to my post in Wiesbaden, Although concern for refugees was not my assignment, I had a compelling inner urge to find those refugees. My time in Berlin, however, was running out.

Coming to Europe I had brought with me several addresses found in a 1938 German Mennonite yearbook. One was Heinrich van Duehren, lawyer and deacon of the Berlin congregation. Within a few days of my arrival in Berlin, I set out to find him. I found the Duehren residence in Dahlem, but on the streets in front were parked army jeeps. This was obviously property requisitioned by U.S. military. A U.S. officer told me that Germans were living across the street in a basement. I knocked on a window and a young woman appeared, the daughter of van Duehren. She reported her father had died. She told me that a Mennonite congregation met once a month and the lay pastor was Erich Schultz, an architect. She gave me his address. After four or five unsuccessful attempts, I found him at home. He greeted me as a long lost son. We talked late into the evening. Yes, he knew of a group of refugees housed with a J. J. Kroeker on Viktoria Luise Platz. No, he had not visited them. That troubled me as pastoral neglect.

Then followed the most intense two weeks of activity in all of my MCC service in Germany. On top of the relief assignment, I felt called to assert myself as a kind of MCC commissioner for refugees. On the day following my visit with lay pastor Schultz, I went to Viktoria Luise Platz. In a mixture of past and present tense, I pick up the story day by day. Here I make use of my files of letters and memoranda from those distant times.

*Wednesday, April 10, 1946.* After an hour with the refugees, J. J. Kroeker arrived, a character out of a book of fiction: a refugee from Russia some 25 years ago, who in the 1930s lived in Newton, Kansas, left his family in 1939 to return to Nazi Germany to do research for the *Auslands Institute,* a broken, alcoholic, disheveled figure, a man of multiple imperfections. And yet this battered, faltering person had gathered and offered a refuge for more than 200 Mennonite refugees who had slipped into Berlin from the surrounding Russian Zone. I thought of the wonder of God's ways–how he makes use of all kinds of persons his purposes to perform.

*Thursday, April 11.* I returned to the Kroeker refuge. I brought with me every item of food and clothing I could spare. Kroeker told of how he traded with Russian soldiers three cartons of cigarettes for 3,200 marks, enough to buy 100 pounds of bread. This time I had a better opportunity to inspect the rooms: bare but clean, clothing on neatly stacked piles, in the middle of each room an improvised brick stove with a stove pipe to the nearest window, waste paper used for fuel. In these rooms lived 23 refugees.

Kroeker told me how they arrived illegally in Berlin from the Russian Zone, each carrying a few possessions on his or her back He estimated that five to six thousand Russian Mennonites from the Soviet Zone had been forcibly returned to Russia. He thought not more than 1,200 Mennonite refugees were still in hiding in the Russian Zone. He showed me the rubber stamp he imprints on little slips of paper which are distributed to the scattered refugees:

Menno-Centre
Prov. Representation of the
Mennonite Central Committee
J. J. Kroeker, Manager

The amazing thing is that rail officials permit the refugees to come to Berlin on the presentation of this phony, unauthorized slip of paper. He acknowledged that U.S. security had imprisoned him recently for two days and has been keeping him under surveillance.

Kroeker told me that their protector was a Major Thompson in charge of Displaced Persons in the American Sector of Berlin. Through his efforts in March 211 refugees had been transferred from Viktoria Luise Platz to an UNRRA Camp in Zehlendorf in the American Sector of the city.

*Friday, April 12.* I headed for the Telefunken Building to see Major Thompson. When I entered his office he leaped out of his chair and greeted me enthusiastically, "You have the lost combination to my safe. I have been waiting for a Mennonite to unlock this case." He told me that he comes from Allentown, Pennsylvania, has Mennonites as neighbors, speaks Pennsylvania Dutch, visited Paraguay for the State Department, knows the Mennonites in the Chaco. A hearty, loud-voiced, self-confident man, he declared, "If I had my way, I would charter a half dozen transport planes, fill them up some night with all these Mennonite refugees and take them to safety in the American Zone."

He explained how the American authorities have been under terrific pressure from their Russian allies to turn over the 211 Mennonites in the UNRRA camp. He said that both he and his superior, Major Barker, Commander of the Berlin Military District, are much concerned that they be kept out of Russian hands, to use his phrase, "saved from extermination." He said that he had given the Russians the deadline of April 15 to register a written claim to the Mennonites. He was betting that the Russians would not dare to go public with such a request. Major Thompson said U. S. authorities desperately needed immediate assurance that some country would accept these people as immigrants. I gave him a copy of a letter of March 20 from Orie Miller, MCC Executive Secretary in Akron, PA, to Sam Goering, MCC European Director in Basel, Switzerland, outlining MCC commitments to aiding Mennonite refugees. With the letter was a copy of the 1921 Paraguayan Privilegium offering immigration privileges to Mennonites. That night and the following day I sought without success to reach by phone Sam Goering in Basel, Switzerland, and Howard Yoder, MCC Director in England.

*Saturday, April 13.* I spent the day writing letters to MCC officials in Basel, London and Akron and dispatched a cable to Orie Miller in Akron, asking for a response on Paraguay and Canada.

*Sunday. April 14.* Early in the morning we flew from Tempelhof to Frankfurt for a CRALOG-German relief agency conference in Stuttgart. I felt guilty leaving Berlin with the refugees in threatened status–so many loose ends. I had hoped to meet Sam Goering in Stuttgart to get instructions, but no luck. Dr. Eugene Gerstenmeier of *Evangelisches Hilfswerk* in Stuttgart offered to help the refugees in Berlin but *Hilfswerk* had little to share. I contacted an International Relief and Rescue Committee representative in Frankfurt who offered to help process Mennonite refugees in the American Zone for immigration.

*Friday, April 19.* Back in Berlin, I returned to Viktoria Luise Platz to find that now, instead of 23 refugees, 95 were crowded into Kroeker's apartment. They have no ration cards because they are in the city illegally. A few months ago they could barter clothing and possessions for food, but now at the end of the winter there is so little with which to barter. The words of the Lord's Prayer leap out, "Give us this day, our daily bread." I had brought a rucksack full of food items purchased at the PX–so little, just "five loaves and two fish." Kroeker introduced me to Abraham Fast, a recent arrival from Mecklenburg. When Kroeker was out of the room, he whispered to me that Kroeker was not to be fully trusted. (Later Fast expressed his displeasure with me. He thought I, an American, could work quick miracles.)

As I left the refugees I felt a drag of discouragement–the problems so complex and I so helpless. But when I returned to the office a cable from Orie Miller in Akron was waiting:

PARAGUAY CONFIRMED READINESS RECEIVE ANY ALL EUROPEAN MENNONITE SETTLEMENT ANY PART PARAGUAY ALL PRIVILEGES EXEMPTIONS 1921 PRIVILEGIUM APPLYING.... KLASSEN ADVISES NO OFFICIAL ASSURANCE CANADA POSSIBLE NOW BUT UNOFFICIAL WORD THAT NEAR RELATIVE WILL GET CONSIDERATION SOON.

My spirits soared. I called Major Thompson to report the good news. I phoned Peter Dyck, MCC director in Amsterdam, whom I knew was in close touch with the refugee situation. He reported that 450 Mennonite refugees had come into Holland with about 600 congregated along the Dutch border in the British Zone.

*Saturday, April 20.* Knowing I would be leaving Berlin in a few days, I took Claude Shotts, chief of mission for CRALOG in Berlin, with me to see Major Thompson. Shotts, a Quaker, could be my conduit to American officials once I was far away in Wiesbaden. Thompson reported that he had won his gamble with the Russians. They had not filed a claim by the April 15 deadline. I gave him a copy of Orie Miller's cable. This, he said, met his first need. Second, he explained he hoped he could get the Mennonite refugees to be declared as "stateless" so that they could be handled as Displaced Persons. Third, he asked that we procure for him in writing a copy of the current Paraguay immigration offer and a statement from MCC that it would assume full financial responsibility for the transportation of the Mennonites to Paraguay. Thereby the refugees' transit status in Berlin could be established and protected. Thompson said that he would be ready to fly to Amsterdam to pick up the Paraguay statement. I suggested to Thompson that a tent camp be established for the Mennonite refugees continuing to arrive in Berlin. Maybe a good idea but he stated that was beyond his authority.

In the afternoon I visited the 211 refugees at the Zehlendorf UNRRA camp. I brought with me a CRALOG colleague who spoke fluent German. We met with the committee of four whom Pastor Hylkema of Holland had appointed in a visit several months before: Jacob Loewen, John Janzen, Peter Huebner and Wilhelm Diester. They wanted to know about Paraguay. I told them about the crops and the problems they would confront in a primitive setting. They all said with enthusiasm that they were ready to face the challenges of pioneering in Paraguay. People crowded around us in that small room. In a letter I wrote: "From them, like a dozen mountains streams, gushed their stories–violence, collectivization, banishment, murder, starvation." I observed evidence of a faith that had survived 25 years of oppression and even threads of a commitment to nonresistance. In my notes I reflected: "These are the kind of people we want to build the new postwar world." As I left them, they spoke appreciatively of the simple, crowded UNRRA camp–"never in our life more comfortable."

*Sunday, April 21.* That weekend I wrote letters to MCC in London, Basel, Amsterdam and Akron. Kroeker called to report that at 1:30 that morning a truckload of 13 refugees had arrived from Saxony with a steep fee demanded by the driver. Now there were 108 in Kroeker's apartment. I finally reached by phone Howard Yoder in London. He said that if I could secure permission from the U.S. authorities, he thinks that MCC could send someone to Berlin. Despite this ray of hope, I felt the gravity of the refugee plight in Berlin. I recorded these thoughts: "I am led to believe that only a miracle of God can save these people. No problem I have ever confronted is so hopelessly complex–and then tomorrow evening I must leave for Wiesbaden, the job here unfinished. The need of the refugees casts a shadow over my whole spirit."

*Monday, April 22.* After breakfast I procured a jeep from the army car pool to take me to the Friends Ambulance Unit (Quaker) in Spandau in the British Sector. I met with Neville Coates, head of the FAU unit. He knew of the plight of the Viktoria Luise refugees, adding that they had wondered whether Kroeker was "saint or racketeer" but were inclined to believe he was a "tarnished saint." They offered transportation to bring in food concentrates for the Berlin refugees if we could get supplies to their British Zone base at Vlotho. I phoned Peter Dyck to see whether MCC could ship food from Holland to Vlotho. I discovered there was a holiday when I sought an appointment with Major Saltonstall in the British Military Government. I turned to the Dutch Military Mission to see a Captain Waltvonpraag. There I was invited to join a group of eight having a late breakfast. Through Mennonite Pastor Hylkema they knew the Mennonite refugee problem. The captain warned me not to lean too heavily on Kroeker; he said their security men were watching him. He added that it was difficult to work with Russian officials, who, although cordial, had to check every detail with Moscow–"always Moscow, Moscow, Moscow." Dr. Wurhoof of the Dutch Red Cross, who was present, commented that there were other stranded refugee groups in peril in Berlin like the Mennonites, an example, Hungarians. He encouraged me to think that we might be able to establish an MCC supply line to Berlin via the Dutch Red Cross.

That afternoon arrived a cable from Orie Miller in Akron:

> MENNONITE CENTRAL COMMITTEE GUARANTEES FULL FINANCIAL RESPONSIBILITY FOR TRANSPORTATION AND OTHER EXPENSES ENROUTE MENNONITE MIGRATION PARAGUAY ALSO FOR ARRANGING SETTLEMENT THERE.... EXPECT YOU CONSULTATION... GOERING ARRANGE MOST ECONOMICAL PASSAGE POSSIBLE KEEPING US ADVISED.

I recorded: "...great news and strengthens my hand." A letter from Orie Miller urging that the refugee "concern be kept at the top of the... priority list." At this distant MCC outpost I sensed being affirmed. Orie Miller and the MCC were entrusting this inexperienced 27-year old with highly sensitive and crucial responsibilities. In those cables from Orie Miller I sensed a kind of "laying on of hands." However, viewed pragmatically, did MCC have any other choice?

That Monday afternoon I attended a service of the Berlin Mennonite congregation, 130 meeting in a Lutheran chapel, Mr. Schultz reading a sermon on the theme, "Not my will but thine be done." Although much of the message eluded me, given the status of my German, it was just what I needed. Many, including some refugees, crowded around after the service "to hear the good word from America." In my notes I reflected, "It's difficult to walk the fence of giving hope and assuring them of our efforts and yet cautioning them that the picture is still dark and not to expect too much."

*Tuesday, April 23.* I called Major General Barker's office for an appointment. He replied that he would be happy to see me at ten. As Commanding General at the Berlin District he is next in line to General Lucius B. Clay. Major Thompson has kept him informed of the Mennonite refugee situation. I sensed immediately his pro-Mennonite attitude. I reported on the invitation from Paraguay and showed him Orie Miller's cable promising full financial coverage by MCC of ocean transportation and resettlement for the refugees. He responded: "Now we must act quickly. Three things are required. First, the financial commitment which we have. Second, a copy of an official document of invitation from Paraguay. Third, a promise of shipping space on a particular ship at a particular port on a particular date." I broached the idea of establishing a tent camp for the growing Mennonite refugee community, but that did not appeal to him. Knowing I was leaving the city the following morning, I asked for authorization for an MCC person to come to Berlin to oversee the refugee task. He was reluctant to approve "an unattached man coming to Berlin to float around." However, he was open to the transfer of an MCC worker under UNRRA in Italy being transferred to Berlin. He would agree to Sam Goering, MCC's European Director, to come for a week. Although I was elated leaving the General's office, I learned he would soon be leaving his post. I immediately cabled Orie Miller in Akron, PA:

> WILL YOU CHECK POSSIBILITIES FOR TRANSPORTING 200 REFUGEES FROM NORTH EUROPEAN PORT PREFERABLY LE HAVRE OR BREMEN TO PARAGUAY PERHAPS ARGENTINE SHIPS AVAILABLE FOR MAY AND JUNE SAILINGS HOWARD YODER CHECKING TRANSPORTATION POSSIBILITIES FROM THIS SIDE.

Tuesday after lunch I had an appointment with Major Thompson, who was delighted to read the cables to and from Akron and eager to receive a report on my meeting with General Barker. With the major was Lt. Col. Stinson, who on May 7 replaces Thompson, who departs on a 45-day leave. I felt sorry for the colonel who had so much to learn about the complexities of Berlin. I recorded, "Stinson will not be the fighter that Thompson is." (I assessed him incorrectly: perhaps not a fighter, but he turned out to be solidly supportive of the interests of the refugees.)

I reported to Thompson the information from Kroeker that the German housing authority in Berlin had given him until April 25 to evacuate his apartment. Hearing that, he blazed with anger, grabbed the phone, called the housing head, and lashed him unmercifully. "Nonresistant person that I am," I commented in my notes, "I trembled at the violent repercussions to the report I had relayed."

I returned from the conference feeling that "the battle seemed won–at least the first skirmish." But I had a throbbing headache. That evening I worked late typing reports on the events of the ten days past. I phoned Howard Yoder in London, who would begin the following day to seek a ship for ocean transport. I called Peter Dyck, asking him to procure the Paraguayan document from the Paraguayan Consul General in Amsterdam. Finally, I got through to Sam Goering in Basel, who said the next weekend he would bring a jeep to me in Wiesbaden. Further, he would be prepared to go on to Berlin to follow through on the work I was leaving unfinished.

In a memo probably of this date to Peter Dyck, I write among other things:

"In the UNRRA camp all are ready to go to Paraguay if the way looks difficult to Canada. I hope that we record on paper the problems they will confront in Paraguay, the general situation they will encounter–so that they will be braced psychologically when and if they arrive. No matter how candid we are verbally, I fear that when they arrive they might say, 'Why didn't someone tell us these would be the problems.'"

*Wednesday, April 24.* Following breakfast I met Kroeker at a subway stop near Niemoeller's church. Seated on a street bench I related to him the developments of the last several days. As in the past, I gave him no copies of documents. He reported that he had prepared a list of the names of all refugees at Viktoria Luise Platz and at the UNRRA camp, together with the names and addresses of their closest relatives in Canada. He reported that Protestant Innere Mission had approached him to be their agent in bribing Russian officers to permit the Mission to bring food into the city for its welfare programs. This, another glimpse into this weird city of clandestine activities. I thought that Kroeker could model a character to be included in that Tolstoyan epic novel on the fall of Berlin. I phoned Major Thompson to report my Tuesday evening phone calls with Yoder, Goering and Dyck. And then to Tempelhof airport and the flight to Frankfurt and my CRALOG assignment in Wiesbaden.

*Thursday, April 25.* Now in Wiesbaden, 30 miles from Frankfurt, I worked on CRALOG relief tasks by day and on the loose ends of the Berlin refugee problem at night. I wrote to Miller, Goering and Yoder, "Now I can move to the sidelines.... I have no illusions that the Berlin problem is solved. Hundreds of Mennonites in the Russian zone may never reach safety. Only the wondrous and unseen hand of God can rescue these people."

*Thursday, May 2.* Sam Goering and son Robert arrived with a jeep for my use. Then two days of repeated phone calls to Berlin and scurrying from office to office to get travel orders for Sam to go to Berlin. The final hurdle was to find a typewriter with a Russian keyboard and a person who could type a travel order in Russian. On his departure Saturday, May 4, I gave Sam a two-page letter outlining persons to see, addresses and telephone numbers in Berlin.

*Saturday. May 11.* Sam Goering returned from Berlin reporting that our friends, Major Thompson and General Barker, had returned to the States. Their replacements, Lt. Col. Stinson and Major General Keeting, promised to carry out their predecessors' policies. The best news was that he arranged that "transit ration cards" would be issued to the Viktoria Luise Platz refugees. He found the Kroeker-Fast leadership "the kind that neither can one get along with nor get along without." To my great disappointment, he had neglected to arrange for another MCC worker to come to Berlin to continue the search for solutions. It meant that I needed to start over again with letters and phone calls to Berlin.

In the afternoon we drove to Karlsruhe to see Benjamin Unruh, whom I had visited eight years before on a cycling trip in prewar Europe. I remembered from 1938 his glowing words of praise for Nazism and Hitler ("a simple country boy like Menno Simons"). Unruh, renowned leader in the Mennonite migration from Russia in the 1920s, was as eloquent and flamboyant as ever. Soon after our arrival he voiced his displeasure with efforts to identify the Mennonite refugees from Russia as stateless or of Dutch ancestry. He declared, "They are *Reichsdeutsch* and always have been." He did not hide his interest in securing some MCC portfolio, but his political record is too spotty for MCC to use his services officially.

*Monday. May 13.* Howard Yoder in London and Peter Dyck in Amsterdam had been looking for an Argentina-bound ship for the Berlin refugees. Good news: Peter phoned to report that space for 110 persons was available on the S.S. *Esperanzo*, a Spanish ship leaving Barcelona, Spain, bound in late June for Uruguay and Argentina. I immediately phoned Lt. Col. Stinson, Major Thompson's replacement, in Berlin, and followed up with a letter.

In the afternoon Willis Weatherford of the Quakers called from Berlin to report that Col. Stinson was ready to open a camp for Mennonite refugees in Berlin if a source of food can be secured. He confirmed that he accepted the Friends Ambulance Unit supply line from Amsterdam.

*Friday, May 17.* At an MCC leaders' conference in Basel I met for the first time Peter and Elfrieda Dyck. I described Peter as one who "has confidence, and is very creative. He looks like one of the top [MCC] workers we have in the game." I added, "I would welcome at times his aggressiveness." P. C. Hiebert, MCC chairman, and his wife had just arrived from the States. At this conference it was understood that Peter would visit Berlin.

*Monday. May 20.* In a letter to Peter I reported that Lt. Col. Stinson has authorized his coming to Berlin on a temporary permit. I outlined the detailed steps required to secure a permit in Paris, a process that may require four weeks. I added that Stinson has approved a supply line for the shipment of three to five tons of food a week from Holland to Berlin and that by Thursday a permit will be in the hands of Dr. Wurhoof of the Dutch Red Cross. My Quaker friend, Claude Shotts, is to be the courier. In a phone call to Irvin Horst, the new MCC director in Holland, he reported that the food is ready to ship.

*Tuesday, May 21.* In a letter to Lt. Col. Stinson I reviewed our mutual understandings and fabricated a title for Peter: "the newly appointed 'Refugee Commissioner in Europe for the Mennonite Central Committee.'"

*Tuesday, June 4.* In a two-page letter to Peter I outlined the names of persons to contact, addresses and telephone numbers for his arrival in Berlin June 13. I concluded with these words: "You are now confronting one of the most difficult of MCC assignments. May His Spirit sustain you and grant you wisdom in this mission."

Then follows the dramatic story of the Berlin exodus that Peter and Elfrieda Dyck have told in the book *Up from the Rubble*. With Peter and Elfrieda's coming to Berlin I breathed a sigh of relief and uttered a prayer of thanksgiving.

As I, now fifty years later, review these events, I think of all the persons, who at critical moments–in small and large ways, aware and unaware–appeared in an unfolding drama that suggests the workings of providence: C. F. Klassen, a young woman in a basement apartment, Erich Schultz, a boy on the street, a *Hausfrau*, J. J. Kroeker, Major Thompson, Major General Barker, Lt. Col. Stinson, Major General Keeting, Claude Shotts, Willis Weatherford, Neville Coates, Dr. Wurhoof, Capt. Waltvonpraag, Sam Goering, Howard Yoder, Orie Miller, Peter and Elfrieda Dyck, Irvin Horst, Siegfried and Margaret Janzen, and so many more. The mystery of God's ways are past all understanding.

*Robert Kreider visiting school in Hesse, Germany, summer of 1946, site of CRALOG child feeding program.*

# 1946: The People Have a Gnawing Hunger

*Written when Kreider, representing the Mennonite Central Committee and the Council of Relief Agencies Licensed for Operation in Germany (CRALOG), was stationed in Wiesbaden, Germany.* Printed in War Sufferers' Relief Bulletin, *December 1946.*

"...that bread should be so dear, and flesh and blood so cheap!"
–Thomas Hood.

I see a ragged lad steal from an open truck a large cabbage. A father sends his children onto the streets to pick up cigarette butts–these to be exchanged for turnips. A maiden sells her virtue for a bar of chocolate. They who dwell in cities live in a wasteland of wreckage. Hopelessness and apathy chain down their spirits. In this Germany of 1946 no problem of life looms larger than the aching, seeking, all-consuming quest for daily bread and shelter. And even now that war has long since ended on European soil, life is cruelly cheap.

Eleven and four-tenths per cent of all babies born in this province of Greater Hesse die at birth or soon thereafter. The city of Hanau reports that the mortality rate for persons over seventy years of age is now twenty-six per cent, an increase from eleven per cent in prewar years. In Kassel nearly 1,000 children show signs of rickets. The Medical Director of Province Greater Hesse states: "In school the malnutrition leads the children to fatigue quickly. The teachers complain that pupils lose their ability to concentrate even with short lessons.... Anemia has made a sharp increase.... Also startling are the highly nervous children."

Adding to the plight of the land is the influx of thousands of refugees expelled from the East. There are now more hungry mouths at the table. With the bomb damage, the return of prisoners of war, the arrival of refugees–the housing situation is alarming. An average of 1.63 persons are housed in each habitable room in Hesse. In the city of Kassel the population density is four persons per room.

This is the Germany of 1946 to whose needs our Mennonite Central Committee now seeks to minister. Our churches have given liberally, with the result that the MCC is one of the major relief contributors to Germany. In the American Zone our contributions have flowed to *Evangelisches Hilfswerk*, the relief agency of the German Protestant Church. To illustrate the operation of this program, let us trace the journey of twenty tons of white flour given by a community in Kansas. The flour is shipped to New York City where it is loaded on a ship, the S/S "American Farmer." Twelve days later the ship arrives in bomb-ravaged Bremen, the

U.S. port of entry for Germany. The flour is unloaded and stored temporarily in the CRALOG warehouse at Bremen. Several days later the sacks of flour are loaded into small European freight cars. The shipment moves by rail south across the British Zone to Frankfurt. In Frankfurt the twenty tons are received into an *Evangelisches Hilfswerk* warehouse. The warehouse is a huge, thick-walled concrete structure–a wartime air raid bunker. The shipment is allocated among three subdistricts–ten tons going to District Wiesbaden where the Mennonite flour is stored inside an old chapel.

A capable, highly-dedicated staff of workers gives direction to the relief work in Wiesbaden. They have surveyed the field of need in their district and have decided that the limited relief supplies at their disposal will be sent especially to certain areas: bombed-out cities, regions where agriculture is unproductive, industrial regions where there is no farming or gardening, regions with high tuberculosis rates, and large cities where the rate of child malnutrition is high.

Except in rural districts, hunger is universal. To whom, then, shall this flour be distributed? The Wiesbaden office of *Evangelisches Hilfswerk* has instructed their co-workers in the field to give preferential consideration for the needs of the following: the acutely ill, those recuperating from serious illness, pregnant mothers, undernourished children whose health is endangered, tubercular patients, and ill or undernourished babies.

*Evangelisches Hilfswerk* has committees established in each community charged with the responsibility of distributing equitably relief supplies. The local committee is composed of five members: the pastor of the parish, a representative of the church council, a representative of the refugees, a physically handicapped person, and the community nurse (responsible for the whole welfare work).

The work of this committee is not easy. They must investigate need, especially of the "modest poor" who are reluctant to request aid. Representatives of the committee are directed to make a home visit before giving any individual assistance. Thrust upon the committee are those agonizing decisions as to who is to receive this lifesaving aid. Frau Bolz of the Wiesbaden office of *Evangelisches Hilfswerk* gives this illustration: "The Deanery of Herborn has received nineteen sacks of flour. With these nineteen sacks we have to help 34,227 persons in the area. This is impossible. Therefore, we have to select only those cases where the need is most urgent. The community, for example, must assist one hundred children of severely endangered health condition. But living in the same community are fifty old people who are sick and who are in danger of starvation without additional food. Who should receive the first help?"

It may be that *Evangelisches Hilfswerk* chose to distribute our twenty tons of Kansas flour, not through the local community committees, but directly to the joint child-feeding program of Greater Hesse. This is a co-operative enterprise in which all German relief agencies share in the feeding of 72,000 school children in eight cities. Our twenty tons of white flour will provide for 20,000 school children a large, nourishing 100-gram (238-calorie) roll or *brotchen* three times a week for a full month. The children tell us with delight that in all the school feeding the *brotchen* they like best—"It is better than cake!"

Daily come thank-you letters from the grateful recipients of our gifts. We quote from only a few letters:

•Our heartfelt thanks for the help which comes of Christian mutual love. These love-gifts lend us new confidence and strengthen our faith that the spirit of Christ's love transcends human passions and the will for reprisal.

•Mrs. F. is alone with her children. The husband and father is a prisoner of war in Stalingrad. All the years long she never lost courage. By a mistake of the authorities she received one ration-card more than to which she was entitled. The temptation to keep the card was great. But the mother succeeded in convincing the children of the wrong in keeping the card. Soon after the ration-card had been returned to the food office, the flour contribution arrived.

•The returnee had tears in his eyes. He said: "You cannot know how much good this love does, especially if one has been pushed around for two years and has felt like a bad defendant who has no right to lead a human life. That my family would receive me with love, I expected. But that I should receive relief supplies from the former enemy-country, I feel humbled."

*Robert and Lois, Berlin, Germany, 1947.*

# 1955: The Chains of Conscription

*A statement of concern to the Committee on Armed Services of the United States Senate on H.R. 3005 and H.R. 6057 amending the Universal Military Service and Training Act, presented at a public hearing, June 9, 1955, at Washington D. C. on behalf of the Mennonite Central Committee.*

I am Robert Kreider, Dean of Bluffton College, Bluffton, Ohio, and a member of the Mennonite Central Committee, a relief and service agency representing the Mennonite and affiliated churches of the United States who number over 140,000 baptized members. I speak in behalf of these churches, who through four centuries have declined to participate in military service and who in discipleship to Christ have labored for the peaceful resolvement of personal and inter-group conflicts. Since 1683, when the first Mennonites settled in Pennsylvania, our people have sought and found in America opportunity to serve God and man free of the inhibiting chains of conscription, militarism, and political absolutism.

I appear before you to record our opposition to the extension of the draft act. We would not minimize the dangers our nation faces in a tense world community. We are sensitive to the perplexing problems which confront you who share responsibility for the safety and security of our land. Out of our varied experiences as a people we are led to question, however, whether mass conscript forces give us that security for which we long. The peril of conscription in this age of atomic warfare may be that it gives a fictitious sense of national security. We believe that conscription itself contributes to the tensions which disrupt the peace of the world.

In our time universal military conscription appears to have become an integral feature in every major military program and essential to the successful prosecution of any broad military operation. Military conscription diverts men from peaceful and productive callings–from raising crops, manufacturing clothing, building houses, teaching children, healing the sick. To us it seems a tragedy that these years of creative energy for millions of young men in this and other lands are dissipated in the anti-social arts of war.

At this moment in world history when there is promise of a relaxation of international fears and animosities, it would seem that our nation is called to assume a decisive role in moral leadership. We have witnessed with satisfaction the efforts of the President and the Congress to halt the drift toward war and to seek reconciliation between the world's antagonists. We have been grateful for the

President's far-sighted proposals for the international control and inspection of nuclear production and the sharing of atomic energy among nations for peacetime purposes. As a sequel to this type of testimony, we urge that before this draft be extended for another four year period this Congress together with the President appeal to the nations to renounce the method of military conscription–knowing that without mass conscript armies major wars would not likely be fought and knowing that with the abandonment of conscription millions of young men here and abroad would find their way into more creative and productive pursuits. We place upon your hearts the concern that in this moment of decision concerning the extension of the draft our nation seize the opportunity for a bold, clear call to peace to all nations caught in this sterile dialogue of answering military might with military might, conscription with conscription.

We wish to conclude our statement by expressing our gratitude that the principle of Christian conscience is respected in this legislation. We are confident that in the future in all legislative enactments the Congress will continue in this great tradition of recognizing the convictions of those, who because of the dictates of their conscience, are of the minority.

# 1962: No Caterpillars For Now, Thanks

*The last of a series of ten articles on Africa written in 1962 for* The Lima Citizen, Lima, Ohio, *mailed enroute on Kreider's ten week trip in Africa–a mission in behalf of the Mennonite Central Committee to establish the Teachers Abroad Program.*

Our French U.A.T. plane took off from Dakar, the lovely sun-drenched capital of Senegal. We skirted the western edges of the Sahara, touched down in Mauritania, and pointed north to the chill clime of northern Europe. A day in London and home. The Africa safari is ended.

A flood of impressions: two months of travel on this fabulous continent of Africa… 24,000 miles in Africa alone–mostly by air–enough to circumnavigate the globe… setting foot in 19 different countries… flying at altitudes of a mile to five miles over a dozen additional countries–countries with exotic names like Mozambique, Rio Mundi, Dahomey, Gambia… traveling on a dozen airlines, each newly independent African state renting and operating one or more airplanes–a national airline, an important status symbol.

Seeing more parts of Africa than Stanley and Livingston and Kitchener ever saw–thanks to aviation… 60 takeoffs and 60 landings–fortunately only one experience of pilferage–only two shirts snatched from my suitcase at the time of a midnight disembarkation at Brazzaville… staying in a score of different hotels–most with comfortable accommodations… putting up for the night in homes of missionaries in the bush–a hot bath in a galvanized iron tub and an outhouse of mahogany… the nightly gymnastics of crawling under a canopy of mosquito netting and searching for any hostile mosquitoes who might be lying in wait to attack… being spared those twin enemies of the white man–malaria and dysentery… no trouble with customs clearance–in two months my suitcase opened only twice for inspection.

Learning to drink tea five and six times a day in countries under British influence… eating strange and delightful foods–bean cakes, ground nut stew (peanuts to us), fried plantain, Guinea corn cereal, millet cereal, boiled cassava root, stewed goat, and–best of all–fresh fruits every meal of the day–pineapples, papaya, oranges, bananas, grapefruit, mangoes, passion fruit, guava, pomegranates, avocados—all tree ripened and often picked that morning in the garden… passing up the dubious joys of eating roasted caterpillars which were being served in one school dining hall visited.

Hearing a babel of languages: Hausa, Swahili, Ibo, Sintabale, Tanga, Chagga, Luo, Yoruba, Twi, and scores more–most of them pleasing and all incomprehensible to the ear… learning to do two things in the vernacular: (1) singing hymns with the help of hymn books with phonetic spelling and (2) gesturing in the vernacular–waving to passersby–one exception being in Northern Nigeria where the clenched fist is the sign of greeting–a bit frightening when first encountered.

There were the unforgettable sights and sounds: the lingering sunset on slopes of Mt. Kilimanjaro... the cool, lush green beauty of the highlands of Kenya... the fishermen on outrigger canoes just off sandy beaches of Zanzibar... the quiet of night in a clearing in the Congo jungle... giant granite boulders–strewn, like marbles over the Motopo Hills of Southern Rhodesia... 10,000 black butterflies fluttering to life along a Congo road... a midnight ride along a sandy road through palmnut forests, a canopy of palm fronds silhouetted against the full moon... the throbbing drums at midnight on the Calibar Coast of Nigeria.

The magnificent harbor of Freetown in Sierra Leone, the finest harbor of all Africa, the city clinging to the sides of the precipitous "Mountains of the Lion" and high on the crest of the mountain, the new university of Fourah Bay... a harvest festival in a rural village of Ghana, with two hundred villagers gathered around a multicolored mound of fresh fruits and produce, their thanksgiving gifts... the languid loping of a dozen giraffes in Tanganyika's great Serengeti game reserve... the gray blue haze of the harmattan–the dry, dust-laden winds bearing south into Nigeria from the Sahara....

There was the unexpected: six inch lizards scampering about nonchalantly on the living room walls of even the best of homes–the hostess oblivious to my initial dismay... gleaming new Texaco, Shell, Esso, Mobil filling stations all over Africa... a frozen custard drive-in on the outskirts of Bulawayo, Southern Rhodesia... a principal of a teacher training college in the bush at Eghi, Nigeria, up near the west branch of the Niger whose boyhood home was Lima–J. B. Custer... the almost universal cordiality that people feel toward Americans... the cool climate of so much of Africa....

Most significant of all were impressions of the spirit: the throbbing, insistent desire of Africans for freedom... the Africans' passion for education... the expansive dreams and plans for the future... the gaiety and friendliness of Africans... the beauty of movement of Africans bearing burdens so gracefully on their heads... the biblical sensitivity and poetic gift of African preachers....

Hemingway said Africa is like a woman. If you fall in love with her, you are hers forever.

# 1962: The Teachers Abroad Program

*Printed as a flyer for the Teachers Abroad Program, Mennonite Central Committee, first appearing in* Mennonite Life, *April 1962.*

"When we win our independence, we shall devote one-half of our national income to education." These were the words of Solomon Kululu, Chairman of the Education Committee of the United National Independence Party of Northern Rhodesia. I was conferring with this ex-schoolteacher in the shabby party headquarters in Lusaka, Northern Rhodesia. This story I heard everywhere from the new African leadership during the course of my two months of travel throughout Africa.

In five years a score of new countries have achieved their independence in Africa. These emerging nations are eager to compress a century of development into the span of a decade. Highest priority among national objectives is given to educational development. Each new country is launching a crash program for the expansion of school services, especially concentrating on secondary schools and teacher training colleges.

*Come and Help Us*

I was impressed by this hungering and thirsting after education. I saw it in the desire to roll back the level of illiteracy which in the countries of Sub-Sahara Africa ranges from 60 to 98 per cent. I saw it at a secondary school in Tanganyika which had seven hundred applications for the one hundred openings in the entering class. I saw it in the eagerness of Africans to buy literature from missionaries as we waited together on river banks for the sluggish ferryboat to come. I saw it at a middle school in Kasai Province in the Congo where dormitories were filled to capacity but the boys came and built their own thatched-roof huts to assure themselves of a place in the student body.

The new countries of Africa are desperately in need of college-trained leadership. When independence came to the Congo on June 30, 1960, only fourteen Congolese were college graduates. In the mid-fifties there were only fourteen Northern Nigerians out of a population of twenty million who held baccalaureate degrees.

Wherever I visited in Africa I heard church leaders and government officials say in effect, "Come and help us." As secondary schools and teacher training colleges double and triple their intake of students during the next several years, the need for additional teachers will be particularly urgent for the mission and church-related schools. Eighty to ninety per cent of the schools in Sub-Sahara Africa have been church-related. Church schools will need short-term teachers from overseas to supplement missionary and African teachers–this for the next five or ten years or until African teachers are available in sufficient numbers to staff the schools. This becomes a type of Macedonian call to come to help the church in its educational ministry at a critical moment in African history.

The Mennonite and Brethren in Christ mission programs in Africa, held in high regard by other mission groups, have created a receptive attitude toward the proposed Mennonite Central Committee (MCC) teacher placement program for Africa. The ministry of the MCC in Algeria, Morocco, and the Congo is widely known and appreciated and contributes to the climate of receptivity.

The pattern for a teacher placement program for Africa is derived from the MCC experience these past eight years where approximately one hundred teacher volunteers have been placed as teachers in the schools of the United Church of Canada in remote villages and coves along the Newfoundland and Labrador coasts. Several of the Mennonite conferences have developed programs for the use of short-term teachers in their mission schools.

At the annual meeting of the MCC in January 1962 a report of the two-month Africa study was presented and approval given for a Teachers Abroad Program (TAP) for Africa. This program will be launched in a modest way in late 1962 with anticipated growth the following years. An advisory committee, composed of MCC, Mennonite college, and mission board representatives, will be responsible for developing the policy for this new arm of service.

The four areas of Africa where TAP teachers may be placed in 1962-63 include: Kenya in East Africa, the Congo in Central Africa, Northern Rhodesia and Nyasaland in South Central Africa, and Northern Nigeria in Western Africa. With the exception of the Congo, where French is spoken, English will be the language of instruction. No TAP teachers will be placed in Mennonite or Brethren in Christ schools; here our mission boards are able to secure teachers. These volunteers will be serving in schools of other denominations–Presbyterian, Methodist, Friends, Anglican, and others. This program is for the purpose of undergirding and sustaining the educational ministry of the church in Africa.

The overseas expenses of the TAP program are to be covered by the salary grants made available by the governments to church schools. The salaries will be pooled in a common TAP treasury and these funds used to cover transportation, room and board allowance, personal allowance, medical expenses, vacation allowance. Administrative and orientation costs at home are being borne by contributed funds.

Most teaching assignments will be for a three-year period. An A.B. or B.S. degree with a major in a high school teaching field is required. A master's degree is desirable but not required. Teaching experience is also desirable. Teachers in the fields of physics, mathematics, biology, and English are in great demand. Couples, where both the husband and wife can teach, are sought. Candidates are being sought who are well qualified academically and who are able to give a clear, Christian witness.

In July, immediately prior to their departure by air for Africa, the TAP volunteers will participate in an orientation school of two weeks. Additional orientation will follow on the field.

Teaching in an American or Canadian setting has its problems. Teaching in Africa, with a radically different culture, presents an added dimension of adjustment and challenge for the TAP teacher. During the course of my travels in Africa, I jotted down in a notebook suggestions of missionary and African educators for the young teachers coming from overseas. A formidable list of fifty-two suggestions was accumulated. A few of these suggestions are listed below and may serve to capture the spirit, sensitivity, and cultural imagination required of the volunteers.

*Hints for TAP Personnel*

1. Overseas teachers start out teaching too fast. Take care of your vocabulary that it is not too unfamiliar. Begin deliberately, speaking slowly and distinctly. Your students probably are having more trouble with your American accent than you with theirs.

2. Be willing to take part in extra duties, not being overly protective of your time, e.g., working on yearbook, supervision of campus improvement, supervision of store, taking turn in conducting chapel, supervision of study hall, supervising practice teaching, adviser to student clubs, coaching a sport, etc. And yet avoid being so busy that you do not have time to talk with students and fellow staff.

3. Be patient. Do not be disappointed in students who do not measure up to your high standards of performance. Above all, do not show irritability and anger. Students lose confidence in an irritable, angry teacher.

4. Do not forget that neither English nor French is the mother tongue of your African students. They are only recently out of primary school where they began to use English. It is particularly important that you use the best English. Whatever your field,

English may be the most significant subject you teach directly or indirectly.

5. You will make mistakes. One might say to his students, "If I am wrong, you correct me."

6. In classroom refrain from sarcasm, irony, extensive telling of jokes, subtleties of understatement or exaggeration. Students are deadly serious. They will miss the point of your humor and may return the anecdote as fact on the next examination paper.

7. Do not expect Africans to be waiting eagerly to learn new methods of teaching, new approaches to your discipline. They are satisfied with their systems. Any changes must be introduced gradually.

8. These schools are being built for a rapid expansion with plans to double and triple size in a few years. One must accept improvisations in classrooms and laboratory facilities.

9. Remember that there will be misunderstandings among staff members even in a mission school. Cultivate scriptural methods for resolving these intra-staff tensions.

10. Remember, you come from an affluent society with all kinds of creature comforts. In Africa, you will have to live more simply and you will have to spend more time with the mechanics of living–shopping, repairing, etc. "In the tropics everything is more difficult."Avoid flaunting American affluence.

11. Learn the customs and manners of the people among whom you live and work. For example, in East Africa receive your caller into the house and offer him a seat. Do not meet him at the door and ask what he wants.

12. You will be the best teacher abroad if you go not only as a teacher but also as a student. Read before departure the books recommended. Read books on the area to which you arc going. Familiarize yourself with the geography of the area. Read up on current events so that you know the names of leaders, political parties, and recent major events. Ask questions. Keep notes of information acquired, particularly of cultural practices of the people of your area.

13. Avoid the use of words which suggest attitudes of condescension and paternalism: "native," "heathen," "savage," "darkest Africa."

14. Do not be shocked by ingratitude. You are not serving abroad to earn appreciation. The African is eager for expatriate teachers, but may resent his dependency on them. Appreciation is often present but largely unexpressed. Frequently this appreciation comes to the surface only after departure.

15. Working in underdeveloped countries where so much remains to be done, we must remember that in the United States and Canada we inherited the society we are in. For a century we were creditor nations. Our development was made possible in no small part by a massive influx of foreign capital. Let us not despair of the future. We are guests of a country to be of service to the people, not to write them off.

16. The greatest thing we can bring to our institution of assignment is Christian character. Academic ability, empathy, character–all these are important, but the greatest of these is character!

The Teachers Abroad Program presents expanded opportunities of service in an Africa which is now experiencing its most exciting decade of development. Some will hear this call: "Come and help us."

*Kreider family with residence in background, 1965. Seated on rail fence, left to right: Joan, Ruth, Karen, and David. Standing: Robert, Lois, and Esther.*

# 1965: Form, Faith, and Scholarship

*Inaugural address as President of Bluffton College, October 15, 1965, the ceremony held on the campus green.*

We are grateful that you have come today. Not so much to honor a man, nor even a particular college, but to honor the academic community which unites us–a community bound together by many threads of common need, common concern and common mission–a community which embraces Bluffton and Bowling Green, Ohio Northern and Earlham, Bethel and Dar es Salaam.

We accept the responsibilities of office in this college, knowing that we shall be sustained by this wider community of scholars, the brotherhood in Christ, and a loving, forgiving, guiding Providence.

In this period of history a college president inescapably is a builder. The president would prefer, perhaps, to savor great ideas and lead the academic troops into the fray against ignorance and error. But build he must–development campaigns... projection of the college image... bricks and mortar. We are told the frightening tale that as many college buildings will be built in the next fifteen years as in the past 330 years of American higher education. The new college president cries out for some purpose for all the time he must devote to such material things as buildings and blueprints.

This week I resurrected an article I had written twenty years ago when I was so young and prophetic:

> A good institution must be more than buildings. It isn't all just brick and mortar. A good institution must have an atmosphere, a soul. The soul of an institution is to be found in the men and women who serve there. They create the atmosphere.

Suggested here is a sharp dichotomy between the physical–a lower order of being–and the social–a higher order of being. But twenty years later I wonder whether this was not too pat a distinction. Form and function are interrelated. In the Biblical way of thinking, body and soul cannot be separated. As Winston Churchill once expressed it, "We shape buildings and then they shape us."

We have withdrawn this afternoon from college halls to this lovely green in the woods to reflect on form, scholarship, and the ways of God with men. This world of architecture is the most social of the arts. Scarcely an hour of the day passes without association with a building. With two buildings on the drafting board for our campus and two more in the program stage, we have been thinking much about the art of architecture. To my delight I discover that the ideas of architecture relate to basic concepts of the liberal arts as well as to central affirmations of the Christian faith. This, then, may be something a bit irregular for an inaugural address–a triangular conversation involving three disciplines–architecture, higher education, and applied theology. The poet John Ciardi has made the attractive observation, "Meaning begins in analogy." We speak of architecture and scholarship and faith. Perhaps we could speak as well of music and biology and faith. Or history, mathematics and faith. One sees the hand of the Creator God, the Lord of all disciplines, in the recurring rhythms, similarities and differences, analogies and patterns linking these several fields of inquiry.

Our faith springs from One who was a carpenter and who dignified the arts of architectural design and construction. He spoke of "the house upon a rock... the house upon the sand" ...the builder sitting down to count the cost before building.

This generation has been blessed with great architects: Mies van der Rohe, Le Corbusier, Frank Lloyd Wright, Eero Saarinen. What of the controlling principles in their art? One notes the motifs of discipline, restraint, respect for the particular, integrity, wholeness, and more.

First, good architecture involves disciplined skill. The artist-architect must learn the disciplined language of line, form, shape, texture, color, space, time, light and shadow. There is not one language to choose, but several. The Apollonian way–formalism. The Dionysian way–dynamism, feeling. The Judaeo-Christian way–appropriating both but acknowledging the dimension of divine judgment on every discipline. As architecture has its disciplined language, so the liberal arts have their disciplines. And to be a follower of Jesus is to be a disciple–one who accepts the discipline of Christ.

Second, good architecture is the art of restraint. Simplicity and dignity. As Mies von der Rohe says: "Less is more, more is less." Or Robert Frost states it another way: "Anything less than the truth would have been too much." Quality architecture is natural, artless. It resists ornamentation, the dazzling, the contrived, the pretentious. "Playboy-architecture" as Giedion calls it. Good architecture is as the lily of the field. This is also the key to good style in writing–cutting, pruning out the excess verbiage, paring the prose down to the muscular core.

A quality education shows these marks of restraint. It is known by the modesty of its claims. It "vaunteth not itself, is not puffed up, does not behave itself unseemly." The educated person is not a snob. He is reluctant to parade his learning. A good college is to be known not by the multiplicity of its courses but as Robert

Hutchins says, "by what it refuses to teach." In many church colleges we are afraid to say, "No." We seek to be all things to all men–the temptation to play God.

Third, good architecture is a creative encounter with the particular. It accepts annoying obstacles and limitations–a site sliced by a railroad track or a deep gully or a building program with a tight budget. It is the particular solution of a particular architect-artist to a particular problem. That solution must be sought with patience, discernment, skill and devotion. James Bixel, whose choral composition we heard earlier in this service, has observed: "when you are restricted, you can be most creative." Dr. Joseph Sittler states it in a related way: "The artistic way to the universal is the way of the particular. The way to make a thing significant is to make it precise; the path to excellence is the lowly path of artistic obedience to the historically particular." Robert Frost has a line: "Triggering the big meanings from tiny things." I like that.

When a solution comes it is to be viewed as a gift placed in the hands of an artist. A gift to be received in gratitude. A kind of incarnation analogous to the Great Gift–"The Word became flesh." An intuitive grasp of reality. There is the letter written by Mozart to a friend:

> When I am, as it were, completely myself, entirely alone, and of good cheer–say, traveling in a carriage, or walking after a good meal; it is on such occasions that my ideas flow best and most abundantly. Whence and how they come, I know not. This is perhaps the best gift I have my Divine Maker to thank for.

When we speak of a creative encounter with the particular we mean approaching with reverence and seriousness that subject in all its beauty and deformity. To the scholar it is total absorption with the question which haunts him. This view of the creative encounter with the particular is suggestive of the Biblical view of agape love–complete identification, vicarious feeling for, entering into the mind and spirit of another. Warren Kliewer, a poet at Earlham, asserts that "in reading poetry one must become a poet." Identification. It is the servant motif–"Christ emptying himself and taking on the form of a servant."

This means that good architecture is a love affair. The world of scholarship is a love affair. The life of faith is a love affair. Beyond learning and skill there must come a conversion experience, a leap of faith and commitment, a surrender. There is a story about Louis

Armstrong who said when he was asked how one learns to understand jazz, "If you don't dig it when you hear it, man, there's nothing I can say about it to help you." A great choir director is quoted as saying that one is converted to music, one doesn't learn it. Understanding music is more than reading the program notes. After surrender comes understanding and then joy.

One characteristic of creative architects, seminal scholars and men of faith is that you cannot predict them. They do not repeat themselves in obvious, conventional ways. This is not unrelated to the role of the Holy Spirit moving through the obedient community–the windows open, full of surprises, responding imaginatively to the particular.

Good architecture is skill, restraint, loving encounter with the particular. Fourth, it calls also for integrity. This is to be found in two senses: wholeness and straightforwardness. First, wholeness. The architect relates form, shape, mass, texture into a cohesive whole. An architect seeks an internal unity in the structure itself, working from the inside of the building out, but also from its surroundings in. He respects the space between buildings. He seeks to relate sensitively the new to that which is old, that which is given. The individual building is important as it enhances the ensemble. On this campus it may be the woodland and stream and the red brick and white trim of the Georgian style. As man needs historical security in a changing age, the architect nurtures these bonds of continuity. He also seeks to anticipate the future. If he is building a science facility, he asks, "What may we anticipate the shape of science to be in 10, 20, 30 years from now?" The architect is sensitive to the fourth dimension–not only depth, breadth, height, but also time–viewing understandingly the givenness of the past and keeping the doors open to the future–a John-the-Baptist attitude that there may be ones coming after me who may be even greater than I. "He must increase, but I must decrease." Joseph Schwab of the University of Chicago writes of this crisis in ideas:

> Our scientific and scholarly establishment is now so large. We can expect radical reorganization of a given body of scientific knowledge, not once in the coming century but at intervals of five to fifteen years…. This means… that our students will confront at least once in their lives what appears to be a flat contradiction of much that they were taught about some subject.

Open to a future trembling with surprises and the unexpected. Integrity also means straightforwardness. The architect must be faithful to the truth and communicate it with skill. Like the medieval Gothic cathedral with its exposed ribbed vaulting and flying buttresses, it is not ashamed; it may choose not to hide its engineering. There is an avoidance of imitation and deceits. One seeks honesty–a let-your-yea-be-yea-and-your-nay-be-nay quality. Long before there were blueprints, men knew that scholarship and integrity were one, that faith called for utter honesty in the awful presence of God.

The good architect respects his materials and all living things in God's creation. "And God saw that it was good." The architect takes inexpensive materials and treats them with care and finds them honorable. One of the great architects of post-war Germany was the late Otto Bartning who erected 48 small rubble churches, called *Notkirche* reclaiming rubble brick from the wasteland of war. Of this he wrote:

> We have learned to know the Wasteland, the outer and also the inner.... The *Notkirche* develops its own silent statement, that, often without our knowing it, has convinced us to build firmly and sparely, neither too massively nor carelessly, neither over enthusiastically nor emotionally, but simply and honestly.

And so too in the good academic life there is a grateful respect for the humble materials of scholarship–an earnest mind, the frayed book, the clean white paper and the sharpened pencil, the well-written paragraph, the sincere question, the log and two friends seated in conversation.

And so too is the life of the holy community. One finds integrity in working with humble materials–sinful men but rich in potential. An architect friend, Edward Sövik, has written:

> We forget too easily that when God had a choice of where to enter the world He chose a stable, an earthy and a humble place. We forget too easily that the physical element of baptism is not perfumed oil, but simply water; and that the communion food was the simplest of fare–ordinary bread and ordinary wine. Here are the best symbols of the search for truth and the willingness to receive it.

Good architecture is skill, restraint, loving encounter with the particular, integrity, wholeness, straightforwardness. It is more. It is the most social of the arts. It begins in a dialogue among architect-artist, the client, the site, the material at hand, the controlling purpose. Scholarship, although it has its periods of solitude and withdrawal, also is a social art. The graduate student having probed the fascinating frontiers of knowledge is pent up with desire to share his discoveries. He must write. He must teach. This is also the picture we have of the disciples at Emmaus. Having been made aware that the stranger, their guest, was Christ Himself–they immediately rose, hastened back over the road to Jerusalem to report their exciting discovery–"the Master made Himself known to us in the breaking of the bread."

A good building extends an invitation. It does not halt conversation. It is drawn to human scale. It is not monumental and overpowering. It is not autonomous. It is not the last word. It offers fellowship. The liberal arts also are invitational–an invitation to dialogue. Conversational tones. Listening as well as talking. Seeking understandings as well as sharpening distinctions. And where there is dialogue–in building, scholarship, and Christian fellowship–there are intriguing diversities, varieties, surprises and delights.

The good architect is never satisfied—a restless discontent. Mr. Manning Patillo of the Danforth Foundation says that one of the marks of a good college is that it is perpetually dissatisfied with itself. The Apostle Paul shared this divine disquietude: "Not as though I had already attained.... I press toward the mark." This divine disquietude seems less directed toward "they," "the structures," the "Philistines," "the pagans," "the illiterates," and more toward me, us. The divine discontent focuses on me–like the Negro spiritual, "It's not the deacon, nor the preacher, but it's me, O Lord."

There are other motifs which link architecture, scholarship, and the faith which we could have explored: freedom and order, the rational and the intuitive, variety and continuity, action and repose. I would ask you to view this as an exercise in inter-disciplinary conversation–tentative, exploratory, suggestive. The informal patterns of this discourse suggest an invitation to a continuing conversation. Members of the small Christian college, nurtured by the liberal arts tradition and a heritage of Christian commitment, have a special opportunity to engage themselves in serious and significant conversation on the great issues of life. I yearn for many things for this college. One is this–that we experience here good conversation in a loving and accepting fellowship about man, his world, and his destiny. Then might the words of the Apostle Paul be said of this campus:

And now, my friends, all that is true, all that is noble, all that is just and pure, all that is lovable and gracious, whatever is excellent and admirable–fill all your thoughts with these things.

# 1965: L. L. Ramseyer–the Golden Years

*A tribute given at a Bluffton College Alumni Banquet in 1965 honoring retiring President L. L. Ramseyer of Bluffton College, Bluffton, Ohio.*

I have been asked to scan the public addresses of President Ramseyer and to distill the essence from twenty-seven years of public addresses. I am awed both by the volume and by the consistently high quality of his public presentations. I have asked my colleagues, "Which of Prexy's speeches do you remember as the best?" Invariably the response is, "Those impromptu, off-the-cuff remarks made at banquets, receptions." These are examples:

• At the reception when the bomb was dropped–the announcement of the engagement of President Ed G. Kaufman and Edna Ramseyer: "We've always had trouble with Ed Kaufman invading our territory."
• The alumni banquet honoring Dr. Ramseyer's 25 years in the presidency–a surprise affair: "I don't know who is going to pay for all this. It surely isn't in my budget."
• The Appreciation Day this spring: "Somebody has been doing things behind my back–without consulting me.... When an administrator loses control over his staff it is time for him to quit."
• At a recent Booster Banquet Jim Ehrman, Methodist, was toastmaster; Warren Eastman, Methodist, was chairman of the program committee; Jim and Jean Szabo, Methodists, presented special music. After seeing all this Methodist talent, Prexy commented: "John Wesley would be very proud of us tonight." That evening Doctor Frank Rodabaugh, Methodist, added: "One can relax when Prexy gets up to speak. What he says is just right."

One of the intriguing characteristics of Dr. Ramseyer's public addresses were the titles. Take, for example, his baccalaureate sermons. Here are sermon topics with the theme of building: "Foundation Stones," "Let Us Rise Up and Build," "How Firm a Foundation." There is a motif of working: "Workers Together with God," "Having Done All, to Stand." There is the motif of Christian love: "Christian Love and Human Freedom," "An Understanding Heart." There is also the motif of vision and expectancy: "Looking Forward," "Hands to the Plow," "Lift Up Your Eyes," "Who Will Go for Us?"

One observes many other characteristics to Dr. Ramseyer's talks and sermons.

•*Timing.* He can drop a chapel talk into a 13-minute time spot–not a second over, not a minute short. Like the timing of Cassius Clay, he can call the round. To change the imagery, his speeches are precisely timed like a 14-line sonnet.

•*Compactness.* He speaks with short, punchy sentences–good, clean Anglo-Saxon words. Thursday he delivered the high school commencement address. One man was overheard to say, "He got more said in twenty minutes than anyone I have heard in a long time."

•*Straightforward, candid.* He always gives a sense of integrity. For example, he spoke thus: "I have no swan song to sing. I have heard too many of them to bore anyone else by another one. My relationships with the Board of Trustees, with the alumni, with the church, and with the community have on the whole been pleasant ones."

•*Humor.* Here is an example: "You have heard of the retiring Mother Superior who prayed, 'With my vast store of wisdom it seems a pity not to use it all–but thou knowest, Lord, that I want a few friends at the end'." Another example: "I am sure that I will not always agree with the decisions that will be made in the future. As someone has said, when two people think alike one of them is unnecessary (or really doesn't think)."

•*Practical.* In a recent commencement address he advised the seniors to (a) read a good daily newspaper, (b) read a news magazine, (c) read a book a month. He is good in his use of practical illustrations. He used illustrations from football with particular delight.

•*Ethical concern.* In all of his talks one finds a sense of calling, Christian vocation, discipleship, service. "The basic quality of the Christian life is a life of service. The true Christian spirit is not a self-centered spirit. We are too likely to ask the question, 'What can I get out of it?' rather than asking, 'What opportunity for service does it give me?'"

•*Gratitude.* The note of thanksgiving is found in his talks–for example: "Surely Mrs. Ramseyer and I can say with the psalmist, 'The lines have fallen to me in pleasant places; yea, I have a godly heritage.' (Ps. 16:6)"

•*The Note of Expectancy.* In 1950 he spoke thus: "Over the horizon of the future of humanity I see the sun. Some say it is a setting sun, the end of an age, the evening of a civilization. You can, if you will, with God's help, make of it a rising sun, breaking into the brightness of the noonday of a new golden age, an age when Christian Faith and practice, emphasizing concern for spiritual values, will defeat the forces of materialism and evil. Over the horizon of the future of the church college, too, I see the sun. Some say the evening of Christian education approaches and the day of state domination of education is at hand. Others, with a willingness to sacrifice and a firm belief in Christianity and its place in education, affirm that a new and brighter day is about to dawn, that the sun is rising on a new golden age of the church college. It depends upon the willingness to sacrifice of you and others like you as to whether that sun is rising or setting."

In that address he concluded: "The golden age must lie in the future. The sun which we see must be a rising sun." This theme he has repeated on other occasions.... "The golden age is not in the past, not in the present; it must be in the future."

I am grateful to Dr. Ramseyer for leaving us this heritage.

# 1966: A Climate of Conversation on Campus

*An article in the* Bluffton College Bulletin, *1966, announcing plans for the introduction of an all-campus inter-term study of a major societal issue.*

One hears ominous voices predicting the decline and fall of liberal arts colleges within the next generation. Jacques Barzun, provost of Columbia, decries the trend of students and faculty toward narrow professionalism and specialization. At Hofstra University in 1963, he declared: "the liberal arts tradition is dead or dying."

President Wallis of the University of Rochester wrote in the November 1965 issue of *The Atlantic* that "colleges which confine their efforts to undergraduates will find themselves relegated [to] good preparatory schools. The best students will go to universities." President Howard Lowry of the College of Wooster replied in the March 1966 issue of *The Atlantic* that the climate of a good undergraduate institution can be as exciting and rewarding as the university graduate school.

The inter-term experiment at Bluffton College is a way of affirming that the liberal arts tradition is very much alive.

Someone has said that the only thing which unites many an institution of higher learning is a common grievance about parking. The petty annoyances of institutional life or the exploits of the team on Saturday afternoons may be all that sustain campus conversation. But this is thin broth to nourish the good conversation in a community of scholars. The inter-term is designed to encourage what may be the most significant activity on a liberal arts campus: good conversation.

The inter-term is designed to narrow the student-faculty communication gap. It brings students and faculty together in planning sessions and in a host of informal ways of joint field trips and study and intimate discussion. The symbol of this now is the Policy Review Committee composed of twelve students and twelve faculty. In January the symbol of this interaction should be the little clusters of students, faculty, and off-campus guests–scattered all over campus each absorbed with one another in earnest conversation.

Snugly fitted between two conventional semesters, the three and a half week inter-term should afford a welcome change of academic pace. Instead of four or five courses, only one. Instead of a scramble for an "A", "B" or "C,"–only "pass" or "fail." Instead of students row on row in the classroom and learning in neatly structured ways–the student is personally responsible for his own education. All this may be unsettling, of course, for those who like their college neatly and predictably packaged. The unsettling quality of this experience may be precisely its best feature. The student is more on his own, working out his own educational salvation but encompassed about by a wealth of educational resources.

The inter-term is designed to involve students at all stages in planning, directing, and evaluating the study. In a sense all students become both faculty as well as students and all faculty become students as well as faculty. Students have poured hours of preparation into the 1967 inter-term. Long before the beginning of the inter-term it has already become for many a significant educational experience.

The inter-term is designed to stimulate study which crosses departmental lines—the music major investigating election misconduct in the cities, the chemistry professor directing a seminar on the urban church, a director of development probing water pollution in urban areas, etc.

The inter-term is designed to affirm that true learning is not simply a well-structured procedure of textbook, workbook, quiz, and exam. It can involve a casual but integrated pattern of field trips, interviews, convocation addresses, films, independent research projects, bull sessions, art exhibits, and reading. There will be too much going on for everyone to do everything. From the academic abundance each student will need to choose his own program.

The inter-term is designed to break down the real or fancied isolation of the college from the community. In the inter-term study of "The City," the nearby city becomes a laboratory. Judges, politicians, businessmen, city church workers, social workers will be coming to Bluffton and bringing the laboratory of the city to this rural, wooded campus.

The inter-term is designed to pose the big issues. These issues are to be more than idle, entertaining exercises of the intellect. The issues address themselves to the core of our vocation as persons, a college, the church. This is symbolized by the coming of fifty leaders in city church work to participate for a week in this study of the city. The inter-term is speaking to issues out there where the church is in mission.

There is no magic in this inter-term experiment. This is no gimmick which unlocks certain long-lost self-generating educational principles. It will not succeed simply because it is a great idea. Like anything worthwhile, it will take work to be rewarding. We can ill afford the luxury of sitting back in detachment and saying "This better be good." The inter-term study will test our resourcefulness, energy and eagerness. If we can create a climate of contagious enthusiasm, then there is assurance that this experience will be significant.

I think this inter-term trial run is the type of experiment a small liberal arts college is uniquely qualified to make. The lines of communication are more direct on a small campus. Decision-making is simpler. Perhaps this inter-term experiment is one way of saying that the liberal arts college is not dead. It is now very much alive. And what better indication is there of this academic vitality than that here thrives good conversation about the great issues of life and human destiny?

# 1969: The Murder of Helen

*A convocation address given at Bluffton College, March 21, 1969, following the death of Helen Bohn Klassen.*

One week ago, perhaps about this hour of the morning, a woman, aged 41, mother of four daughters, was murdered in her home on County Road 21 near Elkhart, Indiana.

At 4:10 p.m. that Friday afternoon I received a telephone call from a secretary at Oaklawn Psychiatric Center, Elkhart, asking me if Dr. Otto Klassen was on our campus and if I would inform him that his wife had been killed.

Death has come very close to many of you this past year. Some of you have lost a father, a mother, a brother, a sister, a close friend. For all of us, the death of Jim Evans was a shattering experience. Earlier in the year the violent death of Robert Kennedy, the assassination of Martin Luther King Jr.–these were as immediate as the unexpected death of a member of the family.

This morning I want to report as accurately as I can about the death of Helen Klassen and the response of persons like you and me to death. This, in a sense, is a case study of a death and how it touches a thousand lives. It is a study of how one family met death. William Douglas in his book, *Of Men and Mountains,* says, "Only those are free who have no fear of death."

The woman who was found dead was Helen Klassen, the wife of Dr. Otto Klassen, the psychiatric consultant who visits our campus once a month. Helen and her husband Otto both graduated from Bluffton College, the Class of 1949. All of Helen's six brothers and sisters attended Bluffton. Stanley Bohn, her younger brother, is pastor of the First Mennonite Church in Bluffton. Otto's three brothers and one sister all had graduated from Bluffton College.

Helen's father, E. J. Bohn, taught philosophy for many years at Bluffton. He and his wife are now living at Goshen, Indiana. Otto's father and mother, the J. P. Klassens, live in their home at the north end of the College Farm. Prof. J. P. Klassen, the artist, now in his eighties, was honored last November at Homecoming with the dedication of the Klassen Court. John Klassen, sophomore, is a nephew.

I had been troubled that day with the question of why I felt led to leave early a two-day meeting in Pennsylvania to fly home, why I had canceled plans to fly to Kansas City for a recognition banquet. I was feeling guilty that I was supposed to be in two other places and here I was back in Bluffton.

At 4:10 p.m. when that fateful call came, I asked the secretary in Elkhart, "Was she killed in an automobile accident?" The answer: "No, she was killed in her home." I asked her to check with a psychiatrist or the Administrator of the Psychiatric Center, Robert Hartzler, how they would advise that this awful information should be conveyed to her husband. The secretary said, "I will check and call back in a minute."

Meanwhile, we sought to reach by telephone Stanley Bohn, Helen's brother.

The phone rang. The secretary from Elkhart called to report: "They want you to tell Otto. Helen has been murdered. Dr. Rupel has left for the house. Their daughter found her mother when she returned from school. The staff suggests that somebody accompany Otto on the drive back." I promised to go to Marbeck Center immediately where I knew Otto was in conference.

Dean Houshower accompanied me. Two faculty members were meeting with Dr. Klassen in Banquet Room A. I entered and asked permission that I might talk with Otto alone in the adjoining room. I closed the doors. We sat down and I explained slowly and quietly that I had never had a more difficult task. I said: "I have just received a phone call from Elkhart reporting that Helen is dead... killed... found by one of your daughters returning home from school.... Dr. Rupel has left for the house." There was the look of shock, of disbelief. "No, this can't be true." I repeated slowly and in a low voice the message and then added the word "murdered." He seized my hand and for the better portion of a minute Otto didn't say a word. Then he said, "I must go home. The children will need me."

He said then, "It must have been Susie, the youngest, who found her. She always comes home first." He wanted to know whether I had told him everything. I said that I had. Almost as though he were talking to himself, he said: "We have had a good family life. Now this." After a few minutes we rose and left the room. Stan Bohn, his brother- in-law, had just arrived. Dean Houshower had told him. The two–one a psychiatrist, the other a pastor–said nothing. They returned to the small room and sat down side by side. All Stan did was just place his hand on Otto's knee. He said nothing. They wanted me to retell the story. Then Otto said, "We must go." Stan responded, "I'll go with you." I asked what I could do. Otto said, "Will you tell my parents?"

That evening just before eight o'clock Otto and Stan and Anita Bohn arrived at his home in Elkhart. The body had been removed from the home only a few minutes before.

Meanwhile, I had talked with the Administrator of Oaklawn Psychiatric Center by telephone. He explained that it had been a violent death, that the area around the house had been cordoned off by police.

I drove out to the elder Klassens, who fifty years ago in South Russia had known so much death, starvation, and terror in the days of the Russian revolution. They had lost close friends and family members. Mrs. Klassen invited me in. She called her husband, who was working in the basement on one of his sculpture works. We talked of small things. After a wait of perhaps five minutes, he came up the stairs slowly, entered the kitchen. We sat around the kitchen table. I explained that Otto had asked me to tell them the dreadful news–that Helen had been killed, murdered in their home. I needed to repeat the message several times. Mrs. Klassen broke down. But soon she was thinking of what should be done to inform Otto's brothers and sister. She began looking for addresses and telephone numbers, her grief absorbed in her busyness in these little tasks. Prof. Klassen sat there motionless. Finally he said, "This violence, it comes from war." Mrs. Klassen began to recall her conversation with Otto that morning. He had spent the previous night with his parents before his round of consultations with Bluffton students. Otto's mother recalled how pleased Otto had been with a new tie he had been wearing, a tie Helen had selected to go with his new jacket.

That evening a few hours later I visited the elder Klassens again. Jim Bixels, their neighbors, had run some errands for them. Prof. Klassen that evening did not talk about the death. He wanted to show Jim Bixel and me some of his works of sculpture which he thought we might not have seen before. He wanted to know whether we would like to go downstairs to his basement studio to see his large wood carving of the Good Samaritan. We agreed and went with him. Prof. Klassen in his grief had found solace and healing in his art.

That evening there were a dozen phone calls and considerable anxiety about how to locate Otto's sister and husband who were camping somewhere in Florida.

That night the news of the murder was on radio and television. It was reported that a suspect, a 23-year-old Elkhart factory employee, who had been a patient at Oaklawn Psychiatric Center earlier that week, had been taken into custody at 7:05 p.m. He had created a disturbance at the clinic Thursday afternoon when he could not get in to see the medical Director, Dr. Klassen. The man was released after questioning.

The following day, Saturday, the Elkhart, Goshen, and South Bend newspapers carried big headlines of the slaying along with major articles and pictures.

Sunday morning Stanley Bohn was back with his congregation in Bluffton. He spoke only briefly about the tragedy. He expressed his gratitude for the help of friends. Everyone knew the burden of grief he bore.

That same Sunday morning in Elkhart, Otto and his four daughters attended services at the Hively Avenue Mennonite Church, their home church. A friend writes of the service:

> The pastor "reminded us of how last spring the Otto Klassen family... had gone to Camp Friedenswald and picked wild flowers and that her Sunday School class had passed them around to all members of the congregation.... So today again, in memory of Helen, the children of her Sunday School class (for whom this has been extremely difficult for they loved her so much as a teacher) passed to members of the congregation a white mum.... We closed the service with the hymn "Jesus, still lead on...."
>
> It was a "weepy" congregation, but we also felt love and warmth and sympathy.... After the service Otto came up to the pastor and said something like "that was a good service." It touched me deeply to think that he who probably was wounded the most would come and remember to give words of appreciation to the pastor.

That Sunday afternoon there were long lines waiting to visit the family at the Yoder-Culp Funeral Home in Goshen. In the evening we visited the funeral home. It was thronged with people. There was Otto and his four daughters: Susie, Beth, Frieda, and Ruth.

In talks at the funeral home we pieced together more details of the event. Susie, aged 12, returned home from school and found someone on the floor beaten. She ran around the house calling for her mother. She could not believe that the person on the floor was her mother. She called her aunt, Doris Bohn, a few houses away. Doris first called a neighbor, Marilyn Klassen, then the doctor and then Oaklawn Center. Marilyn went over immediately, was there alone with Susie until the doctor came. The doctor soon came and they phoned the police. Then Marilyn Klassen called her husband, Dr. William Klassen, who had just begun his class at the seminary two miles away. He dismissed class and hurried to the Klassen home. Bill was one of those who saw the body. Helen had apparently been interrupted while sewing that morning. She had been beaten, strangled, raped, and as she lay dead on the floor she was shot four times. She lay in disarray in a pool of blood. Bill Klassen said it was "pure Boston Strangler." That was the scene that 12-year old Susie saw when she opened the door of her home.

Susie's three older sisters had not yet returned from school. One of Susie's first concerns was this: "We mustn't let my sisters see this." Susie is the only one who saw. Twelve years old.

Local, county and state police investigators searched the home and environs for every shred of evidence they could find. They copied thousands of fingerprints which needed to be studied–separating out those which were not prints of family members. They scoured the house for the lead of bullets and found five slugs, but no cartridges.

That Friday night the family stayed at their uncle's home, Alden Bohn. Otto arrived at 8 p.m. Although Stan and Anita Bohn accompanied Otto on that three-hour drive back to Elkhart, he had insisted on doing the driving. He felt he must do something.

At the funeral home that Sunday evening, Otto Klassen seemed to have strength and composure beyond that of others. The four girls were there. From time to time the father sat down and talked to his daughters. He greeted visitors.

One felt in that funeral home that those who had come to help Otto were helped in turn. There were people of all ages at the funeral home. He commented: "It is amazing how many lives are touched by a person." He shook his head, "This is a crazy business. Somehow we must find ways to live with it."

To someone who came up to him and exclaimed: "We don't know what we can do but we want you to know we are available," he responded, "But, you are here." Their presence was enough.

Ruth, their 17-year-old daughter, came up to us and said, "I want to thank you for what you did for Daddy. You were with Daddy, weren't you?" She smiled in gratitude. I responded that her father's first thought was of the children: "I must go home; the children will need me." Ruth said simply. "That's right. We did need him."

The first night the Klassen family stayed in the home of the Alden Bohns, neighbors. Otto's brother Karl reported how Otto had thought it important on Saturday afternoon to return with his family to begin living again in the house where the death had taken place. To reestablish for the children the familiar patterns. Not to flee the scene. The father thought that there should again be a lot of activity in the house. That there be a lot of coming and going. That it again be a happy place.

At the funeral home were a number of psychiatrists, psychologists, social workers from Oaklawn Psychiatric center moving about among the crowd. One of the social workers commented that they came expecting to help the visitors in a kind of group therapy, but rather they the professionals were helped.

There was conversation at the funeral home which touched subjects we are normally reluctant to discuss. Harold Hartman reported that his wife Katie, sister of Helen, awakened him at 3:00 in the morning and exclaimed with a sense of discovery, "Now I understand Jesus and God. She's gone; but she's still alive... her ideas... her way of doing things. Jesus died but he still lives."

There was much speculation as to who it could have been. A patient with hostility toward Dr. Klassen? A calculating killer? A random, Russian roulette type of killer? Otto said firmly, "It could not have been premeditated." One of his colleagues observed that Dr. Klassen is already thinking of how sometime he might be able to help heal the sick mind of the killer–that he needs to keep himself ready so that he can treat this person if he is called upon.

A neighbor woman at the funeral home asked, "Why Helen? Maybe he was intending to get me. Maybe he got the wrong house. Why was it Helen and not me?"

Otto was concerned about Susie, aged 12. He said, "She wasn't old enough to have had fights with her mother. Every child needs to have quarrels with his or her parents."

Someone said that the high school Sunday School class the previous Sunday had discussed what one would try to do if one were physically attacked. Otto said that their children had brought home the question last Sunday and they had discussed it as a family.

That evening as we were leaving the funeral home Bob Hartzler, the Administrator of the Psychiatric Center, explained that police and detectives in plain clothing were mingled among the crowd watching the coming and going of everyone. Perhaps there was a remote possibility that the killer might make his appearance here. But most of us were unaware of this surveillance.

On Monday morning the memorial service was held in the Chapel of the Sermon on the Mount. On the austere wall of brick in the sanctuary were these words carved in wood:

Thy Kingdom Come
Thy Will be Done
On Earth as it is in Heaven.

The congregation sang "A Mighty Fortress is Our God." An elderly pastor with a deep resonant voice read slowly the 23rd Psalm, the 121st Psalm, and other appropriate passages of Scripture. Scattered through the congregation were present and former patients. The pastor spoke:

We have all experienced sorrow.
We have all experienced anger.
We have all experienced fear.
We have all experienced doubt.
We have all experienced the warmth, the depth, the healing of
    love.
We have lived as in a storm.

It was a brief service. The congregation filed out into the morning sunshine.

That afternoon we drove out to the home on County Road 21. Children were playing ball in the front yard. The Klassen house is new. It is built on the site of their house which had been completely destroyed in the Palm Sunday tornado just four years ago.

A friend was with me who has visited Vietnam many times. He said that this death gives him the feeling of sadness he gets when he views the death and destruction outside Saigon.

That is the story of a death which occurred just seven days ago and which touched many of our lives. It poses the question of how long we have and how we will respond in each of our lives to the fact of death.

# 1969: A Case for Intercollegiate Athletics

*Printed in the* Bluffton College Bulletin, *November 1969.*

Athletics is one of the most important activities in the life of young people in their formative years. Physical competition is vital for a growing child in understanding his body, his capabilities, his limitations, his sense of physical and self worth.

Athletics provides a heightened experience in fellowship–teamwork under tense, competitive and publicly exposed circumstances–in victory and defeat, when no one expects you to win and when everyone expects you to win.

Athletic competition can help a youth to define, nurture and test ethical principles and attitudes. Here the coach has a tremendous opportunity to lead and shape young lives. Precisely because of this, a church-related college should prepare students for coaching.

Athletics affords all kinds of issues where one can stand up and be counted: smoking, drinking and the abuse of the body; respect for or exploitation of the athlete; honesty in financial and other understandings; racial respect or discrimination; clean speech and integrity of relationships; a sense of first things and secondary things.

Athletics provides a body of experience where one can see the relation between long-term, systematic preparation and the results. One can see clearly the consequences of hard work, conditioning and discipline–also the results of negligence and indolence. One sees the pay-off of good planning. Coaching is an art with an accent on long-range planning.

In athletics one can observe the importance of leadership, the need for the acceptance of authority and responsibility. You can see that you are your brother's keeper. You make mistakes and your team suffers. You ignore the coach's instructions and the team suffers.

In athletics one can learn how crucially important are the psychological factors in defeat and victory. This is no arena for the cynic. Victory belongs to the confident ones. Motivation, attitude, self-respect are crucial.

Athletics is particularly intriguing today when old patterns of authority and decision-making are being questioned. Here the big question is posed: How can coaches accommodate to change without losing control? There are related questions. How can one involve young men in the decision-making process without losing team cohesiveness? How can one be responsive to dissent and yet have a unified team?

Athletics is voluntary activity. It is a privilege. No one has a right to the position of first-string quarterback. No one is compelled to play intercollegiate football. It is a challenge to preserve the sense that athletics is fun and voluntary.

Intercollegiate athletics is such a publicly-exposed activity that it has more than the average number of risks, temptations and perils. One of its major perils is the temptation to become commercialized: to buy players, to use any gimmick to win, to try to get athletes into the pro ranks, etc. Precisely because it has such risks, it is an intriguing activity to place in a college community in the context of a host of competing values.

Intercollegiate athletics has a significant role on the campus because it is exciting, great to watch and to discuss–a refreshing answer to boredom, a kind of community catharsis. Simply stated–it's fun.

# 1970: "Rite of Spring" or Another "Campus Riot"

*A college president's effort in the* Bluffton College Bulletin, *April 1970, to report and interpret to alumni and friends of the college a campus crisis.*

On the morning of April 9 I read in convocation a statement on the events on our campus of the previous night—events which had received widespread publicity in newspapers, radio, and TV. I reported: "We understand that after eleven o'clock there was a water fight in the men's residence hall area of the campus. The scene shifted to Ropp Hall where there was an attempt made to get into the inner court of Ropp. All this was accompanied by noise and shouting. Local police appeared on the scene. Meanwhile, someone in the community called the Allen County Sheriff's Office and perhaps some other out-of-town law enforcement offices. Perhaps six car loads of sheriff's deputies arrived in Bluffton after 2:00 a.m...." Six students were booked on charges of disturbing the peace.

I concluded my statement at convocation: "I hope we all can profit by the experience—concerned that fun be kept within the bounds of respect for others, that police authority be exercised with care and restraint, and that friendships be cultivated where there is hostility."

Following the April 8-9 affair our personnel staff interviewed students, townsmen, town officials, and staff members to establish the facts. The six students appear to have been observers of the excitement who did not flee when approached by the police. The Associated Press sent out an article about "600 to 800 students... roaming the streets." We had phone calls from anxious parents.

In my report I had spoken of only six car loads of sheriff's deputies. The total may have been fifty sheriff's deputies from as many as six counties and two city police departments. In the mayor's office in the presence of the Police Chief and the Sheriff it was stated and not disputed that there were probably no more than fifty students on the street or outside Ropp Hall at any one time.

Most of us would never have heard a word about the noisy but playful water fight and the thwarted invasion of Ropp Hall if sheriff's deputies had not been summoned. Many students slept through the whole affair. The incidents that night were not unlike those which have occurred many times before on our campus and other campuses. Such affairs run their course and are quieted down locally with the help of students and staff.

To many of us this was a disturbing case study of the escalation of rumor and exaggeration. It reflects a public's hunger to believe the worst. It is an example of how in reporting, exciting falsehood drives out dull truth. It illustrates how it is more exciting to report "600 to 800 rioting students" than to acknowledge that it was approximately 50 students making a lot of noise in one of the rites of spring.

It provides a frightening parable for this technologically interrelated world–that is, the chain reaction that can be released by pushing a button. Someone phones the sheriff's office and within minutes fifty deputy sheriffs and police from six counties are headed for the scene of "the riot." A playful water fight and a noisy campus scene becomes by definition–with the introduction of carloads of police–a new species of being–"a campus riot." Again a stereotyped image of college students is confirmed in the minds of many. This experience is analogous to other situations–for example, the whole missile system push a panic button and a chain reaction locks into place and one cannot escape the awful consequences of a radically new phenomenon.

In reflecting on this experience, I am reminded of Mark Twain's comment: "The news reports of my death have been greatly exaggerated."

# 1970: Camping in Europe on Three Dollars a Day

*Excerpts from an article sent home in December 1970 for publication in* The Bluffton News.

After four and a half months of camping in Europe, the Middle East, and North Africa we are ready to recommend that camping is a great way for a family to travel abroad. We have found it the best, perhaps the only, way for our family of seven to see a score of countries, travel 15,000 miles by land and do it on a limited budget.

I had a six months sabbatical leave from Bluffton College and a yen to visit the countries bordering the Mediterranean. This was one of those now-or-never situations if all seven of us were to make the trip together. Esther is 19 and ready to enter college, Joan 17, Karen 14, David 12, and Ruth 9. The children are playing hookey for a semester with the approval of their school authorities. Some text books were mailed and waiting for us in Israel. Lois, assisted by Esther and Joan, are supervising a catch-a-day-when-you-can-study program. The major educational experience, however, comes through our travels. Each has been keeping a journal of his or her experiences. Friday is allowance day: each keeps a record of expenditures in the currency of the country–fifteen currencies so far. The children are even picking up snatches of a dozen languages. Our nine year old commented recently: "Now I can speak a little bit in 12 languages and a lot in one–English."

We ordered a VW nine-passenger microbus which was waiting for us on arrival in Luxembourg [purchase price in 1970: $2300]. A large luggage rack was installed. During the first two weeks we accumulated camping equipment–in Luxembourg a sleeping bag for each, utensils, camp stove with a pressure container of Camping Gaz (universally available on the trip), and a nest of kitchen pans; in Harlingen, Netherlands, a second-hand tent for $50.... At Exmouth on the coast of Devon, England, an old sailmaker sewed together an envelope cover for our luggage rack....

We have camped in 24 locations in 12 countries. At one place–on the Mediterranean beach near Limassol, Cyprus–we camped for nine days under a spreading willow tree, a site offered by a local car dealer.... We camped for four days on the pine-shaded campus of the American Farm School at Salonika, Greece. A favorite site was at the foot of a crumbling 12th century Welsh castle, Carreg Cennen, where a farmer permitted us to pitch our tent on a ledge of green grass amid the crags, sharing this wild, medieval castle with his Welsh mountain sheep.... Another favorite was at a *kibbutz* at the south end of the Sea of Galilee, where we slept 600 feet below sea level on shores Jesus walked and only a few miles from the Golan Heights which have been fought over by Israeli, Syrian, and Jordanian troops.... A four-star site was at Adelboden, high in the Swiss Alps, where each morning we could see the first rays of the sun touch the snow-tipped Wetterhorn and Giethorn and then slowly descend into the valleys....

Some natural divisions of labor emerged. Joan and Karen were the experts in pitching and dismantling the tent. David and I teamed up in packing the luggage carrier. Esther kept the interior of the microbus tidy. Ruth was gifted in finding water and going to local markets to buy fruit and vegetables, using a strange currency and fragments of a strange language....

Camping is not for those who simply want to travel inexpensively and effortlessly. It can be time consuming: packing and unpacking, setting up tent, going for water, adapting to others in tight quarters, using primitive WC's, negotiating traffic in congested, unfamiliar cities.

Apart from the airfare to and from Europe and the cost of VW van [which returned to the U. S. to become the family car], we could live more cheaply in our travels than at home. Three dollars per person a day was enough to cover all food, camp fees, gasoline and car expenses, film, postage, entrance fees, guidebooks and guides, incidental costs, and even the camping equipment. It did not include gifts purchased and air travel and the ferry boat tickets from port to port in the Mediterranean area....

In reflective moments we all concur that this has been one of the great experiences in the life of our family. We all were a little sad when we left our tent and camping equipment with friends in Casablanca, Morocco....

# 1971: Devotionals for the Journey

*Two devotionals written, with the assistance of family members, from experiences of the family's six-month trip around the Mediterranean 1970-1971 published in* Our Family Worships, *Sept.-Nov. 1971.*

THURSDAY, SEPTEMBER 9 *Helping God to Plant*
SCRIPTURE: Genesis 2:15; Leviticus 19:23

God planted trees on this earth: sugar maples, sycamores, giant sequoias, olive trees and thousands more than any of us can name. And He asked man to take good care of His trees and garden.

Ruth and David helped an old Israeli forester plant two pine trees on the barren hills near Jerusalem. The old forester spoke words from Leviticus: "When you come into the land... plant all kinds of trees." He told the children, "You are planting more than a tree. You are planting life."

Ruth and David selected their tiny trees. With a big hoe the forester dug a hole in the rocky soil. They planted the trees with their hands. He asked them to wash their hands. He dried them with a towel and asked them to water their newly planted trees. Then he looked up to the graying sky and offered a prayer in Hebrew.

Thank God for gardeners who plant and cultivate the gardens and for foresters who protect the forests.

WEDNESDAY, SEPTEMBER 15 *Let the Children Come*
SCRIPTURE: Romans 6:23

As our car came to a stop in the town of Saimbeyli in the mountains of Turkey, a crowd of children gathered around us. They laughed and shouted, pleased to see these visitors from America. We smiled at them and they smiled back. Although we could not speak each other's languages, we were friends.

More and more children gathered around our car. They ran out from houses, came down mountain roads. Some brought us gifts of fruit and flowers.

Then some men of the town came to the children, spat on them, and tried to force them to leave us alone. But the enthusiastic children came back to us. We remembered how Jesus loved the children. He had said that to enter heaven, even a grown-up must be joyful like a child.

Thank God for the joy of being a child. Ask God to help us not to be annoyed but to love all children.

# 1973: Things Hidden From the Wise

*Commencement address given at Goshen College, Goshen, Indiana, April 15, 1973.*

As you are about to embark on a journey, I have come to tell you stories of ordinary people I have met in my journey this past year.

Several months ago in a Manitoba blizzard I obtained a ride with a family driving from a place called Winkler to Winnipeg, where I was to catch a flight. This was a Kleine Gemeinde Mennonite couple in their sixties and their daughter, an elementary school teacher. Because of the blizzard we could not see far in any direction; as our car crept along we talked. The daughter told of returning recently from two years of voluntary service in Toronto. She had had health problems before and was hoping for a nice, conventional eight to five job–away front the emotion-saturated life of the classroom.

She arrived in Toronto and learned that her job, together with another new volunteer, was to be head resident for eight emotionally disturbed teenage girls, dropouts, some hooked on drugs, some on probation after skirmishes with the police–loose in their morals, mixed-up kids. The day before the leader of the unit collapsed from nervous exhaustion and had to leave. Monday morning, less than two days after arrival, two green girls were to take charge. She said: "We were scared–real scared–we knew the girls would test us by trying everything. That morning before seven I got a phone call from my folks. They said they knew this was my first day and that they were thinking of me and that they had prayed for me and wished me well. That was like a miracle. I felt better."

She went on to describe her experiences with those girls–drugs, abortions, fights with boyfriends. She added: "Sometimes I got so mad at them that I found myself shouting at them, even swearing at them–me, a nice Mennonite girl. But you know, those were the best two years ever. You couldn't have paid me to take such a job, but I found myself happy in doing it for no pay. I really learned what it means to forgive, to love nasty people, to turn the other cheek." When we reached Winnipeg I thought to myself what a gift it is for these simple, rural parents to have a daughter who opens doors and windows for them to a world of hurts. And what a break to have such understanding parents.

A second experience: recently I in turn gave a hitchhiker a lift. It was near Harrisburg on the Pennsylvania Turnpike and growing dark. He was Boston Irish; his grandfather having attended Boston Latin School with Joe Kennedy. He had a casual blue-jean appearance, an Afro-Irish mop of a hairdo. He confessed to a so-so high school performance, a year at a city college to establish his academic reputation, and now attendance at the Wharton School of Finance for a career in business. In our six hour drive our conversation ranged over many subjects: lacrosse, the Kennedys, the girls of Boston, a course on Marxism which caused some anxiety for his dentist father, a summertime lawn-mowing business with six young employees. At one point I asked him: "What do you hope to be doing five years from now?" His answer: "To be honest, I hope I'll still be in school. I am beginning to see that business is not my first love. I really would like to get into orthopedic medicine and work with crippled children. But I've never been too hot in science. This summer there'll be no lawn mowing, just science courses to see whether I can cut it." He added—"This idea goes back to when I was a kid and a young orthopedic doctor in our neighborhood, one of the nicest men I ever knew, died suddenly. I've always wanted to be like him." Give a lift to a hitchhiker and there is a young Peter Pendergast—with so much to teach me, a man twice his age.

A third experience. Out in Colorado in the Wet Mountain Valley up against the Sangre de Cristo range lives a rancher Jim Berry. When we first met him a year ago our car had just broken down. He towed us 14 miles to the nearest garage and then loaned us his new 4-wheel drive pickup until our car would be repaired. He never goes to church. He likes the bottle. But for us he was a living paraphrase of the Good Samaritan parable. And at dusk one evening be took us up above his ranch buildings to see some of the most beautiful mountain meadows. In the speech of a rancher: "I'll tell you one thing—according to my way of thinking, there isn't a more beautiful place in the whole world than this valley." And with the eyes of a True Believer, I think he is right.

Three experiences. What is the common motif? We who are college graduates—or in a few minutes will be college graduates—and live in the world of books and computers and test tubes are susceptible to the virtues of elitism, academic snobbery, hauteur. We may view with boredom and indifference those whom we think are of lesser breed—who really can't do anything for us. We might have been among those who asked with ill-concealed contempt: "What good could come out of Nazareth?" Or in contemporary phrasing: "I can't stand it to go back to X town; there's absolutely no one to talk to." I am impressed that from Chaucer to Frost, the gifts of so many of the great poets flowed from their mingling with ordinary people. They found among the people "things hidden from the wise."

There is an old Talmudic legend that the world is held up on the shoulders of ten ordinary men–ordinary, that is, nameless, dependable, unassuming, devoted men–ordinary, but really very extraordinary. On them the world depends. These ordinary people sometimes bring gifts of ideas like poets and prophets unawares.

An illustration: In California I met a social worker who works with the retarded. He commented to me: "You know, I realized recently that I receive more from the retarded than I give them." He went on: " I have come to see the retarded in a new light. They are a resource rather than a problem. Too long we have been thinking of them as problems."

A second illustration: Down the road from us (or up the creek, if you travel by water) lived until recently an old artist, born in South Russia more than 80 years ago. The Russia he knew as a boy predates Stalin and Brezhnev, predates World War I, the Revolution, the civil wars between the Reds and the Whites, the great famine in Russia. As the family was packing up boxes and boxes of sketches, paintings, sculptured objects, ceramic pieces–we were shown a collection of penciled drawings–thousands of tiny little drawings–sketched 55 years ago on the cheap paper of World War I–scenes of the artist's childhood: children playing leap frog, boys herding sheep, women baking, washing, men harvesting, cutting wood, an old man playing the balalaika. Here was a record of a folk culture, soon lost forever, except in the memories of old people and these artistic fragments of an old artist.

A third illustration. One of the profoundly moving spiritual experiences for me this past year was our attendance at the annual meeting of Mennonite Disaster Service at Morton, Illinois. This had been the big year of disaster: Corning, Elmira, Wilkes Barre, Buffalo Creek, Harrisburg, Rapid City. And this had been for MDS their finest hour: in 1972 a total of 50,000 work days from perhaps 6000 volunteers. Mennonite Disaster Service is a kind of folk movement: lay-led, decentralized, little administrative machinery, non-reflective (the phone call at 11 p.m. that workers are needed; at dawn the following morning two carloads of volunteers are on their way to the disaster), a spontaneous kind of lay evangelism (workers covered with mud listening to disaster victims unfold their stories of tragedy and trying to respond with words of encouragement that are not too pat). The annual meeting at Morton was almost like a Wesleyan camp meeting: one layman after another rising and telling his disaster experience–and the recurring refrain: "We came to help and we received more help than we gave." And variations on the theme: "There but for the grace of God go I." There was, for example, Big Eddy. He tells of being responsible for disaster cleanup operations in Elmira, New York. The National Guard was there. Local people had to line up to wait their turn for food, water, clothing, blankets–people tired and irritable. Fighting broke out in the lines. A Red Cross official came to Eddie: "MDS has got to police those lines." Eddie responded: "But the National Guard–why don't you use them?" "No, that won't work; things will explode.... You only need to send two fellows. Have them wear the MDS insignia and talk to the people in the line." Two were sent and they talked to the people in the lines. And the lines quieted down. Eddie, the Mennonite Disaster Service man, said: "That Red Cross official–his confidence in the Mennonite peace witness was a lot stronger than mine.... I was ashamed."

These are several illustrations of insights picked up along the way from ordinary people–"things hidden from the wise."

The great movements of history have been movements which have gone to the people: the Early Church–"and the common people heard them gladly"... St. Francis and his barefoot friars out among the people being instruments of his peace; "where there is hatred, love; where there is injury, pardon; where there is doubt, faith"... the Swiss Brethren who poured out of Zurich in 1525, called to carry the Gospel to weavers in guild halls, farmers in upland fields, tradesmen in marketplaces–anywhere where two or three could be gathered together to hear and study the word.... The stirrings of social conscience among young Russian intellectuals in the 19th century known as the *Narod* (Return to the people). Alexander Solzhenitsyn in his novel *August 1914* describes sympathetically this movement in the person of young Isaakii who "loved his native village of Sablya and their farm six miles distant... who loved the work, and during the holidays... never shirked his share of the scything and threshing... who thought of himself as someone who had received an education to use for the benefit of the people and who would go back to the people with the book, the word, and with love."

"To the people" movements are the stuff of which gentle reformations and radical revolutions are made. Often defeated, frequently aborted, sometimes ignored, going "to the people" is a way of testing great ideas. It is the village tinkerers approach to technological progress. Make it, take it out, and test it.

By going to people we can acquire new ideas "hidden from the wise." We can also observe new ways of doing things.

An illustration. Some weeks ago I was driving from Colorado Springs to Wichita and stopped for lunch at a restaurant in Meade, Kansas. I entered one cafe but quickly left without ordering–a slightly forbidding place. I walked down the street and found a hotel restaurant–new decor, the place throbbing with activity. The manager stopped by to inquire how I found my lunch. Through him I learned that the restaurant had just been opened three days before, that several months ago the then rundown hotel and restaurant had been up for sale; ten couples formed a corporation and bought it, pitched in, refurbished it, brightened it up and restored it as a center of community life. They planned to renovate the basement into a youth center for weekend use. All this, I learned, stemmed from a shared Christian concern that God's people ought to be hospitable people. I like that–a return to the medieval monastic vocation of providing inns for the weary traveler.

Another illustration–learning from people doing things. In South Dakota I met a mother, who in watching TV saw a Chicano youth, a confessed killer of four, who had been condemned to 290 years in prison. This young man looked like her son and her heart went out to him. She wrote to the prison warden for permission to write to the convicted murderer. The answer was "No." She wrote to the Chief Chaplain. The answer was "No." She wrote to an assistant chaplain. The answer came back: "The list of those permitted to correspond with him is filled." She persisted. In time she got on the list. She has been corresponding with the young man and with other members of his family. She has been encouraging him in his law studies, his painting, his Christian life. A caring, tenacious mother can penetrate that grey eminence of the penal system.

As a sometime-intellectual and a sometime-administrator, I like things tidy and orderly, procedures regular and deliberate. I have a distaste for brash action, the blurted remark, the knee-jerk reaction. But as I mellow with age I must acknowledge that the Spirit may often speak in people's blurted remarks, in their impulsive reactions.

An example: Martha Mitchell has so often annoyed me with her blurted, impulsive comments to the press–phone calls in the night–an embarrassment to an image-conscious administration. But then this loquacious, uninhibited, slightly blowsy woman from Arkansas in all her folk wisdom breaks through establishment niceties to blurt out last summer after the breaking of the Watergate case: "I told my husband I'll leave him if he doesn't get out of politics… all those dirty things that go on." A folk conscience more sensitive than that possessed by all the spiritual and intellectual advisors around the throne.

A second example. A Daniel Ellsberg, one of those "best and brightest young men" of the Kennedy and Johnson years who helped orchestrate the liberals' and intellectuals' war in Vietnam–who drew back in horror at this sordid mess, and all the lies being pumped back to Washington to document the official line. He is now on trial. His defense might well be that of another weak man long ago who became a strong man, a rock: "I ought to obey God rather than men."

Parenthetically, one of the most deeply disturbing books I have read this year is David Halberstam's *The Best and the Brightest*, the story of how brilliant, liberal, pragmatic young men (the smoothest and the glibbest), with all their impeccable credentials, led us into the most sordid, shabby war in American history. Again one remembers the folk wisdom comment of House Speaker Sam Rayburn, who said to his protégé Lyndon Johnson (then Vice President) when the latter rhapsodized about this team of the "best and the brightest": "Well, Lyndon, everything you say may be right, and they may be every bit as able as you say, but I'd feel a whole lot better if just one of them had run for sheriff once."

As we were saying, the Spirit sometimes moves in the blurts of folk wisdom,"things hidden from the wise."

A philosopher friend of mine–he, too, with impeccable academic credentials–says that he has come to be less interested in carefully structured propositional truth, that in seeking and speaking truth we need to devote more time to telling and listening to stories, telling and listening to parables.

He tells his own story. An Oklahoma farm boy, he volunteered for MCC service and was sent to Vietnam and as a 22 year old was given large funds and great responsibilities. He wrote impassioned letters back to the central office detailing his administrative plight and begging for instructions. He comments: "Either in their naivete or in their infinite wisdom, they sent back bland, no-answer letters." And he adds, "Then a Catholic priest helped me to see that implicit in those no-answer letters was a message to me that I was responsible, that they had no more ability than I to wend through the thicket of complexities, that I was to act and to report. I was to act."

Another illustration of storytelling. I was intrigued with the cover story in the current issue of *Time* on Senator Sam Ervin, who someday soon is headed for a showdown at High Noon with the president on presidential power versus congressional power. Sam Ervin, who is a top constitutional lawyer, is another one of these folk-wisdom people, and a teller of folksy stories from his native Burke County, North Carolina. He says, "I found that an apt story is worth an hour of argument… a good way to relieve tension." Sam Ervin, with his bagful of stories, will be a most formidable adversary as those Watergate hearings move to a showdown with national television coverage.

A third illustration of storytelling. Perhaps you, like me, read Art Buchwald's newspaper column. He comments on the current Washington news in parables. Contemporary Pharisees are no more enthusiastic about these parables than they were about another one who once told it in parables. Take this parable:

> The good news in Washington last week was that crime had dropped in the capital 50 per cent.... However, housebreaking at the Watergate was up 100 per cent. Illegal bugging of politicians increased 73 per cent.... Shredding of crucial evidence increased 33 per cent.... While street crime was down, crimes associated with executive privilege were up by 13 per cent. The smuggling of cash contributions across state lines for immoral purposes increased by 74 per cent.

A parable.

We have been talking about things hidden from the wise... drawing deeply on the resources of ordinary people–the fine art of listening... the gift of curiosity, asking questions... storing up memories. John Steinbeck, the novelist, in his delightful book *Travels with Charley in Search of America*, wrote:

> Once I traveled about in an old bakery wagon, double-doored rattler with a mattress on its floor. I stopped where people stopped or gathered, I listened and looked and felt, and in the process had a picture of my country the accuracy of which was impaired only by my own shortcomings.

In discussing the search for wisdom I do not wish to deprecate the scientific discipline of experiment and analysis, nor the paths of reasoned discourse, nor the solitary arts of meditation, prayer, and reading. In fact, the book is a door to understanding people. As I have thought about this subject, "Things Hidden From the Wise," I have found help from a variety of books: from Bill Moyer's *Listening to America* to Robert Coles's *Children of Crisis* to *The Foxfire Book*–the latter the recorded experiences of a teacher and his students in the mountains of Georgia. And the Bible. This whole idea of going-to-the-people to find things hidden from the wise is a motif written large in the four gospels. As I have read again Matthew, Mark, Luke and John there is everywhere this to-the-people theme. Listen to these words from the New English Bible: "he went journeying from town to town and village to village"... "when he was seated there, crowds flocked to him"... "and the whole town was there, gathered at the door"... "crowding in upon him to touch him"... "he could hardly breathe for the crowds"... "when Jesus was at table in the house, many bad characters–tax gatherers and others–were seated with him"... "then he said to his host, 'When you give a lunch or dinner party, do not invite your friends, your brothers or other relations, or your rich neighbors... but when you give a party, ask the poor, the crippled, the lame, and the blind.'"

The Gospels also record the sobering data of the cowardice of the people, the demagoguery of the people, praises turning to curses: then the disciples all deserted him and ran away... the crowd cried: "crucify him, crucify him".... And the theme of story telling: everywhere he went he spoke in parables... in fact he never spoke to them without a parable... the Kingdom of Heaven is like... the Kingdom of Heaven is like...

One senses, too, that Jesus drew deeply from the people for his own spiritual needs: the sight of the people moved him to compassion... the two blind men sitting at the roadside (near Jericho).... Jesus was deeply moved and touched their eyes... the poor widow observed at the temple treasurer: "I tell you this, this widow has given more than any of the others, but she with less than enough, has given all that she had to live on"...

And finally: Jesus exulted in the Holy Spirit and said, "I thank thee, Father, Lord of Heaven and Earth, for hiding these things from the learned and wise, and revealing them to the simple..."

To you who are about to receive degrees–our gratitude, our blessing, and our love... and go forth seeking those "things hidden from the wise..."

Go in peace. Keep the faith. Serve the Lord.

# 1973: Influenced, but Not Imprisoned, by Our Heritage

*Printed in* The Mennonite, *September 25, 1973, and in several other publications.*

Many of us walked taller as Mennonites upon reading Harold S. Bender's presidential address delivered in 1943 at the American Society of Church History: *The Anabaptist Vision.* It began with the soaring, perhaps extravagant, affirmation of Rufus Jones:

> Judged by the reception it met at the hands of those in power... the Anabaptist movement was one of the most tragic in the history of Christianity; but judged by the principles which were put into play by this reproachful nickname, it must be pronounced one of the most momentous and significant undertakings in man's eventful religious struggle after the truth.

The Bender address symbolized for many of us a Mennonite coming of age. It spoke to our identity problem. It helped us overcome our Mennonite shame.

I suspect that every sensitive Mennonite goes through life with a backpack of ambivalent feelings about his people and heritage–a sense of embarrassment in being a peculiar Mennonite and yet a sense of pride in being heir to a great, creative Anabaptist heritage.

We have known embarrassment: a small, rural, quaint, irrelevant minority, mistaken for the Amish and the Mormons, identified with the violent and radical left, confused with the fundamentalists, lumped together with crackpots, linked with prudery and legalism. It is no fun to be a member of a queer, "backward" group in this modern, enlightened, emancipated world.

We have known pride. A minister of education in Kenya, a desk officer in Washington, a program director in Ottawa–all speak glowingly of Mennonite programs and performance.

The halo begins to fit uncomfortably when one remembers the words: "Beware when all men speak well of you."

Again and again I have been renewed in my appreciation for my Mennonite identity and heritage by stepping outside and looking at the Mennonites from a slight distance: going away to the university and looking back, working with other agencies and comparing, traveling abroad and reflecting. Distance, and the perspective it gives, often makes the heart grow fonder. This is the biblical formula for renewal through withdrawal and return.

Sometimes one's heritage comes alive through the written and the spoken word. When I was a boy I was intrigued in reading P. C. Hiebert and Orie Miller's book, *Feeding the Hungry*–the story of the MCC relief effort in South Russia. As a child I remember the coming to our community of the Epps, the Klassens, the Schmidts, and the Warkentines, all Mennonite refugee families from Russia. Hearing their stories we sensed what it means to be a suffering church.

Recently I have read two provocative books on the heritage question by a Slovak-American, Catholic author, Michael Novak: *Ascent of the mountain, Flight of the Dove* and *The Rise of the Unmeltable Ethnics.* He pleads persuasively for a new appreciation for the ethnic dimension of life: "Dignity comes not simply from money or occupation, but also from belonging to a culture.... Ethnic consciousness can, like modern science, lead to evil as well as good." People who are secure in their identity seem to act with greater freedom and openness to others. Mr. Novak states it another way: "We believe that people who are secure in their past and joyful in their present cannot but be hopeful in their future." This he calls the "new ethnicity."

Some of the best writing anywhere on the heritage and ethnic self-understanding question is to be found in a collection of essays written in honor of J. J. Thiessen and published by Canadian Mennonite Bible College: *Call to Faithfulness.* Among the chapters which speak to the issues before us are ones such as these: "The present in dialogue with the past," "Mennonite families: Foundations and launching pads," "The struggle for recognition," "Adaptation and identity," and many others. This book deserves wide reading.

Others are speaking to these issues. A young woman, Sharon Curtin, writes with sensitivity and insight these words in her recent book, *Nobody Ever Died of Old Age:* "My grandparents were an integral and important part of the family and of the community. I sometimes have a dreadful fear that mine will be the last generation to know old people as friends, to have a sense of what growing old means, to respect and understand man's mortality and his courage in the face of death. Mine may be the last generation to have a sense of living history, of stories passed from generation to generation, of identity established by family history."

The best educational treatise I have read this year is *The Foxfire Book,* a book of experiences of a teacher and his students in a mountain community, Rabun Gap, Georgia. The students, with the teacher's help, gathered stories from their mountain neighbors on hog dressing, home crafts and foods, planting by the signs, home remedies, log cabin building, and other affairs of plain living. Listen to these words from the author's introduction:

> Daily our grandparents are moving out of our lives.... These grandparents were primarily an oral civilization, information being passed through the generations by word of mouth and demonstration.... When they're gone... the eloquent and haunting stories of suffering and sharing and building and healing and planting and harvesting–all these go with them, and what a loss. If this information is to be saved... it must be saved now; and the logical researchers are the grandchildren, not university researchers from the outside.

The author states that to reconstruct one's heritage does something for the gatherer of the information:

> In the process, these grandchildren (and we) gain an invaluable, unique knowledge about their own roots, heritage, and culture. Suddenly they discover their families–previously people to be ignored and in the face of the seventies–as pretelevision, preautomobile, preflight individuals who endured and survived the incredible task of total self-sufficiency and came out of it all with a perspective on ourselves as a country... something to tell us about self-reliance, human interdependence, and the human spirit that we would do well to listen to.

To be a Mennonite is to be a member of an ethnic group. We may insist that Mennonites are a religious group and stand above ethnicity. What is an ethnic group? Michael Novak says that it is "a group with historical memory, real or imaginary."

In part you are born into an ethnic group; in part you choose it. "Given a grandparent or two, one chooses to shape one's consciousness by one history rather than another. Ethnic memory is not a set of events remembered, but rather of instincts, feelings, intimacies, expectations, patterns of emotion and behavior; a sense of reality; a set of stories for individuals–and for the people as a whole–to live out."

These heritage convictions and instincts are often below the level of consciousness and part of a chain of transmission not easy to root out. Ethnic memory may be conveyed in food, language, patterns of speech, ways of having fun, jokes, tastes. Heritage memory may be carried by these and by other means–family reactions to volunteering to need, openness or restraint in discussing faith issues, patterns of giving.

Mennonites are a cluster of subethnic groups. Among (Old) Mennonites are lingering evidences of differences between communities of Amish background and those of Mennonite background. The glory and the burden of the General Conference are its multiplicity of subethnic groups: Hutterite, Swiss, Volhynian Swiss, Pennsylvania Dutch (Swiss via Alsace or the Palatinate), Dutch from West Prussia, Dutch from Poland, Dutch from South Russia (those of the 1870s, others of the 1920s, others post-World War II), Bavarians. Each has its differences of food, speech, customs, family names, and patterns of church life.

This year I have been going about Canada and the United States asking people about their heritage. One cannot talk about heritage without finding it in autobiographical form.

Recently we asked Tom Gish, editor of the *Mountain Eagle* of Whitesburg, Kentucky, what gives him hope for eastern Kentucky where are located four of the poorest counties in the United States. He answered: "The strength of the people. They know who they are. A person knows where he comes from, who his father is, who his grandfather is."

Another man, born and bred in the hills, added: "There's not three persons I meet in a day whom I don't know." This public official continued: "Something goes wrong for you around here and there are all kinds of people you can call on."

A few months ago a middle-aged Mennonite university professor commented to me: "I am working on the spiritual capital of my parents. They gave me a powerful heritage–a memory of suffering in Russia, exodus, tragedy and deliverance, and then an ethnic thing (German language and all) to rebel against; what spiritual capital am I building into my kids?... We can't live for long on the heritage of the early 1920s."

A Mennonite Brethren teacher and ex-MCC worker, reflecting to me on the MCC, said: "MCC is half in and half out of an ethnic culture. It provides a place for innovation–a testing ground for those things which work and those which do not." My friend went on to say that our ethnic-bound ways can be a resource for the church: "An ethnic group accommodates itself to dissent. A fundamentalist church of true believers will throw or freeze out the offbeat youth in its ranks. An ethnic Mennonite Brethren Church is reluctant to throw out your cousin's oldest son. It hangs in there with him and keeps on caring." Martin Marty, writer, historian, Missouri Synod pastor, said to a small group: "As a Missouri Synod Lutheran, three groups are most helpful to me in understanding myself: Jewish novelists, post-Vatican II Catholics, Mennonites." He explained that all have a strong ethnic consciousness, take their past seriously, take their faith seriously, and yet are trying to move into the modern world, translating their heritage into new forms to respond to contemporary needs. He finds it refreshing to meet people in touch with their past even if they have transcended and reinterpreted it.

Ladonna Harris, a Comanche Indian and the wife of former Senator Harris of Oklahoma, told some of us in a recent meeting in Washington that a minority ethnic group like the Mennonites might have a gift, a mission in understanding other ethnic groups. If you savor the uniqueness of your heritage, you can be more sensitive to the subtle ways in which others differ. She put me on the trail of an Italian Catholic priest, Monsignor Geno Baroni, whom I then went to see.

The priest told me he had had an inner-city parish where he became deeply involved in the civil rights movement–the black struggle for ethnic recovery. He found that his Italian parishioners were not following him in his activism. He discovered that his people were not supporting the blacks because they themselves had so little sense of ethnic self-worth. He changed course and began to concentrate on helping his people to restore their threatened sense of self-identity. He feels that as his Italian people come to appreciate their peoplehood they can be helped to understand the peoplehood of blacks, Jews, and perhaps even Irish Catholics.

Michael Novak and others are telling us that the American people have been badly served by the myth of the American melting pot. It has been an Anglo-Saxon, English-speaking, largely Protestant ethnic group's effort to homogenize us all into a bland all-American type. James Farrell calls the melting pot an "Anglo-Saxon effort to rub out the past of others." The Canadian tradition, fortified by a powerful French-speaking bloc, offers a better alternative–the idea of a cultural mosaic. Each ethnic group is to be respected and cherished, each contributing in richness of color its past to the total picture.

The Apostle Paul speaks of varieties of gifts and said that they were good. Is it not appropriate to think that varieties of culture are also good in God's grand mosaic? We are not to be ashamed of our ethnic and heritage peculiarities. They are gifts, resources. Let us encourage other peoples in their yearning for ethnic identity: the black, the Navajo, the Italian-American, the Chicano. Let ethnic sensitivity be a resource, an opening in our ministries of evangelism and reconciliation.

I am intrigued how the biblical writers cast their message in familial (ethnic) terms. Stephen standing before his accusers and stating his case for Christ and conscience declares himself not to be ashamed of his ethnic past and spiritual heritage. He begins his statement with the story of Abraham and conducts his hearers step by step through the pilgrimage of the Hebrew people.

Scholars seem to have found new meaning in the Hebrew consciousness of peoplehood– "the people of God."

I am of the conviction that Christ speaks to the sickness of our society by translating the gospel into familial (ethnic) terms–on being a good neighbor... on being a brother... as a father cares for his children.... "Woman, behold thy son" and "Behold thy mother"... of celebrating a wedding feast together... on eating together... of not coming to destroy a heritage but to cherish a heritage.

I am of the conviction that our heritage speaks to the sickness of our society. Here are people who take seriously the biblical record and their dramatic Anabaptist-Mennonite heritage. This heritage expressed in the language of family, smallness, neighborliness might offer answers to the ills of our society with its vacuum of the soul, its value-free chatter, its rootlessness, its restless movement, its mindless conformity, its buy-use-and-throw-away approach to things and people, its dreary sameness, its temporariness, its bondage to public opinion, its pressures "to be with it," its manipulation of images.

If the Mennonite heritage is to speak to the needs of people today, it cannot be a slavish imitation of Mennonite traditions. It calls for fresh translations of our heritage into the language of our day. Our need is not for a copying of surface characteristics, but rather for a living out in fresh ways of ideas and themes within the tradition.

This is only a start. We, of course, have not faced up here to some of the hard questions. How does one reconcile the biblical affirmation of family and peoplehood with the scriptural calls to spring loose from the ethnic: Jesus' question, "Who is my mother? and who are my brethren?"... Paul's words, "there is neither Greek nor Jew..."? Is not a reaffirmation of Mennonite peoplehood a throwback to the *Volkskirche* which our Anabaptist forefathers rejected?... Does not an Anabaptist believers' church call for a melting and fusing together of cultures?... Is it fair to call Mennonites an ethnic group; are they not rather a religious people above ethnicity?... Can you have pure peoplehood of God without cultural expressions of it?

We need not be ashamed of the gospel of Christ, nor of our Mennonite heritage.

# 1974: The Best and the Brightest

*A book review of David Halberstam's* The Best and the Brightest *(1973) that appeared in* The Mennonite, *January 22, 1974.*

I first read David Halberstam's *The Best and the Brightest* when it appeared in hardcover a year ago. This is a deeply disturbing record of the Vietnam War and how the Kennedy, and more particularly the Johnson, administration fearful of being tagged with the charge of "being soft on communism" or "weak presidents," slipped step by step into a shabby war in Southeast Asia. I have again read this book, now just out in paperback, and it gets better, more significant with age.

Mr. Halberstam describes how in the presidential employ was a stable of the "best and the brightest," pragmatic, amoral, ambitious young men (the smoothest and glibbest), all with impeccable credentials. This loyal ingroup, in uneasy alliance with the Pentagon and the CIA, optimistically improvised plan after plan which backed us blindly into the Vietnam War. They filtered out unpleasant truth from Vietnam and told lies to cover the step-by-step descent into a political hell. With only a few faint voices leaking their doubts, no one had the courage to break with the system of deceit, no one standing up to resign, to protest.

The bright ones close to the throne could rationalize that they "must go along," to compromise, to be there to shape policy for the good of the nation at a later date—not knowing that that noble hour would never come, not realizing the corrupting character of deceit, nor the habit-forming drug of power. The story begins in the honeymoon days of Kennedy and ends with the fall of Johnson.

Substitute the name Nixon for Johnson; substitute Ehrlichman, Haldemam, Dean, and Colson for Bundy, McNamara, Rostow, and Taylor; substitute "the plumbers" for CIA; substitute California advertising men for men from MIT and Harvard; and finally substitute Watergate for Vietnam and you have two tragedies cut of the same cloth. It's the fabric of sin and misgovernment.

Here is "the arrogance of power," "the imperial presidency," a common distrust of the people, Congress, and the press. Watergate, following on the heels of Vietnam, makes this a doubly significant book.

The records of both Vietnam and Watergate are associated with words and phrases like these: power, remaining No. 1, toughness, image, winning, never being a loser, hard-nosed realism, toughing it out, covert operations, information control, government by manipulation. Just as Vietnam destroyed Johnson and the best and the brightest around him, so Watergate is slowly destroying Nixon and almost all those around him.

I suspect that if the Lord spares our country a few more decades we shall look back to the Vietnam-Watergate era and see it as a continental divide in the history of American society. When I first read *The Best and the Brightest*, I had been reading the Book of Jeremiah. I saw striking parallels between the warnings of this Old Testament prophet and David Halberstam's critique of American military policy in the middle and late sixties. He doesn't use theological language, but he had much to say about the demonic forces, the princes and principalities of darkness of our day.

David Halberstam's book offers good corrective reading for those who think that deceit and coverup began with President Nixon. It is uncomfortable reading if you have affection for John Kennedy and his men of Camelot and worse, if you have a lingering admiration for Johnson, Rusk, and McNamara. In any event this is highly absorbing reading—rich in fascinating personality sketches.

As the United States is now in danger of being drawn step by step into a war in the Middle East, we owe it to ourselves to see how we slipped and stumbled into a war in Southeast Asia.

From the self-perception of America as the No. 1 defender of the free world, we easily adopted the idea of fighting a clean technological war without Americans dying. This led to a plan of simply furnishing war materials, America confident of its industrial power and technological genius. Observers were sent, who soon became advisors. Then airplanes and bombs were sent and these needed advisors and maintenance people. The security of the airfields must be protected and so battalions were sent to protect the bases.

One began to hear less about "protecting the free world" and more words like these: "No fourth-rate Asian power is going to push Americans around." More troops arrived. The enclave plan emerged with U.S. forces concentrated in coastal bases with limited objectives. Soon this led to an aggressive "search and destroy" strategy, then to a war of attrition.

Step by step America was in a full-scale ground combat war. We spoke less and less of defending freedom-loving peoples and more and more about "protecting our boys." More bombers to "protect our boys" and more boys to protect our bomber bases. Through this "escalating war by stealth" Americans were being fed an optimistic diet of manipulated data, which found its most obscene form in "the fake body count."

David Halberstam describes how in Washington the Vietnam War created a climate of suspicion. In the presidential circle friendly doubters became doubters, doubters became critics, critics became enemies, enemies became traitors. The only alternative was total loyalty. Halberstam describes the last days of Johnson: "He had a sense that everything he had wanted for... his offering to history was slipping away, and the knowledge of this made him angrier and touchier than ever; if you could not control events, you could at least control the version of them. Thus the press was an enemy. Critics of the war became his critics; since he was patriotic, clearly they were not." Does this not have sounds of Watergate?

Mr. Halberstam, for many years a *New York Times* correspondent, is one of America's most respected journalists. *The Best and the Brightest*, which has been for almost a year in the top ten best-sellers in nonfiction, is a book to be taken seriously—a sad book, a prophetic book, a readable book. These are like pages torn out of the books of the Hebrew prophets. Jeremiah, I think, would have approved this book with its call to national repentance.

# 1974: Letter to Richard M. Nixon

*In the September 3, 1974 issue of* The Mennonite *appeared the following resolution drafted by Kreider and adopted by the General Conference Mennonite Church in triennial meeting at St. Catharines, Ontario, July 26, 1974. Henry Gerbrandt, Elmer Neufeld, and Robert Kreider were asked to present this letter in person. On October 25, 1974, in* The Mennonite *appeared a letter from Kreider reporting on the multiple efforts to reach the recently resigned President and reflections on what words of additional counsel might be spoken to a man of Quaker affiliation.*

Dear Mr. President: We are meeting here as an international body of General Conference Mennonites. Today came news of the withholding of evidence and the intensifying national crisis.

We who stand afar off can sense only in part the anguish and turbulence of soul which must be yours these days and months. We confess that among us is pain and sadness, among some anger, others a sense of betrayal.

And yet our hearts go out to your family, your colleagues, your advocates, and you. Our prayers are attending you. And we pray for ourselves who bear guilt for systems of government which come to be pervaded with evil forces.

We invite you to place your burdens in the hands of God who loves, cares, and forgives beyond all human capacities.

We encourage you to seek anew to draw deeply from the life-renewing and cleansing spring of your Quaker-Christian heritage–with its affirmations of forgiveness, reconciliation, and obedience to Christ; its invitation to listen attentively to the still, small voice of his Spirit; its call to the life of peace, simplicity, and truth.

We encourage you to pause and read anew in the Scriptures of the acts of the great and mighty men–men who have stumbled and fallen, who have strayed from the paths of God, who repented of their ways, received forgiveness, and then became a blessing and a strength to their people.

As the walls of your world close in on you, we beg of you to stand before God and then your people and to say with simplicity and truth–"Here am I.... Forgive me. And from now until the end of my days, guide me along the paths of faithfulness."

We, too, stand ready as a Mennonite people to be used as an instrument in the cleansing, healing, and restoring of our systems of law and government which we have allowed to become captive to evil. We, too, ask for forgiveness.

# 1974: To Give But Also To Receive

*Appeared in* The Messenger, *October 1974 and in several other periodicals. This is based on Robert and Lois' around-the-world trip in 1974 for the Mennonite Central Committee.*

By virtue of the label, "North American," we are perceived by Africans and Asians as people of self-confidence, people with information and know-how. In their eyes we are problem-solvers, movers and fix-it persons. North Americans appear this way overseas even in interchurch relationships. For example:

- An emerging church is establishing a new central office. Do they need a telephone, car or duplicating equipment? No problem – we can provide.
- The young church is starting a program of evangelism or is interested in sponsoring an agricultural development enterprise. No problem–we can find evangelism consultants and trained agriculturalists.
- A complex, apparently insolvable issue arises. No problem–we will appoint a task force to study it and make recommendations.

A heady feeling of self-satisfaction envelops us as we respond to overseas peoples in their need. This may be good and healthy, and yet it may be laced with pride and a sense of superiority. We attend a worship service and are disappointed if we are not called on to speak. We see our faithfulness measured by the number of people we send overseas. We are the haves. We are the givers. We feel satisfaction for we know that "it is more blessed to give than to receive."

I once knew a dear overseas missionary and relief worker who was always busy doing good for others. However, it was difficult, almost impossible, to help her. Her sweetness was a tyranny of kindness. Some of our ministrations overseas also suffer from a tyranny of kindness–goodness that goes down a one-way street.

What can we do about it? As we traveled recently in Africa and Asia, we became aware of one answer to our inflated pride in being the giving people: our friends overseas have many gifts to give us if we can lower our defenses and let them help us.

First, our Christian brothers and sisters in Africa and Asia can be our visual interpreters of the biblical world. They, more than we, live in a biblical world–in societies where people walk great distances, wash dusty feet, draw water, and offer blood sacrifices. As we study the Bible through their eyes, it comes to life with a new immediacy and freshness.

We visited the Bihari refugee camp on the edge of Dacca, Bangladesh. Three hundred refugees live together in an area no larger than a small basketball court. As we entered the area, dozens of thin but bright-eyed, curious children crowded around to see, to touch, to hear. Adults came up and angrily tried to chase them away. In that moment the words of Jesus seemed so real: "Suffer the little children to come unto me."

On another occasion, threading alleys and passageways in a poor section of Calcutta, we climbed stairs to an upper room where a Hindu wedding feast was waiting. Our thoughts went back to a supper many centuries ago in an upper room. As we had been invited only that morning, we recalled Jesus' parable of the host going out to invite strangers to his wedding feast.

Approached by beggars on the ferry boat, in the street, literally everywhere, we were haunted by the admonition of our Lord: "Give to him that asketh." The hundreds of people sleeping on the concrete floor of Hawrath Railroad Station in Calcutta evoked the image of "the Son of Man having no place to lay his head."

We saw people carrying enormous loads on their heads and backs and heard the scriptural injunction, "Bear ye one another's burdens." And in noting others carrying heavy loads from a yoke borne on the shoulders, we remembered Christ's words: "Take my yoke upon you."

Second, the peoples of Africa and Asia can teach us something about the grace of the simple life and the art of survival. Tasty meals are prepared from simple vegetation gathered in the fields. For many meat is a rarity in their diet. Children create ingenious toys from discarded wire. In Southeast Asia people live in 90 degree heat day after day without air conditioning and without complaint. They are accustomed to walking long distances because only the rich can afford cars. A family of seven can live comfortably in a bamboo structure with less floor space than a one-car garage.

In Southeast Asia death is constantly present in daily experience. No Vietnamese family is without memories of violent personal tragedy. For a generation the war has careened back and forth across the scarred countryside. And yet these durable people carry on.

The people God has created in Bangladesh, India and Vietnam have learned how to survive with only a few possessions, how to produce a family's food requirements on an acre or less and how to share the little they do have. If a nuclear holocaust should lay waste the earth, these people may be best prepared to survive.

Third, the peoples of Africa and Asia have stories to tell if we are ready to listen. Like the ancient Hebrews, these are parable-telling peoples. To emphasize or clarify an idea, a worker in Zaire used stories his grandfather told as the family sat around its fire in the evening. A Javanese pastor told us stories of living through a generation of crises–the Dutch colonial period, the Japanese occupation, the war of liberation from the Dutch, the Indonesian civil war–and how the church grew despite opposition. A pastor of the Mennonite Church in Japan recalled his life in the Japanese navy, his thoughts of suicide and the Christian joy he found in a fellowship group meeting for Bible study in a garage at Kobe, Japan.

Wherever we went, we heard stories which should be written down and shared with friends in North America and elsewhere because they would enrich our devotional and Christian education literature. We often thought how helpful it would be if the stories of war and peace and reconciliation experienced by our Asian friends could be gathered into a common spiritual treasury for us all. How good it would be to collect a devotional storehouse with contributions from brothers and sisters of many countries. Perhaps as each contributor drew from his respective cultural and spiritual pilgrimage, we would sense the richly varied dimensions of the worldwide Christian fellowship.

Finally, our Christian friends from Africa and Asia can bring us gifts in the art of worship. We attended a service in Lubumbashi, Zaire, where we understood not a word of the Swahili but felt at home. All guests that morning were invited to come forward to be introduced and welcomed into the fellowship. Standing beside us was a young man who was welcomed back from a term in prison. The offering was no formal, routine affair as in North American churches. We all filed past the communion table and placed our gifts one at a time in the offering bowl while the eyes of the congregation focused upon each one. The joyous singing and clapping ceremony of gathering the offering came as the celebrative, culminating point of the worship service. Here stewardship was a worship act of high seriousness and exultation.

In a remote valley of southern Swaziland we attended a weekend of meetings by independent churches worshiping in a mud-walled meeting house. When we entered the clean-swept church with its dirt floor, we all removed our shoes. We heard those lines of scripture, "Put off your shoes from your feet for the place where you stand is holy ground." When we prayed (and the congregation prayed frequently), we all knelt on hands and knees. The doors and windows were closed for they are attentive to the scriptural injunction, "When you pray, enter into your closet and when you have shut the door pray to your Father which is in secret." As we prayed, audible prayers rose simultaneously from many in the congregation. No sermon continued longer than five minutes, but there were several sermons and testimonies. Accompanied by clapping, hymn after hymn in the African musical idiom rose to the thatched roof. They were taking seriously the biblical encouragement to "clap your hands all ye people."

Our circuit among African and Asian peoples made us aware again that God has given the people in North America certain gifts which we must share. But we have only some of the gifts. We are also called to admit our emptiness. We need to accept with gratitude the good gifts which brothers and sisters overseas offer us. Perhaps then we will know the blessing of having received.

# 1974: The Sixties–Things Fall Apart

*Printed in* The Mennonite, *November 12, 1974, and in several other publications.*

Things fall apart; the centre cannot hold...
The best lack all conviction, while the worst
Are full of passionate intensity...
William Butler Yeats

Something hit us in the 1960s. For some of us a neat, comfortable, stable world fell apart. Some of us are bewildered and guilt-ridden: "What happened? What did we do wrong? Why did our family fall apart? Why did our children reject us–after all that we had done for them?" These are the words of not a few parents. Perhaps these are your words. Listen to these experiences drawn from good Mennonite homes, experiences which cropped up in the late 1960s, a few spilling over into the early 1970s:

*Item*: "Divorce in our family? No chance. I always thought other kinds of people had divorces. Now it is right in our own family. Two of our children are divorced. What did we do wrong as parents?"

*Item*: "We returned with our children from the mission field. Our daughter was a top student. Then she began to change–more withdrawn, irritable. One day a neighbor woman came to my office and blurted out that our daughter was on drugs."

*Item*: "The oldest daughter attended a Mennonite college, transferred to a state university, broke with old friends and found new friends whom she did not introduce to her parents. Then she disappeared. Two years later she surfaced to return home and to face criminal charges."

*Item*: A pastor comments, "We really have two families–the older children who graduated 10 to 15 years ago are all top students... and then the younger children who rebelled against home, church and college. Our family has been quite a burden to the college... how much are we to blame as parents?"

*Item*: "We were having a congregational meeting to decide on building a new parsonage. Some of us committed enough funds to make it possible. Some students came home from college and seminary and spoke against the plan in the meeting. They said that the church ought to use the money for something more significant. That hurt. It wasn't their money. It really hurt."

*Item*: "You ought to talk to my Mom. We three older children are all conventional, good, high-achieving Mennonite children. The younger children aren't interested in respectable Mennonitism.

They're into Eastern Mysticism. Mom and Dad wonder where they failed with the second half of our family."

*Item:* "I was a part of the Sixties–not one of the far-out guys–but I felt good about many of the changes taking place then... and I still feel good about much of what happened."

*Item:* "I, too, am a son of the Sixties. I returned in the Seventies to teach in our college only to find that the scene had changed drastically. Students were more vocational and conventional, less aroused about issues beyond themselves."

All these are Mennonite experiences out of the 1960s. One hears from many parents this haunting, guilt-ridden refrain: "What did we do wrong? Things just fell apart." It is hard for parents and elders to sort out their feelings: anguish, bewilderment, shame, loneliness, anger. They read the thoughts of fellow church members as gossipy and critical. One parent commented: "People are so awkward in knowing what to say to us. I have to force myself to go to church and face everybody."

One hears other parents say in effect: "Things haven't fallen apart for us; however, there but for the grace of God go I." And then too we hear others who are smugly self-congratulatory. As one man told me: "My children all turned out good–no long hair, none who smoke or drink, no crazy ideas. All have good jobs and are married and attend church regularly."

There are also the voices of the youth alumni of the Sixties. A young Mennonite who was in college in the Sixties comments: "Take away some of the not so nice things, one has to admit that much good happened in the Sixties. I still don't think people heard or are hearing what we were trying to say." Perhaps now we are ready to listen more sympathetically to the voices of the last decade.

The Sixties present a complex collection of issues which calls for wisdom and grace. Here are brotherhood issues, pastoral counseling issues, salvation issues, society-wide issues. The task I wish to undertake is to sketch the broader picture of our society so that these stories of alienation and brokenness might be more lovingly understood. The guilt-ridden need not feel so guilty; the smug need to feel a bit of guilt. Those who saw things clearly but were hurt need our support. I submit that we have just come through one of the most turbulent and revolutionary periods in the history of our society and we still may not be out of the tunnel. Perhaps we have just seen, less the terrors of the night, than the dawn of a new day and we perceived it not. Henry Steele Commager has been helpful in putting it all in perspective:

It was the Sixties that broke, dramatically and even convulsively, with the world that had been fashioned in the previous three quarters of a century. It was then that Americans–and others everywhere on the globe–moved into a world that was new, dangerous, and perhaps unmanageable.

He says that the Age of Confidence, born of the 1890s, gave way to "the Age of Disillusionment, perhaps even the Age of Despair." Let us be cautious to generalize about the Sixties. We don't know quite what happened. The data is not all in. Also, let us not absolve ourselves of personal responsibility by decrying sinister forces in control of society. Social or economic determinism is too easy an explanation. I do believe that in the Sixties God was trying to tell us something and we were too blind to see and too deaf to hear. If we scan the horizon perhaps we can see the dove and the olive leaf in this turbulent ocean of change.

In 1960 the United States still dominated the world scene. Some still talked of "the American Century." A decade later who would be so presumptuous as to claim abroad that this was "the American Century?" The decade began with a crescendo of idealistic talk–leading onward and upward from the New Frontier to the Great Society. But the grand phrases turned to ashes in our mouths. Assassination followed assassination. We backed into a major war in faraway jungles against "a fourth-rate power" because "no one was going to tag us with being soft on Communism." The United States fought a big undeclared war to meet domestic political needs. President Johnson offered us simultaneously the Great Society and a great war–the latter on borrowed funds. We ended up losing the war, losing the Great Society, and reaping a runaway inflation and a quarreling, angry society. In the late Sixties things were falling apart. Or were they also just being born?

Volcanoes of fear and anger erupted in all our major cities: Los Angeles, Newark, Detroit, Cleveland. Explosions of student wrath spread from university to university: Berkeley, San Francisco State, Columbia, Cornell, even venerable Harvard, and a few weeks after the invasion of Cambodia, the most tragic of all, Kent State. Overseas 50 new nations appeared on the world stage mounting a chorus of criticism against the age of colonialism. The message was not lost on groups in our society who had long been silent. Now was their hour for recognition. Black Power. Red Power. Chicano Power. Women's Liberation. Gay Liberation. And above all, youth demanded a slice of the action. Things were falling apart. Or were these the seeds of renewal?

The discontented ones saw negation as the highest creativity. The Sixties were not a good time to reason together. "Confrontation," "non-negotiable demands," "establishment," were in-words. Out of Vietnam we heard an upside-down kind of logic: "We had to destroy the village to save it." Anarchistic students took up the theme: "We have to destroy the university to save it." The men of the ghetto joined in: "We had to destroy the city to save it." In our college, the creativity took milder but nonetheless negative forms: criticism and abandonment of hallowed campus traditions–family-style dining, all-campus cleanup days, men serenading the women's dorm, annual publication of a yearbook, robes at commencement, formal receptions, compulsory chapel, and many others. Leaders dragged their feet against what they feared to be too hastily demanded change. A paralysis of dreaming and action settled in. Confronted by tides of cynicism and debunking, leaders retreated to holding actions. They tried to present the smallest target for criticism.

In the 1960s we were beginning to suspect that we were not as nice a people as we had told ourselves we were. The revelation of the My Lai massacre revealed that some of us were savages and we wondered how many more My Lai massacres there had been which were not reported. This was the first decade in which almost every family had a television set. Every night we had ringside seats for the killing in Vietnam, the plundering in Watts and the assassinations in Dallas and Memphis. Massive doses of sex and pornography were offered in the movies, magazines, and paperbacks. This was the first decade of "the pill"–symbol and perhaps cause of a general relaxation in pre-marital and extra-marital sexual relationships. Things were falling apart. Or was a new day at the dawn?

In the Sixties we came face to face with the prospect that America's days of greatness were numbered. We were shocked to discover that our natural resources were running out. We were a nation of polluters. We built beautiful new buildings and defaced them immediately with graffiti sprayed from aerosol cans. The United States was using up her share of natural resources ten times as rapidly as the world average. For the first time we woke up scared that our well-stocked cupboard would be bare. Things were not only falling apart; they were being eroded away, burned up, poisoned and polluted.

In the Sixties our country was losing its infinite local variety. Uniqueness was erased in the new suburban developments, ribbons of concrete sameness called superhighways, the billions of McDonald hamburgers, look-alike airports and gas stations, look-alike cheerleaders and evangelistic campaigns. A new pre-fabricated, air-conditioned, Xerox-copied, computerized, comfortable sameness everywhere. We Mennonites–we who were or who had once been "the peculiar people," the children of nonconformity–must now be feeling down deep inside a lostness, a loneliness in this look-alike society. Perhaps that is why some of the sons and daughters of Menno who dropped out of it all were reasserting in strange ways an ancient but submerged Mennonite nonconformity.

After Sputnik we rushed to give higher education top priority. For a time a new community college was being built every week. From 3 million students in U.S. colleges in 1960 enrollments skyrocketed to 8 million in a decade. We were caught up in a euphoria of growth–growth mistaken for progress. Suddenly, however, growth was over. Inflation plunged many, apparently most, colleges into deficit operations. Students were disillusioned with the academic life: "Look what the best and the brightest have done in running the Vietnam War." The establishment had failed them in Washington. "The establishment was right here in microcosm on the campus; it must be confronted." The word "dropout" entered our vocabulary. The great bull market in higher education was dead. Here and there one heard parents cry plaintively: "The home has failed; the church has failed; the college is all that we have left; don't you fail us." But colleges seemed to fail as things were falling apart. Or was a new house being built?

With the piling up of youth on college campuses–product of the population explosion of post-World War II–youth became highly visible. They were the children of affluence–more cars, more stereos, more money in their jeans than in any previous student generation. These were the sons and daughters of parents who knew the Great Depression and World War II and they didn't want their children to have to go through what they had gone through. These parents had been less authoritarian than their parents. They didn't want their children to suffer the privations they had experienced. Mothers took second jobs to see their children through college. And then something went wrong. Somehow parents as well as college administrators and politicians were all a part of the establishment. "Generation gap" entered the vocabulary. A cliche made the rounds: "You can't trust anyone over 30." A youth counter-culture arose with all kinds of para-communicative messages beamed out to the establishment: parents and all those over 30. They were perhaps saying something about our Go Getter, upward-ascendent, PR-manipulated, pre-packaged, image-conscious society. They were saying it with all the little symbols repugnant to nice middle class people. They said it with symbols from our past which we were trying to live down: blue denim, long hair, bare feet, beards, peasant dress, rock music and guitars. They said it with the new: the deafening beat of rock music, beads, mini skirts, bikinis, and strange words and phrases. Some showed disdain for the hallowed in our culture: work, money, academic degrees, success, and soap. This was a visceral rebellion to the Great-Go-Getter-American success story. Parents and elders responded with the old cliches but many of the older generation no longer quite believed the old cliches. Parents reminded their children of how tough it had been when they were growing up in the Depression. They dropped broad hints as to how they were sacrificing so that their children would not need to go through what they had had to go through. This helped no more than for the colonialist to remind the new African of all the good that colonial rule had done for him. The elders were reminded that not only was there a "generation gap" but also a "credibility gap."

One looked to the church to hold things together in this shifting, insecure period. Frustration festered in the local congregation. More people seemed to be dissatisfied with their pastors; pastors weren't holding things together. Youth, sometimes in apparent league with the pastor, were making all kinds of strange innovations: guitars and folk music in the worship service, alternative course plans in the Sunday School. Church attendance was declining. Fewer came to an evening service or a series of special meetings. Fewer attended funerals. Church growth seemed to be leveling off and some rural churches were experiencing a drop in membership. This was a difficult time to be a pastor. Pastors and congregations often found themselves at odds as to the pastor's role. Many a pastor failed to get a vote of confidence at the time for the renewal of his term. More took flight from the pastorate–just when congregations urgently needed able pastors. New developments emerged in the Sixties: Death of God talk, the Jesus People, the small group-house church movement, the charismatic movement, non-denominational crusades, sensitivity training seminars, cultic movements–some of these strengthening, some weakening. Meanwhile, divorce and separation infiltrated the fortress of the Mennonite family. Things were falling apart. Or was this the throes of birth?

One looked to national leadership to give the clear word of truth, to hold things together. But in the Sixties from Kennedy to Johnson to Nixon a cult of majesty emerged in the White House–"the President knows best," "the President can do no wrong," "foreign affairs is too complicated for the ordinary citizen," "national security is top secret," "leadership is a matter of image." The outsiders–the blacks, the poor, the young (and many others)–sensed something phony about this imperial presidency. Some groups in society were badly hurt by the "positive polarization" of Agnew-Nixon domestic policy–Agnew lashing out with alliterative invective to harass youth, the peace-minded, blacks, Easterners, city-dwellers, TV commentators. This divide-and-conquer state has left deep wounds in our society. This disparity between word and deed, between public statement and Oval Office practice, eventually came to light in the great tragedy of Watergate–twin to that other tragedy, Vietnam.

The Sixties were years when the men and women of the conservative world received the message that they were people of the past. It was also an era shattering to liberals. Entering the sixties they knew that there was no problem too big that if you just took time, you could not fix it. Poverty, slums, racial inequality, war–all these social sins could be conquered. Vista, Peace Corps, Upward Bound, urban renewal were launched with high expectations. At the beginning of the decade it seemed so much easier to right wrongs. At the end of the decade simple direct action was infinitely more difficult; so often activism appeared counter productive. A beautifully conceived Poverty Fund fell far short of expectations. Things were falling apart. Or were we hearing messages about a new age being born?

Looking back at the last decade we see through a glass darkly. We are still so much a part of these revolutionary changes. Now in this post-Vietnam, post-Watergate era things seem to have quieted down. Is it a return to the apathy of the Fifties? We observe a new inwardness, a doing of your own thing, a new respect (or is it less disrespect?) for authority, a sense of inadequacy or indifference in the presence of the bigger issues, a new vocationalism, a skepticism about master plans and broad action schemes. One sees a new affection for antiques, genealogies, centennial celebrations, ethnic cookbooks. Is this the putting of things together again? Or is this simply a lull in the storms of change?

Or did we hear in the decade of the Sixties the birth pangs of a new day? Perhaps the outworn could not be patched one more time. Perhaps shaky foundations were tested and found wanting. Perhaps a new humility was displacing an old arrogance. Perhaps in the past decade we were glimpsing a new freedom which opened to us vistas for a new humanness, a new faithfulness, a recovery of a sense of hope. Perhaps with the healing passage of time we might be able to say that the Sixties were neither bad nor good but a time when we came to adulthood. Perhaps most of us have not yet sorted out all feelings and understandings. Perhaps the poet, with whose lines we began our writing, may have grasped it when he wrote further:

> Surely some revelation is at hand.
> The darkness drops again; but now I know
> That twenty centuries of stony sleep
> Were vexed to nightmare by a rocking cradle,
> And that rough beast, its hour come round at last,
> Slouches toward Bethlehem to be born?

We may now have enough distance in time from the events of the Sixties that we can discuss these issues with less discomfort. We have sketched here the background of the times. This is an invitation for discussion. What lessons in the wonderful and distressing changes of the last decade are there for our people? Certainly we need some sense of history to help us with our guilt, our pride, and our bewilderment. Only those are free who have a sense of history. All history, all background invites us to be a community of discernment–"to discern the signs of the times"–and to be a caring community in Christ.

That is the heart of the matter–to be a discerning and caring community in Christ. This is a time for caring. Among us are some lonely people–parents and children–who have been hurt badly. They want to talk. They may not feel sure of themselves. Others want to reach out to those hurt but they, too, are not sure of themselves. Simple cookie-cutter answers give little help. A wall of silence does not help. Pat moralistic answers do not help. To stonewall it, to cover it up for a later day–out of sight, out of mind–thinking it will all go away–this is not the way of faithfulness and reconciliation. The church needs to provide fellowship in Christ that reaches out to the casualties of rapid change. The church needs to provide support in Christ for those called to be agents of change.

Are we now ready as congregations to open up opportunities where we in small groups can discuss what we have gone through? Can we provide settings where parents and children and friends can review their experiences, where sins and mistakes can be confessed and forgiven? I see a reaching out for circles of fellowship to listen, confess, forgive, support, encourage, affirm, love, pray, covenant together to be new creatures in Christ.

We have abundant resources for this task. We have the church with its capacity to provide new forms for a community of caring. We have the presence of the Holy Spirit. If we yield ourselves to the leading of the Spirit, in days of rapid change we need not be captive of fear. We have Christ, the Lord of all history and our particular segment of our anxiety-ridden history. The Son of Man is the Man between the ages, who came into the world for just such a time as this. He is the assurance that although things seem to fall apart, through Him all things will be made whole.

This is in the spirit of the Jubilee Year:

> The Spirit of the Lord is upon me, because he has anointed me to preach good news to the poor. He has sent me to proclaim release to the captives and recovering of sight to the blind, to set at liberty those who are oppressed, to proclaim the acceptable year of the Lord. (Luke 4:18-19)

# 1975: Vietnam–Little Peace, Less Honor

*Printed in* The Mennonite, *January 28, 1975, and in several other publications, following a trip to Vietnam in April 1974.*

In Stuttgart, Germany, at the end of World War II, a German prisoner of war (just released from the Russian front) told me a story of having filed daily reports on the doomed position of the German troops at Stalingrad. In time he was called back to headquarters in Kiev or Kharkov where he was shocked to discover that headquarters was turning out a steady stream of glowing news bulletins of German successes at Stalingrad. This former intelligence officer declared, "Up to that point I thought Germany had a chance of retreating, regrouping, and winning, but at that moment all my hopes were shattered. I knew we would lose the war. And we did. You can't lie to your people and win."

Early last year we visited Vietnam and discovered what we had only imperfectly known before: the United States is still at war in Vietnam. The dying goes on–80,000 killed in fighting since a cease-fire in Vietnam was negotiated January 27, 1973. That is 25,000 more than all the Americans killed in a decade of war in Vietnam. Eighty-five percent–perhaps more–of the dollars for the South Vietnamese side of this war continue to be paid by U.S. taxpayers.

The Vietnam story seems to be such an unhappy chapter in our American history that we don't want to talk or hear any more about it. We put it out of sight, out of mind, and cover it up with self-congratulatory phrases like "peace with honor." But there is little peace and less honor. These are a few of the things we saw and heard and they were not good.

We had driven along a river ten miles north of the sad village of My Lai to inspect an area suffering a severe food shortage. Villagers stopped us along the way to tell us that the previous night the South Vietnamese army (ARVN) had shelled a village only a mile away, destroying houses, killing three or four and wounding seven or eight. Much of this area is controlled by the ARVN by day and the Provisional Revolutionary Government (PRG) by night.

That same day we inspected the raw, shell-pocked slopes of what the local people call "artillery hill." Much of the area within a mile radius of this former U.S. army hilltop stronghold is unusable for rice paddies because it is contaminated with thousands of unexploded shells, grenades, and mines.

We were led by a Mennonite Central Committee worker, whom we were visiting, to a spot on that slope where last month a Vietnamese refugee mother of seven had been blown up as her hoe struck a hidden unexploded shell.

A barefooted farmer, also a refugee, came up and told us that he had uncovered thirty unexploded M-79 shells in the half-acre plot which he was preparing for the planting of rice–the first crop in ten years on that land. He took us to an abandoned well where we saw a nest of deadly shells he had gingerly laid there, shells found while hoeing.

Neither the South Vietnamese army nor the American army nor the Vietnamese landlords will risk their lives in clearing these fields. However, the desperate refugees who have been driven from their own nearby fields in the war zone will take that risk. This refugee farmer explained: "My family is hungry; I have no choice but to go on clearing the land."

Our MCC friend is exploring ways in which he and other volunteers from overseas can help the refugees clear their land of unexploded ordinance. U.S. mine sweepers have cleared Haiphong harbor of mines in North Vietnam. In South Vietnam are hundreds, perhaps thousands, of these artillery hills–"Haiphongs on land"–each polluted with deadly shells and grenades. We keep wondering whether that refugee farmer is still alive or whether his hoe too has since struck a live M-79 shell, his family left fatherless.

The following morning two of our colleagues saw two bodies lying along Highway One as they drove south of Quang Ngai–victims of fighting between ARVN and PRG the night before.

Nothing appeared in the Saigon newspapers about these events in the day following. Perhaps this was too routine to bother to report. Or perhaps this was just a routine cover-up. North of Saigon we saw a country under siege–Vietnamese troops everywhere, barbed wire entanglements, highways outside the town closed to traffic at night, armed guards at all bridges, sandbag bunkers at entrances to public buildings.

We picked up reports from MCC workers of their visits to and concern for political prisoners–one a young farm girl who had been seized by police in the market and taken away to be tortured to the point that she became paralyzed from her waist down. Our workers reported to U.S. Ambassador Martin this and other cases of South Vietnamese holding without trial and torturing political prisoners. He simply denied the existence of such atrocities. Ambassadorial stonewalling.

After a week of seeing the war out there in the Vietnamese countryside, we returned to Saigon. We talked about these experiences with a visiting American pastor. He, too, was disturbed to hear our reports. However, the next day, Sunday, he visited friends on the staff of the U.S. Embassy and U.S. Agency for International Development. He returned Sunday evening and admitted that he had received quite a different picture from these U.S. officials. He had been informed that the South Vietnamese government with U.S. help was regaining control of the countryside; peace was returning; the American press was unfairly exaggerating corruption among South Vietnamese officials, the torture of prisoners, the intensity of the continuing war.

We were shocked, saddened. It was incredible that there could be such a disparity between the image-makers in Saigon and what we had just heard and seen.

In the air-conditioned, insulated offices of Saigon, unpleasant information is filtered out, leaving only the pleasant news. A cancer grows on our flesh. Another cover-up? Don't we want to face the truth? Have we not learned? Are we not mature enough as an American people to be given straight from the shoulder the facts of a war that goes on and on?

Now, two years after the Paris Agreements, we urge a fresh and thorough reassessment of the war in Vietnam by the people, the Congress, and President Ford. It is a continuing and tragic war–our war–the war we are paying for–this war with its staggering human, moral, national, spiritual costs: or is it not our war if it is someone else's sons who are dying? Is this our cover-up?

# 1975: The Beautiful Feet

*Printed in* Gospel Herald, *April 15, 1975, and in several other publications.*

"How beautiful are the feet of them that preach the gospel of peace." One hundred years ago this verse appeared as the motto under the masthead of the *Herald of Truth,* one of the earliest Mennonite periodicals to appear in English. In those days it seemed right for Mennonites to declare that peacemaking was one of their prime tasks in kingdom service.

Now one hundred years later is peacemaking still high among our commitments? Would we print the motto "to preach the gospel of peace" under the masthead of our conference paper? On our church bulletin? Or are we a little ashamed of the sign of the conscientious objector written on our backs?

Now that the world says nice things about hardworking and law-abiding Mennonites and writes articles in national periodicals about our disaster service do we play down that offensive conscientious objector image? Are we covering up the gospel of peace?

Imperfectly suppressed from our past are those unpleasant memories of having been called "yellow," " slackers," "unpatriotic." We want to be liked. We want to be accepted. Enough of that "being a peculiar people."

*A Time to Take Stock.* We look around us and find popular, attractive religious leaders who are not burdened by the yoke of peace teachings. Some of us wish to be like them.

And some of us are tired—weary of issues, causes, concerns. Some of us want to be left alone. We want to live private lives. "Weary and heavy laden."

When we see our polite, quiet peace position "soiled" by peace demonstrators and draft-card-burners we want to deny that we have anything to do with them. To our remorse we hear the crowing of the cock. We wish Jesus had not said so much about peace and turning the other cheek. But it is not just peace that gives us problems. We are bothered by His hard talk about money, prisoners, debts, enemies, cross-bearing, being a slave, and forgiving others. We like to spiritualize away the concrete claims of His cross.

Some of us are little different from the world around us. A Mennonite boy is suspected of breaking into a number of houses and stealing. An aroused fellow church member declares: "The next time he breaks and enters someone ought to take a shotgun and scare the living life out of him. That would teach him." No one disagrees.

Some of us carry a burden of shame. A young Christian becomes a conscientious objector with little or no help from any church–just his reading of the gospels and his aversion to the Vietnam War. To his joy he discovers that Mennonites are a peace people. He applies for membership in this peace church but is told by a deacon, "Oh, we don't make much of that anymore."

Clearly this is a time to take stock. Is the foolishness of the gospel of peace something of which we must be ashamed or is it "wiser than men?"

Mennonites look best in crises. Wars bring out the best in us. But now there are no wars–at least no declared wars. There is no conscription. The heat is off. Mennonites have a way of losing their faith, their saltiness, their distinctiveness when all goes well.

This is a time for a spiritual checkup. A concern has welled up among us that we Mennonite and Brethren in Christ need to be more attentive to nurturing our people in the gospel of peace. Children need to be trained up "in the way they should go." Parents need help in being courageous followers of a nonresistant Christ. Grandparents need to tell their stories of trial and witness.

If the biblical teachings of the gospel of peace are to burn brightly in our congregations, we need to rediscover the biblical ground on which our faith is founded.

We see the gospel of peace as no mere optional equipment–but part of the central nervous system of the body of Christ, the bloodstream of the faith. Paul saw it total and undivided when he spoke of "putting on the whole armor of God": truth, righteousness, peace, faith, salvation, the Spirit.

As we search the Scriptures the gospel of peace finds its center in the person of Christ. In Him one sees peace as of the whole fabric of the gospel: as good news–not an annoying burden to be added; as freedom, liberation–"only those who are nonresistant are really free;" as the spirit-filled life–relaxed, yielded, trusting, "peace as a river;" as a gift to those who accept and follow Christ, to those who take the Scriptures seriously.

Peace cannot be separated out of the wholeness of Christ. Peace does not exist alone. Separate peace from the gospel and it becomes a thing demonic. Separate evangelism as a thing apart, and it becomes demonic.

And so in peace we look for linkages in our studies: evangelism and peace, conflicts in the Bible and peacemaking, peace and the work of the Holy Spirit, peace and patriotism, peace and justice, peace and bread, peace and the hurts of the community, peace and Lazarus at the door, peace and the money we give to Caesar, peace and the gifts God has given to our people. As we read the

Scriptures we see everywhere linkages: grace and peace, love and peace, joy and peace, righteousness and peace.

*Peace Is Too Important.* Peace is everybody's business. Peace is too important to leave just to the pacifists, even as evangelism is too important to leave just to the evangelists. Therefore, congregational peace education is concerned with helping larger numbers of our people become peacemakers and teachers of the gospel of peace.

Peace education must embody the spirit of reconciliation. As one reaches out to those who are threatened by, embarrassed by, or apologetic of peace, one cannot shame them into the kingdom. Peace is a knock on the door. Peace is invitation: "Come, let us search the Scriptures together." "Come, take my yoke upon you, and learn of me." "He hath given to us the ministry of reconciliation."

Peace education has an urgency. A war could explode any moment in Bible lands. A secretary of state threatens war to protect the flow of oil to the world's largest consumer. A war, using money from the United States, goes into its third year after the Paris Peace Accord–Americans now paying Asians to die for them. Famine, hunger, inflation, depression hover over the globe. With things falling apart in some of our marriages, congregations, and communities we know that we stand in need of the ministries of reconciliation.

Peace and evangelism cannot be separated. As we visit our people in Canada and the United States we hear those who are ashamed of peace, but we also hear of those who are not. Congregations are growing because men and women are drawn to a church where there are actually Christians who believe and practice what Jesus says about peace.

It might be that we with our peace heritage are called to the kingdom for such a time as this. Peace education in our congregations can equip us to see these gifts which God has given us and which we so imperfectly use.

That motto of the *Herald of Truth* might again be our theme. "How beautiful are the feet of them that preach the gospel of peace."

# 1975: They All Flunked the Final Exam

*Printed in* The Mennonite, *September 2, 1975 and in several other publications.*

I want to tell you about a model teacher I have come to know through a study of the records available.

He faced a tough assignment. He had a three-year job to train a small group of students to be teachers. All of them seemed eager to learn, but some were barely literate. They would not have been admitted to the top colleges or universities. You might call them disadvantaged, or of the lower socio-economic class.

They were a mixed-ability group: several slow learners, several with high test scores, one skeptic or anti-establishment type, one former Internal Revenue agent, several who had been working their way up in their father's business.

From time to time this teacher tried to attract more students, and in some cases he was successful. He had a perennial problem with drop-ins and drop-outs. The ones he invited to join gave him all kinds of lame excuses why they couldn't attend his school: work at home, social engagements. "We're really interested, but can't you give us a rain check?"

He could almost foresee that day, three years hence, when one of his better students would drop out at a crucial moment, a second one for a bribe would squeal on his teacher to the secret police, another would continue to play the skeptic role for three years like an old broken record ("Why?… What is your evidence?… It still doesn't make sense to me.")

As a matter of fact, all of the class flunked their finals. They got scared, actually panicked, and didn't show up for the final exam. Sheepishly they slunk back later and asked for incompletes, which were graciously granted, and presumably they all finished the course except one, who was a terribly mixed-up student. In a mood of depression he killed himself.

The teacher did not have the normal four years to shape up this assorted group of students. He had to telescope his instruction into three years to help them get ready to be teachers themselves. Everyone granted it was an intense, tough study program.

This teacher was unconventional. He didn't build a classroom, a lab, or a dorm. He took a dim view of professional types, trend-sensitive intellectuals who hung around the capital city. He ran into some trouble with status-minded mothers who were worried about his ungraded classroom and kept pestering him with questions as to whether their sons stood at the top of the class. These mothers didn't like it when he told them that the poorest student was the best student and that little children had better understanding than grown-ups.

He achieved better control of the class by taking them away from the hometown, that is, going off-campus. He loved the out-of-doors. He was one whom we would call a naturalist, environmentalist, one with ecological sensitivity. He held his classes in the fields. He conducted seminars by the lake and up in the mountains. He did a lot of teaching while walking, which presented problems for note taking.

He and his students ate together in restaurants and apparently accepted many free meals from villagers. They made field trips into inner cities. He gave them challenging tasks to perform in villages. He believed a student learns best when he is given a chance to be a teacher. Therefore, he was high on internship experiences, practice teaching, on-the-job learning. It was not just experience for experience's sake. He insisted on detailed report-back sessions, "debriefing" of their field experiences. He grilled them with questions.

He used some traditional teaching methods. He lectured, but that was not his major teaching method. Often auditors joined the class to listen to the lectures and even to ask questions. We don't know of any instance where he charged auditors fees; in fact, there is no record of any tuition or lab fees for anyone. He made the lectures more meaningful through follow-up seminar sessions where issues from the field trips were reviewed.

He knew how to relate to students' experiences. He used many illustrations. Always they were drawn from life as the students lived and saw it. If one illustration didn't click, he tried another and another.

During a series of these illustrations, a student would occasionally blurt out: "Oh, now I see." And the teacher would stop and congratulate the student on the spot for his breakthrough of recognition.

Sometimes outsiders were rude hecklers. They would try to trap him with trick questions. He would lead them on and on and finally catch them at their own game. His students delighted in the adroit verbal footwork of their teacher and, of course, in time, they, too, became adept in handling the jibes of hecklers. The most exciting encounters probably were in those places where many people gathered: shopping centers and malls, health centers, or at the docks.

He didn't grade on the curve. He attempted to bring each of his students up to his full potential. Sometimes he got a bit emotional.

A few of his outbursts were almost embarrassing. "Positive reinforcement" of a learner we might call it today. His scolding occasionally bordered on harshness, especially when his students were trying to put each other down or when they forgot basics in which he had drilled them. Those who knew him best were awed by the depth of his emotion. They reported that he was known to cry privately when he couldn't get through to people. He wanted so much to be understood. He was also known to break down and weep about the capital city where conditions were in a mess.

In retrospect, one might wonder about this teacher's competency. No degrees. No credentials. No previous certified teaching experience. He disturbed the segregationists because he was a good friend of the half-breeds who lived in his region. He wasn't careful about those who hung around with him. To put it bluntly: "Would you want your child to be taught by someone who had been seen on several occasions talking to prostitutes?"

Many good people, who would defend him against his many critics, probably warned him: "If I see you talking to another prostitute, I just can't stick up for you one more time." It was exasperating that he didn't take this good sound advice which his best friends gave him for his own good. Stubborn fellow–and yet, people liked him.

Related to this stubbornness was the fact that he was thought to be excessively objectives-oriented. He couldn't be diverted from his stated objectives–whether you agreed with them or not. For example, he passed up several excellent opportunities for popular advancement. He simply wanted to be a teacher and work with his teacher training program.

You would think that living, eating, and sleeping with a group of students twenty-four hours a day would drive a teacher up a wall. Most of us would say, "I've had my fill; I've got to get out of here." He didn't resort to the escapist devices which up-tight people go for today: booze, tranquilizers, drugs, sex, TV, cars, or flight to faraway places. When he had all that he could take, he often took a walk or a boat ride–sometimes alone, sometimes even taking some of his students along. Mountains and seashores were the best of tranquilizers. And he prayed a lot. He wasn't the kind who was ashamed to admit that he needed help from God. After one occasion when he had hiked up a mountain and spent extended time in prayer, his students remarked that they had never seen him more radiant.

We don't have good information on his clothing. He probably would not have made the "ten-best-dressed-men" list because he took a dim view of having more than one outfit of clothes. When they traveled–and he and his class were on the go much of the time–he put up in all kinds of places.

He could sleep anywhere. Once he fell asleep in a boat. His students, too, could sleep anywhere, as they did one night in a park instead of getting ready for the final exam.

He socialized freely with his students, even insisting on taking them along with him on his dinner invitations. Although he may have engaged in some small talk at dinner, he liked to direct the dinner conversation to the big issues. Generally his hosts seemed to be honored by this man who treated them like adults and forced them, in a sense, to stand on their intellectual tiptoes.

In many ways he conformed to the image of what a teacher should be and do. Everyone called him "teacher." His concept of curriculum, classes, and teaching leaned toward the functional and away from the classical. His expertise didn't fit neatly into any one department or discipline. His interests spilled over into medicine, psychiatry, and agriculture. He needed none of the social-distance props of the formal school. He needed no lectern. His course outlines were in his head.

He never used a PA system, because he was known to communicate effectively with as few as a dozen or seventy or could be heard by as many as 5,000–which calls for a mighty strong speaking voice.

He really shook up his students and others with apparently impulsive acts such as volunteering to help with the housework and on one occasion getting down on his hands and knees and washing his students' dirty feet. It was a little embarrassing to everyone, and yet impressive.

Despite his offbeat ways, people liked to have him as a guest at social events. He had an easy, friendly manner–great with children. He also could entertain. Once at a wedding he converted ordinary drinking water into vintage wine. They still talk about that wedding. He had a good sense of humor, which was often directed at himself and sometimes consisted of sharp barbs at pompous leaders.

When he was interrupted, as he so frequently was, he dealt graciously with the unruly and the rude, even when some eager townspeople tore away the ceiling above his head to get close to him. He paid no heed to sarcastic remarks about his hometown (and there were many): "What good could come out of *that* town?" He was content to be known as a small-town boy and the son of a skilled laborer.

The teacher did not marry. He respected women. They loved to talk with him. In fact, many of the auditor students for his classes were women. He never put them down. Women often remarked after a conversation with this teacher that he really made them feel like somebody–gave them a boost in their sense of worth, what we would call "helping them with their identity crisis."

He was a demanding teacher. He was hard on dilettantes–those who nibbled a bit here and there, those who popped into his classes to talk brilliantly but failed to do their homework, those who refused to put their ideas to the test in field assignments. He was so demanding that he had more than his share of dropouts. "Too tough," some said. Others: "Who does he think he is? He wants every minute of your time. He expects too much."

He received considerable criticism for his teaching methods from other professionals in the academic community, criticisms like these: 1. Too demanding. 2. Unsound teaching technique. (Many observers, including often his students, were annoyed by his habit of not answering a question directly. They would present him a problem and would insist on an answer: "Can I or can't I? Should I or should I not?" Instead of giving an answer, he so often asked a question in return or responded with a story. He was accused of sidestepping tough questions. One has to admit that some of his questioners didn't want to have to do their own thinking.) 3. Finally, too popular. (But his critics didn't come out and say just that. Instead they said he was "subversive," "an atheist," "an agnostic," "disloyal," "unpatriotic," "a radical," "an integrationist.")

This kind of carping criticism built up toward the end of his teaching career so that a lot of people didn't know whether it was safe to be seen listening to him in public. When the heat was on, one of his students even denied he studied with the teacher.

This teacher had some real hotheads in his study group. Once when the local police appeared, one of his students panicked and sliced off a policeman's ear. Even though the policeman had come to arrest him, the teacher rebuked his own student right in front of the policeman. With this unruly, emotional group of students the teacher had to spend a lot of time on the problem of conflict resolution. He had abundant patience.

He also had to spend much time on money questions. He was working with young men from low-income homes who could not suppress the hope of making it big financially. One of them had it bad, dropped the course for a big bribe from the secret police. The students knew better, but those old materialistic instincts kept welling up again and again. His students were really hung up on the money question, but in time they got over it.

And so one could go on and on reviewing this case study. This study has focused on teaching methods and academic climate—teacher and student. We have not described the content of his teaching, of which one gets only intimations here. And yet his method and his message were fused. His method was his message and his message was his method.

This case study from two thousand years ago is as contemporary as a morning newspaper. Teaching and learning is a sacred calling because this Master Teacher of whom we speak has touched it with his presence.

# 1976: A Hymn of Affection for a Land and a People

*An article printed in* The Mennonite, *January 13, 1976, and in both the* Wichita Eagle *and* Hutchinson News.

I am critical of America. America has caused me to feel shame, grief, pain. I am critical because I care about my country. I love my country. I don't want it to hurt or be hurt.

Some strange notions circulate these days about the appropriate ways of expressing love of country. One notion is that it is wrong to criticize one's country. Another calls one to declare that our country is No. 1, "the greatest," "the best." Another notion is that patriotism is best revealed in a few prescribed acts of civic faithfulness–the more frequently repeated the better: displaying the flag, saying the Pledge of Allegiance, hearing the "Star Spangled Banner," owning a gun–but especially displaying the flag. Another strange notion–from the opposite pole–is that it is indecent, old-fashioned, small-minded to speak of love of country. Enough of these notions.

I want to tell people that I love my country. How do I love my country? Love is wrapped up in little things.

I love the names of American town and place. There is music in these names: Cygnet, Uniopolis, and Wapakoneta... Shipshewana, Churubusco, and Jim Town... Pawnee Rock, Pretty Prairie, and Yoder... Pecatonica, Tiskilwa, and Pekin... Kickapoo, Kosciusko, and Jubilee... Paradise, Hinkletown, and Sporting Hill... Cotopaxi, Rosita, and Crow Junction... and thousands more.

I love the writers who celebrate the American experience: Ernest Thompson Seton, Willa Cather, Hamlin Garland, Ole Rølvaag, Carl Sandburg, Robert Frost, John Steinbeck, Herman Melville, and Henry David Thoreau. My affection for America has been shaped by books like *Wild Animals I Have Known, Huckleberry Finn,* the *Sears Roebuck* catalog, and magazines like the *National Geographic.*

I glory in our national parks and monuments: Rocky Mountain, Dinosaur, and the Grand Tetons... Mesa Verde, Great Smokies, and Death Valley. My heart leaps up when I think of the Badlands, Kings Canyon, the north rim of Grand Canyon, and a dozen other natural wonders.

Every small American town has its particular charm. Along a Main Street in any town my eyes drift upward from the polished surfaces of storefronts to the neglected upper stories of an earlier era. I look for the gingerbread design of the cornice, the fading outlines of a weathered advertisement of generations past, and especially I delight in finding the builder's date. America, in part, is the savoring of things past.

I love the infinite variety of American trees–the sassafras, the hop hornbeam, and the sugar maple… the flowering dogwood, the hedge apple, and the buckeye, and hundreds more. I am fascinated by American farmsteads and fields–especially fields of corn, wheat, and milo ready for the harvest.

I love to see the great blue heron wading in the creek, Canadian geese flying in formation southward, the barn swallow gliding at twilight, and wild turkeys on Jim Berry's ranch. I love to see in the spring the first spring beauties and violets on the hillside, the jack-in-the-pulpit hiding at the base of a beech tree, clusters of May apples spreading their green umbrellas, the Indian paintbrush along Texas Creek.

America is rich in heroic figures. Among early and even later heroes were these who quickened my affection for America: Peter Altgeld, John Woolman, and Christopher Dock… John R. Mott, Thomas Edison, and John Muir… Jane Addams, Helen Keller, and Jim Thorpe… Charles Lindbergh, Alonzo Stagg, and William Allen White–and a lot more.

In my inner eye are places of rare beauty all over America–a winter dawn along Riley Creek, the greening of a field of wheat in Kansas in April, the rocky coast of Maine, South Brush Creek rushing down from the Sangre de Cristo, the Flint Hills in the spring, tumbleweed blowing across U.S. 54 west of Meade, patterns in the drifting sand of the Great Sand Dunes.

I am intrigued by the ethnic diversity in America. Take, for example, the names in last autumn's World Series of baseball: Evans, Morgan, and Bench, but also Anderson, Driessen, and Johnson, and then Billingham, McEnaney, and Doyle, but also Concepcion, Perez, and Borbon and–beautiful to the ear–Petrocelli, Yastrzemski, and Geronimo. If only there had also been a Reichenbach, Sawatzky, and Tschetter.

I love American food–corn on the cob, ice cream cones, homemade apple butter, baked beans, pickled red beets, lemonade, Lancaster County pretzels, cornmeal mush, fresh huckleberries, peanut butter, rhubarb pie, maple syrup, baked squash, horseradish, and mint tea.

I love church potluck suppers, the joyous sounds of church bells in Bluffton on a Sunday morning, going to church camp at Friedenswald, the variety of church colleges, harvest festivals, crop drives, church-sponsored retirement villages.

I love the diversity among our religious groups: the Hutterites and the Shakers and the Schwenkfelders and the Greek Orthodox and the Dunkards and the Missouri Synod Lutherans and the Swedish Covenant and the Hard Shell Baptists and the Free Methodists and the Moravians and the Irish Catholics and the Amish and a lot more.

I am fascinated with American technology–the Model T, windmills, treadle sewing machines, rural mailboxes, wood-burning cookstoves, bank barns, storm cellars, steam locomotives, farm silos, roller skates, safety pins and zippers, player pianos, covered bridges, rail fences, and the great display of American ingenuity to be found in an 1894 Montgomery Ward catalog.

I am intrigued by American clothing–bib overalls, stocking caps, blue jeans, sweat shirts, corduroy jackets. And then, too, American quilts, samplers, and braided rugs.

I love the household arts–drop-leaf tables, dry sinks, bentwood chairs, ladder chairs, cane bottom chairs, pie cupboards, roll-top desks, rope beds, chests of drawers with marble tops, corner cupboards, and wooden barrels.

I love American music which sprang to life on this soil–Negro spirituals, bluegrass music, gospel music, ragtime, Dixieland, the blues, and the Salt Lake Tabernacle Choir.

I love American sports–football on an autumn evening, Cincinnati in the World Series, Buffalo's No. 32 racing for a touchdown, Joe Morgan stealing second, John Havlicek slicing in for a lay-up, Jack Nicklaus sinking a fifteen-foot putt, children roller skating down sidewalks, and boys shooting baskets through a hoop above the garage door.

Scattered across America are shrines which have a touch of the sacred: Fox Hill and Big Woods... Henry Huber's big red barn and the iron bridge at the bend in the road... the old mill in Westcliffe and remote Smith Park nestled in an upland valley of the Sangre de Cristo... the panorama of Wichita unfolding at Exit 13 on Interstate 135... the distant silhouette of a western Kansas town with several elevators like the image of a European village clustered around the parish church.

I like the crisp, friendly courtesy of immigration officials on arrival at Kennedy International Airport.... I love to drive the streets of Washington, D.C., at dawn before the city awakens.... I watched on television with gratitude and admiration the men and women of the judiciary committee consider the issues of impeachment.... I listen with respect to a state patrolman who is so gracious as he gives me a traffic ticket.... And having experienced so many of the world's bureaucracies, I appreciate the relative simplicities of our brand.... I remember the Amishman walking up the marble steps of the Supreme Court building.

I love American newspapers–the *New York Times*, the *Toledo Blade*, the *Hutchinson News*, the *Freeman Courier*, the *Sugar Creek Budget*, the *Mountain Eagle*, the *Bluffton News*, the *Wet Mountain Tribune*. Half my education I owe to all those readable American magazines: some of a bygone era–*Childlife*, the *American Boy*, *World Tomorrow*, *McClure's*, *Life*–and some contemporary–*Saturday Review*, *Time*, *Newsweek*, *National Geographic*, *Audubon*, *Popular Mechanics*, *Sports Illustrated*, *Post American*, *The Farm Journal*.

My love for American comic strips does not seem to fade–once upon a time the Toonerville Trolley, Katzenjammer Kids, and Mutt and Jeff, and now, Peanuts, Doonesbury, and a dozen more.

I love American humor–Will Rogers, Art Buchwald, W. C. Fields, Robert Benchley, Ogden Nash, James Thurber and, best of all, the editorial cartoonists–voices of the American conscience: Mauldin, Conrad, Oliphant, and a dozen more.

I love to delve into the stories of America–the settlement of Michael Neuenschwander and his family in a clearing in the forest in 1832, the coming of the Atchison, Topeka, and Santa Fe to Harvey County in 1871, the stories of those pioneers who lived in boxcars that first winter in Pawnee Rock, the digging of the Miami Canal in the 1830s.

I am drawn to the works of American artists–Grant Wood, John Curry, Thomas Benton, and Currier and Ives–and American photographers–Gordon Parks, Margaret Bourke-White, and Eliot Elisofon–who celebrate America.

I have a love affair with America. I feel a kinship with others who love their countries–Haitians who love Haiti, Nepalese who love Nepal, Germans who love Germany, Canadians who love Canada.

America is my land. I belong to it and it belongs to me. I am also a citizen of another country whose maker and ruler is God. There is my first citizenship and my first allegiance.

America is also God's country. He loves our land and people. He also weeps for our land and people. God has many countries to love and for which to weep. God rebukes whom he loves. Caring criticism and love go together.

And so I am going to go on speaking out when America errs, hoping for a better America and loving an imperfect America. The greatest of these is loving.

# 1976: America–God Shed His Grace on Thee

Book review printed in The Mennonite Weekly Review, *February 19, 1976.*

On my desk is *America–God Shed His Grace on Thee* by Robert Flood. Published by Moody Press, Chicago, in 1975.

> *America's spiritual foundations and her evangelical thrust over two centuries bear directly, we believe, on the country's general prosperity and its position as a great world power.*
>
> *Was it not of God that both the navy and army should enter the Chesapeake at the same time?*
>
> *But can it be mere coincidence that the most blessed nation on earth has over the years, also been so evangelical? So much so, in fact, that it has come to be known as a "Christian" nation....*
>
> *They live under a "Christian" form of government that many feel most closely achieves the biblical ideal....*

The author speaks of himself as an evangelical Christian. And yet I wonder whether the author knows brothers and sisters in Christ who are not United States citizens. I know hundreds of Christian friends who live under other flags. I could not ask Pastor Djojodihardjo of Indonesia to acknowledge that America is Number One in God's sight, nor could I ask Carl Bruesewitz in The Netherlands, nor Million Belete in Nairobi, nor Henry Poettcker in Winnipeg to declare with the author that the United States is "the most blessed nation on earth."

I think of other brothers and sisters in Christ: Hisae Murokawa in Tokyo, Liesel Widmer in Switzerland, Heinold Fast in Germany, and Mrs. Sarko in Calcutta. They all have lived in America and have affection for America and its people, but I could not call on them to join in a hymn of praise to the United States–this "Christian nation"... with a government that "most closely achieves the biblical idea."

I lift up a prayer, "Father, forgive this author for he knows not what he has done." This beautifully illustrated and exquisitely printed book, is a seductive book. It seeks to speak for Christians in America but is not worthy of a conscientious scholar who loves God's truth above the kingdoms and principalities of this world.

The cult of Cain is glorified: nine pages with illustrations of battleships, four pages with illustrations of cannons, three of soldiers, others of battle scenes, and one of an Israeli tank with presumably the Star of Bethlehem keeping watch over the Israeli soldiers by night. The author glories in victory of the Protestant British over the Catholic Spanish: "It gave undisputed control of the seas, allowing Protestants to colonize the New World.... Had Spain won this battle and retained her supremacy of the waters, she might well have colonized America. And the Pilgrims and Puritans might never have had the chance to carve out the beginnings of religious liberty and democracy in America."

I hear another voice, but not found in this book: "Not by might nor by power, but by my spirit saith the Lord of hosts."

The cult of American riches is glorified: three illustrations of bulging supermarkets contrasted with a hungry naked black child from somewhere over there. The author suggests that America is rich while others are poor and America is powerful while others are weak–all this because of Americas's "evangelical thrust." This book sounds no cry of penitence: "Father, forgive us, a sinful people." There is no word of America having been the greatest slave-holding republic in history. No cry for forgiveness that Americans drove Indian brothers and sisters westward from the forests and the fertile plains and herded them into concentration camps in a strange land. No word of remorse to my brother Takashi Yamada that we killed thousands of his brothers and sisters at Hiroshima and Nagasaki. Here one finds a sweet, satisfied Gospel without humility and penitence.

I have tremendous admiration and affection for Abraham Lincoln, but I squirm with uneasiness with 13 pages of illustrations of Lincoln and the great outpouring of adulation to this hero of the faith. I know of no evidence that Lincoln accepted Christ as his personal savior and identified himself with the Church, the Body of Christ. It is just not honest to Honest Abe to make him a hero of the evangelical faith. Adulation is demeaning and misrepresentation is falsehood. Jesus asks us that our "Yea be yea and our nay, nay." I think Lincoln would have agreed.

The author quotes extensively and appreciatively from Ezra Stiles, president of Yale University, who spoke thus soon after the American Revolution: "Who but a Washington, inspired by Heaven, could have struck out the great movement and maneuvers at Princeton?... To whom but the Ruler of the winds shall we ascribe it that the British reinforcement, in the summer of 1777, was delayed on the ocean three months by contrary winds, until it was too late? What but a providential miracle detected the conspiracy of Arnold." The author sees God on the side of Catholics destroying Mohammedans at Tours, Protestants killing Spanish Catholics in the English Channel, the English language gaining mastery in

North America, Americans killing British in the Revolution. I suspect that God has a different interpretation of these events.

As a Christian I am saddened and angered by this book which purports to give a Christian interpretation of American history. The author would do well to read thoroughly the Prophets and the Gospels and to study what Jesus Christ says of His Kingdom which is not of this earth and whose ways are not the ways of violence and pride and gluttony. He would do well to read carefully the American story, not just the old school book hero stories. Read the American story from the standpoint of the Indian, the black, the immigrants, the little people, the dissenters, and those who walked with God. And then write a history of America so that our brothers and sisters in Winnipeg and Tokyo and Nairobi and Basel can read it and not feel that they are of a lesser breed.

I see this book as like unto a work of pornography which should not be sold in church-related bookstores. I speak with feeling because I love America and I want to be faithful to Jesus Christ who loves America and Canada and Tanzania and the people in every land.

# 1976: Jesus and Grammar

*Printed in* With, *November 1976.*

I know Jesus through adjectives:
beautiful, radiant, and meek... humble, kind, and strong...
holy, just, and true.

I know Jesus through prepositions:
beyond, in, and above... beside, over, and through.

I know Jesus through nouns:
the way, the door, and the truth... water, bread, and the
light...
the Savior, the Christ, and Lord... teacher, master, and
friend...
Prince of Peace, Son of God, and Son of Man.

I know Jesus through conjunctions:
only, thus, and nevertheless... either-or.

But best of all I know Jesus through verbs:
to weep, to laugh, and to sing... to carry, to lift, and to
walk...
to touch, to heal, and to give... to remember, to comfort,
and to mourn.
to suffer, to share, and to console... to care, to rebuke, and
to forgive.
to invite, to send, and to save... to tell, to serve, and to
love...

Words help us to understand Jesus. But all the words of all the
languages of
the world cannot fully describe Jesus.

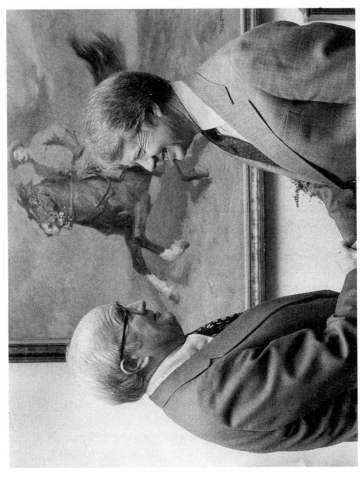

*Kreider with President Jimmy Carter, White House, Dec. 16, 1977.*

# 1978: Shaking Hands with President Carter

*Printed in* Mennonite Weekly Review, *January 5, 1978. Kreider reports his visit with other educators to President Jimmy Carter in the White House.*

When I was a boy Don Smucker, who lived down the street, reported proudly to us one day: "I shook the hand of a man who shook the hand of President Hoover." We were impressed he allowed us to shake his hand and then each of us went about announcing proudly: "I shook the hand of one who shook the hand of one who shook the hand of President Hoover."

That was 50 years ago, and one Jimmy Carter was just then a little boy in Plains, Georgia. Just two weeks ago I shook the hand of this Jimmy Carter, now President of the United States.

How should one view the experience of meeting the President of our country? Here are notes which could reflect four different ways of viewing the President:

*I. Meeting with Mr. Carter–Fellow Citizen*

Appointment with Mr. Carter at 10:00 a. m., December 16 in the West Wing of the White House. Tight security. Prime Minister Begin of Israel meeting with Mr. Carter since 8:00 a.m. Guards at gate check one's Social Security card and driver's license. Issue tags. Twenty of us representing Catholic and Protestant higher education. Guards again check our names against a duplicated list as we enter West Wing. Newspapermen and an African delegation waiting in the reception room. Vice President Mondale brushes past to express graciously to the Africans the regrets of the President that he cannot meet them because of the Begin conference.

Fran Voorde, Assistant Director of Schedules, greets us in the reception room and ushers us into the Roosevelt Room–30 by 40 feet, doors in four corners, long mahogany table needing refinishing in the center of the room, the table surrounded by leather upholstered chairs, the walls decorated with portraits of FDR, Theodore Roosevelt, and TR as a Rough Rider on San Juan Hill, plus two Remingtons, a painting of four frigates from the Revolutionary War, a scale model of a frigate from the War of 1812. A plain pad of white paper, a sharpened No. 2 pencil, and a cup and saucer at each place setting. A Filipino attendant served each of us coffee or tea from silver pots. As we sipped coffee, Fran Voorde, a pleasant 30-year-old woman, explained to us that Mr. Carter would be coming soon. We were not so sure, remembering that African delegation in the reception room which had to settle for a greeting from the Vice President.

A woman in a maroon suit entered and introduced herself as Elizabeth Abramowitz–unusual for a black woman to have a Polish name. She explained that she was the Assistant Director for Education and Women's Issues on the President's Domestic Policy Staff. As she was speaking, about 10:20 a.m., the door opened and in walked Mr. Carter, dressed in a light grey-blue suit with light blue shirt and a dark red and blue figured tie, his blond hair with the dry look. We all stood up....

*II. The President in All His Majesty*

The door opened and there stood President Carter, the 39th President of the United States–head of the most powerful state in the world. Coming directly from his conversations with Prime Minister Begin of Israel, we sensed the awesome burdens of office resting on his shoulders. In his hands he held the fragile peace of the world. And then this man–the ruler of 220 million people, commanding the greatest military power in the world–apologized to us: "I am sorry to have kept you waiting." A man so powerful to be so thoughtful for the small inconvenience of 20 ordinary citizens!

How grateful were we that our President with all the great responsibilities of his office, should grant us an audience. He listened intently to our words in behalf of church colleges and then he said to us simply, "I understand."

(President Carter never attended a church college–in fact only three Presidents in this century ever attended a church-related college: Woodrow Wilson, Presbyterian Davidson; Warren Harding, Methodist Ohio Northern; and Richard Nixon, Quaker Whittier.)

At the conclusion of our meeting he rose from the table and shook hands with each one of us–speaking to each one personally. Smiling in a friendly, caring manner and looking into my eyes, he shook my hand firmly and said, "We feel a kinship with you."

"A kinship?" Because I am a Mennonite and he is a Baptist–both Anabaptists way back? Or because we have a common affection for church colleges? "A kinship"–what did the President of the United States mean? To think that he used a biblical word–"kinship"....

*III. The President in the Web of Systems and Powers and Principalities*

Our meeting with the President was one of a dozen ceremonial meetings the President presided over that day. His manner is flawless. He observes with patience and grace the liturgical patterns of greeting, listening, conveying understanding, and concluding with the warm, friendly shaking of hands with each person who comes into his presence.

But one wonders. How effective is this friendly, attentive, intelligent man? How much power does he really have? Does he shape our destiny? I thought of an editorial I had read only five days before in our morning paper:

> The real power is not in the White House, but in a small scattering of power groups who stay on year after year regardless of the election returns. For labeling purposes, these groups are the oil industry, the press, lawyers, the South, munitions makers, the white suburbs, and some blanket blocs usually lumped as "big business" and "big labor".... What sort of a nation does this power bloc want? One in which big cities are shunned and kept poor. In which we are encouraged to travel, one person to a car if we like, and mass transport is downgraded. In which a huge, huge chunk of federal benefits flows to the South, Southwest and California–the "Sun Belt"..... In which oil consumption is encouraged in all areas, from food production to travel. In which farmers are urged to keep their peace and be quiet.... In sum, nothing much changes. The names vary from time to time, but the attitudes don't. The dollars come from where they came in Ford's day, and in Nixon's, and in Kennedy's.

I left the White House gate and walked alone on the streets of Washington and thought: "One of those 220,000,000 citizens and at once also one of that tiny minority of nonresistant Christians–what can I do to be a faithful disciple and an active citizen?" I hope. Help thou my lack of hope.

*IV. If One Could Really Talk with Jimmy Carter*

Our delegation prepared a three-page statement for the President to read. We also prepared a three-page statement for the President to present to us as a response–the material for this excerpted from his speeches. The President said that he read and approved the statement and the response. Both statements with beautiful, carefully selected, shaped, polished words–but words without life.

Mr. Carter appears as one with whom I would like to talk. I would like to talk with him about our church colleges, but get behind the pretty words and phrases: "liberal arts," "new challenges of service," "assisting students in becoming responsible members of our society and world," etc. To help him understand what church-related colleges can contribute, I would like to invite him to come to our campus (or any one of our campuses)

> • to ask questions of John de Gruchy, our guest professor, about the experiences of his white and black friends in South Africa.
> • to join the campus community in the celebration of Christmas, dining together, singing carols, and seeing "Amahl and the Night Visitors."
> • to talk with Martha who spent an internship year in Jerusalem and Linda, an intern in Bangladesh.
> • to watch Robert Regier's slide presentation, "Prairie Images," and then to talk about the dream for a prairie wilderness area in the Flint Hills.
> • to sit with a group of historians at the occasion of the Fall Festival discussing our church in the American experience.
> • to talk with the students who prepared the toy exhibit in the Fine Arts Center.
> • to talk with our Ethiopian students about their troubled homeland.

Visits to several of our church college campuses might provide helpful information for a president isolated in the endless liturgical acts of his office. Ideas–such as "Christian liberal arts"–can best be understood when they are found incarnate in persons and experiences.

Four perceptions of meeting the president: a straight reportorial account... a hymn of adulation... a cynical view of the powerlessness of a leader caught in the rituals of office... the yearning to break through rigid liturgies to share concerns in a personal way.

I cling to the fantasy that some private, inner meaning lies concealed in those words, "We feel a kinship with you."

# 1978: Thoughts on Reading the Thursday Morning Paper

*Printed in* Hutchinson News, *March 16, 1978.*

Thirty four Israeli killed
on a holiday bus–
Palestinian terrorists and
the politics of desperation.

Israel born of terrorists,
Stern Gang, Irgun, Menachem Begin–
Israeli terrorists and
the politics of liberation.

So goes on
the tired old litany of violence.

How many Palestinians must the Israeli kill
to teach them terrorism doesn't pay?

An eye for an eye and a tooth for a tooth?

Better still–thirty-four villages for thirty-four lives.

It takes a lot more Palestinian dead
to equal one Israeli dead.
Write new decrees
in the ancient writ:
For every slaughtered son of Israel
let a village of Palestinians go down in slaughter.

Jehovah weeps
as the ancient dialogue
of kill and counter-kill
goes on... and on... and on...

No one hears
the still small voice:
They who take the sword,
shall perish by the sword.

# 1978: A. W. Roberson–Peacemaker

*Printed in* Mennonite Weekly Review, *April 2, 1978.*

When I lived in Newton, Kansas, in the late 1930s it was a segregated town–even though it was north of the Mason-Dixon Line. All restaurants and drug stores refused meals to blacks unless they went to the back kitchen door. One exception was the 24-hour Fred Harvey House in the Santa Fe Depot. No black could get a room in a hotel. Itinerant Negro railway workers had to find lodging in private black homes. No Negro child could swim in the public pool. Negroes could not get haircuts in Newton barbershops.

"Negroes" or "colored", as they were called then, were segregated in the Jim Crow sections of the three movie theaters. Black athletes could play on the high school football team but were barred from the basketball team where black skin would touch white skin. No blacks clerked in stores. Those who were employed worked for the Santa Fe Railroad or as domestics and a few for the garbage and street department.

At Bethel College a black debater was not admitted to the national forensic honorary fraternity because of the society's "Africa exclusion clause" in its national charter. The clause did not stop the College from establishing a chapter limited to an all-white charter membership.

Much of the visible segregation has been wiped out. In part this is due to decisions of the courts and federal and state civil rights legislation. Changes, however, may be due even more to persons like A. W. Roberson, a sensitive and courageous black railway postal clerk who moved to Newton in 1944. In time, his patient, persistent, quiet ways moved mountains.

He was born of slave grandparents. He came from Denison, Texas, and soon after arriving began devoting himself to breaking down racial walls. He is one of the host of unsung black heroes and heroines who even predate Martin Luther King. He, like many others, has helped to make Newton a better community in which to live.

A. W. Roberson, seventy-one years old and now retired, has shared with us his story. He is an active member of a Negro Baptist church and the father of two grown daughters. He draws his moral strength from his family, his church and his parents–from whom he derived a clear sense of what was right and what was wrong.

Arriving in Newton late in World War II, he soon became president of a small, struggling local branch of the National Association for the Advancement of Colored People (NAACP), which represented the 400-500 Negroes in Newton. One of his first acts was to apply for NAACP membership in the local Chamber of

Commerce–no black ever having been a member. After several months delay and repeated inquiries, his application for membership was granted. At a dinner of the Chamber of Commerce he was permitted to eat for the first time in the otherwise segregated Ripley Hotel.

He sought help from the integrated Newton Ministerial Association to open for blacks, restaurants and drug store counters. He secured no support. The chairman of the association expressed to him his personal good will, but said that he could not help because so many in his congregation came from the South: "I can't get involved. I'll lose my bread and butter." To this Mr. Roberson responded: "But you know it says in the Bible, 'Go ye therefore... teaching them to observe all things whatsoever I have commanded you: and lo, I am with you always, even unto the end of the world.' Don't you believe that when you do the right thing, God will take care of you?" The pastor replied, "I guess I have too little faith."

The right of blacks to buy a decent meal in Newton seemed a fundamental right to Mr. Roberson. With the help of a small mixed group of blacks and white friends they visited all restaurant-owners and drug store counter managers to persuade them to serve blacks. One half of their group started at the south end of Main Street and worked north and the other half started at the north end of Main Street and worked south. Every restaurant, thus, was visited twice. At the end of the day the two groups compared notes. They were rebuffed at every place. One operator declared, "Before I'll serve you, I'll close up." Three years they waited. Mr. Roberson and others lobbied for a state law to declare these exclusion practices unlawful. With a new law on the books in the early 1950's again they made their round of Newton restaurants and drug store counters. No one wanted a lawsuit. Finally, blacks were permitted to sit at the counters in Newton. Mr. Roberson remembers his white friends–Lloyd Spaulding, Selma Platt (Johnson), and others–who helped them when such action was not popular to do so.

One day Mr. Roberson noted an announcement in the Newton Kansan that the Red Cross was sponsoring swimming classes for children at the public swimming pool. He inquired at the pool, "Does this mean all children?" The response was, "I suppose so but I better check." His inquiries led from person to person, each passing the buck to another until he reached the chairman of the Red Cross. A meeting was arranged at the municipal building with the city council. The council agreed to admit black children if they could secure the consent of parents of white children. The NAACP had difficulty finding persons who would sign their names, but at the Bethel College Mennonite Church they found 22 parents who would sign. That year Mennonite children in the summer Bible school took swimming lessons along with black children. Daily Vacation Bible School was very popular that year. This, however, was only a partial victory for the blacks who were still denied the use of the large pool. Year after year they petitioned that the ban be lifted. Their requests were denied. The third season the NAACP Chapter raised a fund for legal fees and decided to sue the city because of this violation of civil rights. Blacks also were tax payers for this public pool. The city came up with a counter offer making provision for the blacks to use the pool on certain days of the week. This compromise the NAACP refused.

Mr. Roberson and his friends then arranged for five black girls aged ten to fifteen, to go to the pool with bathing suits, towels, and admission money and with a group of parents watching discretely in the background. They were refused tickets and told that they would have to go to the city manager for an answer. The city manager called the city attorney. A special meeting of the city council was called with at least 15 Negroes in attendance. The council adjourned to a side room for an executive session. The city attorney had advised the council, "We can't stand a suit; we'll lose in court." The mayor came back to affirm publicly, "The council wants to do what is right." The pool was opened to blacks and also Mexicans. Fears had been expressed that the presence of blacks would lead whites to desert the pool. The first day 17 black and 729 whites came–the largest attendance on record. The pool has had no incidents since between Newton blacks and whites. Mr. Roberson added: "There was no black takeover. I don't believe there ever was again that many blacks (17) at the pool on one day." Nothing was reported in the newspaper about these events.

Mr. Roberson and his wife were concerned that blacks and Mexicans were confined to a segregated area in the local theater. This, they felt, must be changed. One evening they went to the theater fifteen minutes early while the bright overhead lights were on. They went forward and sat in the fifth row in the center where their blackness could be seen. If anyone came to ask them to move, Mr. Roberson planned to say, "Thank you, we are comfortable where we are." Although his wife was actually a bit uncomfortable, they sat there all evening. No one asked them to move. He and his wife went to the theater several additional times with no adverse action from the management. He then encouraged other blacks to go to the theater, to sit forward in the center, "to be calm, to talk nice, to keep cool, to be quiet, to be polite to anyone asking them to move, to refrain from anger or profanity–agreeing in advance that they would have to be carried out" if they were to be ejected. And so the Jim Crow section in Newton came to an end.

Mr. Roberson tells of going to a Newton barbershop to have his hair cut. Although the barber was not busy, he refused Roberson service stating: "You must have an appointment." To this he responded: "You're not refusing to cut my hair, are you?" The barber cut his hair. Mr. Roberson gave the barber a generous tip and commented, "You know, you did a nice job." He has not heard in recent years of any barber turning a black away. He adds, "A lot of white people don't realize that we only want to know we can do things other people can do if we want to. It's not that we want to take over swimming pools, barber shops, and restaurants. We just want to be free to do something if we want to do it."

Blacks were excluded from the high school basketball team. A black freshman boy who was a brilliant basketball player came to Roberson with his father. He wanted to try out for the high school team. Mr. Roberson went with them to the high school principal. The ban on blacks was lifted and the boy became a star on the Newton team. Mr. Roberson tells of working on job opportunities for blacks in Newton. Now they are teaching in the Newton school system, serving in supervisory positions in city government, and clerking in stores.

Little or nothing of these community conflicts and their resolution were reported in the city newspaper....

For the first three years after coming to Newton, Mr. Roberson and his wife roomed with a black plumber, U. S. Rickman. He tells of their long search for housing. He would call a realtor, who reported that he had a fine property to show him. When Mr. Roberson appeared, the realtor, startled to see a black, would explain not too convincingly, "I'm sorry that since you called that house is no longer available, but we have a nice little bungalow over on... (the black section)." At a tax sale he bought lots in a white neighborhood. Soon he was besieged by phone calls from persons wanting to buy those lots and, thus, keep a black family out of the neighborhood. He found a house five miles east of Goessel and moved it into Newton on to the lot. When finally it was ready for occupancy, he was approached by a man who said, "I'll give twice what you put in to it." He answered: "I'm goin' to live here and die here." When it came time to move in he took off three weeks from his job. He wanted to be sure that his family would not be subjected to harassment. He says that all in the neighborhood today are his friends. "It shows that people are afraid of the unknown." He adds, "I have always contended that the best way to do away with discrimination is to have people come in contact with each other. They find that they are not too bad."

I asked Mr. Roberson what he prefers to be called, "Black," "Negro," or "Colored." He answered, "People don't know what to call us because we've changed so often. None offend me. Still I am what I am. 'Negro' is best of all. Kids like to say 'Black'. The only term which offends me is 'Nigger.'"

When I have met on different occasions with Mr. Roberson, I have asked him in varied ways this question: "What gives you the courage to live as you have lived, the strength to do what you have done?" He speaks of his family and his church. He also speaks of "the principle of the thing." He goes on to say, "I took that from my daddy. I admired him. He was a poor man. He was a laboring man on a railroad maintenance crew. He stood up for what was right. He checked the rails to see whether they were safe. The supervisor once said that they were safe, but Dad stood up and said, 'They're not safe.' I guess I took some of that feeling about right and wrong from my Daddy." Mr. Roberson also acknowledges that his federal job with the postal service gave him an economic security which protected him from fear of loss of job.

Mr. Roberson looks back on his life and is satisfied. "Conditions have changed quite a bit in Newton. I have nice neighbors. However, there is no NAACP chapter now. Things got so much better that people have gotten complacent. Now Newton is more or less integrated, all except the churches. It's sad that the church is the last to take a stand. The sports and entertainment worlds were the first to lead out. And yet, I think I could join any church in Newton today."

As Mr. Roberson tells his stories one senses that his opponents have become his friends. He tells of his conflict with a big, profane, domineering Irishman who became "one of my dearest friends." He speaks of the lessons he has learned, such as, "If you know you're right, don't give up the first time they say 'no'. If you're right, you are likely eventually to get it." Finally, he observes, "I don't believe in violence. Everything can be realized by peaceful means."

Mr. A. W. Roberson has never received any awards as a peacemaker, no honorary degrees for public service, no recognition as a first citizen of his community. I think God, who sees all things, has observed A. W. Roberson and is pleased with this man who has a gift for caring for people's hurts and his ministry of reconciliation. The city of Newton, I am confident, is a better community because this gentle and sturdy man, grandson of slaves, chose to make his home in this place.

# 1978: Verbs of Violence

*A letter to the editor of the* Hutchinson News, *April 4,1978, chiding the newspaper for hyperbole in its language on the sports pages.*

Violence on TV. Violence in professional sports. Even violence on the sports pages of the *Hutchinson News!* Here are verbs of violence gleaned from headlines in several issues of the newspaper I read each morning before breakfast:

nip, rip, clip, flip and strip
down, pound and drown
shell, route and axe
dump, burn and bury
drop, top and stop
trim, trap, tramp, toss and topple
sink, spear and sting
lasso, gag, club and claw
bend, belt, break and attack
pin, floor, whip and wallop
cripple, mangle and slaughter

And then, too, the more elegant verbs:

annihilate, decimate and eliminate
stymie, dissect, nudge, devour, bash and vex

And, also, leaping verbs:

jump over, turn off, cut down, fly over, flip over, roll over, up end, wipe out and squeak by

And, finally, bland old-fashioned verbs:

beat, defeat, undo and–even–win.

A verbally battered reader.

# 1978: A Hymn of Appreciation for Kansas

*Printed in* Hutchinson News, *July 2, 1978 and the* Mennonite Weekly Review, *July 6, 1978* .

"Oh, if it weren't for those monotonous hours crossing Kansas to get to the mountains of Colorado."

The plains of Kansas–monotonous to some, but a land of delight to those with eyes to see. These are the reflections of the road as one drives from Newton to McPherson and then west on U. S. 56 to Lyons and beyond on State Route 96 to Great Bend on the Arkansas and to the "High Plains"–through towns like Ness City, Scott City, Tribune to the state line.

The highway, bordered by the Missouri Pacific, points straight westward, a power line on one side, a telephone line on the other–four parallel lines converging at a point in the distance–an elevator town seven or eight miles farther west.

It feels as though one is driving westward up an ever so gently inclined hill–as if the whole continent were tilted upward toward the setting sun. And it is tilted–from Newton at 1400 feet to one of the last towns in Kansas, Tribune, at 3600 feet.

This is a horizontal world–with gifts of breadth, space, horizons, solitude… opportunities beckoning in the distance, a sense of freedom, no feeling of being crowded, a land with few barriers.

The best part of the day in this horizontal world is the sunrise and the sunset when the life-giving and blazing sun is at the edge of the world–subdued, vulnerable, where it can be viewed with the naked eye–the sun present but neither dominating nor forsaking the plains. Both at dawn and at dusk this land is etched with long shadows which give patterns to the earth.

Piercing upward from this horizontal world in vertical thrusts of adoration to the God of the Plains are the grain elevators–spaced every six or eight or ten miles along the Missouri Pacific–like twelfth-century Gothic chapels on the plains of France, soaring upward in gratitude of the Good Giver of rain and sun and seed and soil.

And as one drives past Conway, Modoc, and Amy with their 500,000 bushel elevators one wonders how many loaves of bread are contained in the grain stored there–grain to be baked into bread and fed to the hungry of the world. One wonders where this grain will go–some to Genoa for pasta, some to Shanghai for noodles, some to Brooklyn for bagels, some to Leningrad for rolls, some through a long and circuitous process into hamburger buns and returned to McDonalds at Great Bend.

Scattered through the fields of wheat are wells pumping oil from the depths of the earth. Grain and oil–these are two great resources–apart from the people–produced from this earth. A road marker reminds us that a little more than a century ago the great resources of these plains were the grass and the buffalo–50 million of them sustained by the tall bluestem grass. But now there are no buffalo.

A century from now what will be the resources of these plains? When other energy resources are depleted perhaps these abundant natural forms of energy will again come into their own: the sun, the wind and the grass.

On a late June evening the roads and landscape are alive with the harvest. Ten-ton trucks are moving toward the elevators. Giant combines are devouring the grain. Huge red straw balers, bearing the name "Hesston," follow in the wake of the combines.

In the fields pickup trucks bring gasoline to the combines and cold drinks and sandwiches to the crews–like pit stops on the Indianapolis 500–a cluster of busy attendants, quickly refuel the big machines which lunge off again. The crews work against the deadline when one must stop because the grain is too moist to be cut in the night air.

Traffic is slower on Highway 96 on an evening as the convoys of trucks loaded with combines and with flashing red tail lights move from one job to the next. These are the crews doing custom combining–following the harvest, beginning in late May in Texas, moving up through Oklahoma, now into Kansas, later on to Nebraska and northward to the Dakotas.

Following the harvest–this must be one of the last great forms of adventure like sailing four-masted schooners around the Horn, trekking west with the Forty-Niners, following the Oregon Trail, crossing the Sahara in a Land Rover.

Following the harvest: brawn, sweat, heat and bone-tired weariness, fighting the elements of the sun, rain and storm, deadlines to meet, commitments to keep, risks to take, listening constantly for any irregular sounds in the operation of the combines and the trucks, watching vigilantly for anything amiss, and–if a breakdown occurs–all pitching in to get the big combines to roll again so one can go on tomorrow when the dew is out of the fields.

As dusk turns to darkness one sees the weighing stations at the elevators glowing with friendly light–receiving the trucks as they come to disgorge their heavy loads. Again one wonders how many loaves of bread a 10-ton truck of wheat carries–how many persons will it feed.

Late at night and early in the morning the roadside cafes are the scenes of the camaraderie of the harvest–pickup trucks parked around the cafe, men in greasy denim and wearing seed or fertilizer caps inside nursing cups of coffee and talking–telling the stories of the harvest and bantering with friendly casualness with the waitresses.

Along Highway 96 one sees the symbols of the region: windmills, stone fence posts west of Lyons, pickup trucks, Massey-Ferguson and Golden Harvest caps, modest farmsteads with a sprawl of small sheet-metal buildings (no large barns), and bales of hay–some one ton cylinders, some like giant loaves of bread, some conventional bales.

The towns on Highway 96 have their patterns. There are the broad streets which recall a pre-automobile age when one could make a U-turn on Main Street with a six-span mule train. Still remaining are Victorian-styled brick and stone storefronts from the 1880s and 1890s–businesses built within a decade of the founding of these frontier towns.

The weathered church on the corner, which was once the First Presbyterian or the United Methodist, is now an independent Bible church with purple Sunday School buses in the parking lot. On the edge of town is the new brick First Presbyterian or United Methodist church set back from the street and surrounded by well-watered lawns.

In the smaller villages may be only a filling station-cafe, but in the larger places business establishments are spun off by centrifugal force to the edge of towns. On one end of town one finds a low white building with its ice cream machines and another half acre of parking space for the ever-present pickups.

Driving through the night one breathes the aromas of the plains–each different and each to be savored. Each smell evokes an image: the smell of straw from newly combined fields of wheat… the cattle feeding lots… fields of freshly cut alfalfa… the strong and heady aroma of hog production industries… oil wells near the road… diesel fumes from passing trucks… the cleansing smell of a fresh rain. One of the joys of farming must be the smells.

There is nothing more dramatic on the High Plains than an approaching thunder storm: brilliant white elevators in striking contrast to black skies, a panoramic view for 10 miles around of ominous clouds, patches of bright blue sky and lightning flashes, perhaps a double rainbow. As one drives along the highway nothing obscures the great symphonic interplay of sights. Here one is enveloped by the elemental forces of weather–drought, storm, and blizzard.

As one drives west to the Colorado border the Missouri Pacific tracks are one's constant companion. At dawn a long freight train passes bearing exotic names of faraway places: Denver and Rio Grande, Chesapeake and Ohio, Southern Pacific, Penn Central, Norfolk and Western, Seaboard and Southern, Pittsburg and Lake Erie, the Lackawana, and–most beautiful sounding of all–the Atchison, Topeka and Santa Fe. One senses the linkages of these high plains with all the rest of the continent.

Driving west on Highway 96 in late June is not a monotonous test of endurance across a flat surface of boredom. It is a journey of infinite delights for those with eyes to see and the senses to receive.

# 1978: Vera Brittain's Testament of Youth

*Book review printed in* Mennonite Weekly Review, *in 1978.*

On my desk is an autobiography full of suspense and tragedy, a book that is now a classic from the World War I era, published just fifty years ago, Vera Brittain's *Testament of Youth* (London: Victor Gollancz Ltd., 1933). This is one of the many books which has been on my shelf which I promised myself I would sometime read. This weekend I started it; I could not stop until I had read all 447 pages.

Years ago I remember reading Brittain's eloquent pacifist and anti-war statement, *Humiliation with Honor.* I did not then know what pain and pathos were buried in her experience. Here is an intelligent, sensitive young woman from a middle class English family who retells with diary, letters and recalled memories of how the Great War destroyed her idealistic, comfortable world.

This, then, is the story of the Lost Generation of World War I. Some called it "the depleted generation." Those of us of the World War II generation can find much in *Testament of Youth* with which to identify, as can probably those of the Vietnam generation.

As the book begins, the gifted Vera Brittain goes off to Oxford, the first guns of August 1914 being only a distant sound. Soon, however, her closest friend and only brother Edward, a skilled violinist and imaginative composer, goes off to war as does Roland, brilliant young poet, to whom she soon became engaged. There is also Victor, almost a brother, and Geoffrey, closest of friends, a handsome young idealist who wanted, after the fighting would end, to be a pastor in a city slum.

These four young students, diverted from Oxford and Cambridge careers, went into the trenches of France believing that "the call of our country was the call of God." They "neither hated the Germans" nor "loved the Belgians," the only possible motive being, as Roland expressed it, "heroism in the abstract."

On March 31, 1915, Roland went to the front. He wrote letters and poems of sad beauty. He described the sunset of a dying summer and added, "it is a pity to kill people on a day like this... or any kind of day." He superintended the reconstruction of old trenches and described it in these words: "in among the chaos of twisted iron and splintered timber are the fleshless, blackened bones of simple men who poured out their red, sweet wine of youth unknowing, for nothing more tangible than Honour or their Country's Glory or another's Lust of Power. Let him who thinks War is a glorious, golden thing but look at a little pile of sodden grey rags that cover half a skull.... Who is there who has known and seen who can say that Victory is worth the death of even one of these?" On December 23, 1915, a day before he was to leave the trenches for a week's furlough with Vera and family, he was killed by a machine gunner's bullet.

Vera had left Oxford in the summer of 1915 "to do something," to become a nurse's aide in the Voluntary Aid Detachment–first stationed at London General Hospital, later for a year on the island of Malta, in 1917-18 at Etaples just behind the British lines in France, and finally back in London. As she decided to enter nursing service in the springtime of 1915 she observed that "it seems that everything ought to be creative, not destructive and that we should encourage things to live and not die."

She gave a woman's view of the war: "the waiting and waiting for news which was nearly always bad when it came," the fretful complaining of aging parents about rations and servants, the estrangement between the world of the trenches and the austere world of civilians across the channel, the constant flow of dismembered and shattered bodies from the fighting fronts, and the heroism of those who doggedly carried on.

In April 1917 Victor was shot through the eyes with a bullet. Less than a week later Geoffrey was killed in crossfire in the trenches. Six weeks later Victor died. Only her brother, Edward, the violinist, was left. After a year of convalescence from a splintered elbow he returned to the front. A year later he was killed by a sniper's bullet on a lovely mountaintop in Italy.

The pages of *Testament of Youth* are filled with eloquent, haunting passages from the letters she received from her friends in the trenches. They sent her lines of poetry, these men who "had a rendezvous with death." She reflected: "How futile it had all been, that superhuman gallantry!"

She described the mass of patients brought in from the big German offensive of March 1918: "stretchers on the floor, the scattered boots and piles of muddy khaki, the brown blankets turned black from smashed limbs bound to splints by filthy blood-stained bandages. Beneath each stinking wad of sodden wool and gauze an obscene horror waited for me...."

She spoke of the heroism of war. "Young men and women, disastrously pure in heart and unsuspicious of elderly self-interest and cynical exploitation, were continually rededicating themselves... to an end that they believed, and went on trying to believe, lofty and ideal."

She worked in an emergency ward serving German prisoners at the front. She held the hands of dying Germans, who may have killed her dearest friends. She commented, "The world was mad and we were all victims; that was the only way to look at it. These shattered, dying boys and I were paying alike for a situation that none of us had desired or done anything to bring about." She spoke of it as "the blind fight the blind."

At the war's end she wrote, "I lost one world, and after a time rose again... from spiritual death to find another." She called it her "resurrection!" She rebuilt her life, finding fulfillment in writing, the feminist movement, the cause of international order, pacifism, friends who had also walked with death, and a husband–a survivor of the war generation who understood.

A particularly moving section of her book is her visit after the war to a bitter, conquered Germany. She recorded in her diary: "I wonder how we should like being a conquered people.... War, especially if one is the winner, is such bad form. There is a strange lack of dignity in conquest; the dull, uncomplaining endurance of defeat appears more worthy of congratulation."

Vera Brittain concludes her book with a line of her poetry:

> But slowly towards the verge the dim sky clears,
> For nobler men may yet redeem our clay
> When we and war together, one wise day,
> Have passed away.

# 1979: Deadly Force Authorized

*Printed in* The Mennonite, *June 19, 1979.*

First Street runs eastward from Main Street in Newton, Kansas, past Bethel Deaconess Hospital, First Mennonite Church, Prairie View Mental Health Center, and then out into the rich black farmland that stretches toward the distant Flint Hills. Eastward for 20 miles are the farms of Mennonites who settled on these prairies 105 years ago–the Andres, Busenitzes, Claassens, Dycks, Entzes, Harders, Harms, Janzens, Regiers, and more. Ten miles beyond Newton is Grace Hill Mennonite Church; then the town of Elbing with Zion Mennonite Church and the Berean Academy. Four miles south is Emmaus Mennonite Church.

On a late Sunday afternoon in early spring we drove through this peaceful countryside. The air was chill and the skies gray. The black and tan fields were interspersed with stretches of velvety green winter wheat. The broad vistas of Kansas prairie conveyed a sense of space, freedom, and peace. It was a day the Psalmist could write about: "The earth is the Lord's and all that is in it."

The Flint Hills is an ages-old hill country gently eroded down to grassy uplands, the limestone thinly covered with soil bearing native grasses such as the tall bluestem. We were looking for a Titan II installation of McConnell Air Force Base. A man pumping gas at a station in Whitewater gave us directions to the site: "A half mile beyond Potwin you come to a blacktop. Three miles north and you're there."

Only one road sign–a letter "M" with an arrow–gave any hint of directions to the site. We followed a gravel road to the hilltop–and there it was, a four-acre plot enclosed by an eight-foot woven steel fence, topped by three strands of barbed wire. We were stopped by a large white sign:

WARNING RESTRICTED AREA
IT IS UNLAWFUL TO ENTER THIS AREA WITHOUT PERMISSION OF THE COMMANDER MCCONNELL AIR FORCE BASE KANSAS. WHILE ON THIS INSTALLATION ALL PERSONNEL AND THE PROPERTY UNDER THEIR CONTROL ARE SUBJECT TO SEARCH. USE OF DEADLY FORCE AUTHORIZED
(Section 21 Internal Security Act of 1950. 50 USC 797)

We drove a hundred feet beyond the warning sign right up to the locked wire gate, again with the same ominous message: "Warning… use of deadly force authorized."

We knew we were in the presence of one of the most deadly weapons ever made by man. Buried in the center of that hilltop is a 147-foot-deep silo in which is poised for instant flight a 103-foot missile (a Titan II) capped with a warhead lethal beyond human comprehension. We were only 75 yards away from a warhead which packs more destructive power than all the bullets and bombs used in all the wars of history. This deadly device is only 21 miles from Newton, 25 from downtown Wichita, and 25 from our house. Here is a Titan II trigger-ready to arch an intercontinental ballistic missile toward targets 6,000 miles, perhaps even 9,000 miles away. The warhead in that knoll beyond the fence holds 5 to 7.5 megatons of destructive fury–a bomb at least 300 times more devastating than the one dropped on Hiroshima.

We sat in our car for a while studying that steel fence enclosing forbidden land. No signs of human life. No trees, no bushes. Some brown grass. A lone buzzard rested on an antenna. Some fresh ruts cut near a driveway. The only movement inside the enclosure was a continuously revolving and blinking green light (like the warning light mounted on a highway patrolman's car) and a rotating wind velocity meter.

In the center of the gravel-covered enclosure projecting up from the hilltop was a low white-domed structure, probably the top of the silo with its 700-ton lid which can be opened in 20 seconds. Scattered throughout the enclosure we saw assorted towers, floodlights, and concrete platforms with strange periscope-like projections. No cars or trucks were parked inside the gate or outside. It was an eerie, lonely place. It began to drizzle.

A gravel road circles the Titan II site. Slowly we drove around the perimeter of the enclosure. Sixteen signs wired to the fence repeated the warning: "Use of deadly force authorized." We wondered whether anyone was watching us, even with sensitive instruments listening in on our conversation. I thought of "Big Brother" in Orwell's *1984*. The only evidence of life was steam rising from a concrete depression near the big white lid on the silo. We understand that down there in the bowels of that multi-million-dollar installation are air force crews who are on 24-hour shifts–tinkering, watching, polishing... waiting... waiting... waiting for the alert and the turning of those two launch keys in the little green box.

We thought of all the things which could release the weapons of terror. Crewmen underground going berserk. In the command room curious air force personnel fooling around with the instruments. Terrorists. A corroded pipe and another chemical spill. A madman in command. Wild blips on a radar screen. An upstart nuclear power using H-bombs as blackmail....

One hundred and ten years ago buffalo grazed on this knoll. Now it seemed that powers, principalities, and systems have built a technological shrine in this solitary place. My thoughts trailed off to another altar on a hilltop: Mount Carmel, where one Elijah was pitted against the 450 priests of Baal. But there were only the two of us in this awesome place.

We left the hilltop and drove down country roads, reading the names on mailboxes. We were a few miles east of the Claassens and the Regiers. The nearest farmhouse to the Titan II site–just a third of a mile away–lived, according to the mailbox, Charles E. Carter. The house in process of being remodeled, sections covered with tar paper, was surrounded by five old cars, a camper trailer, and two dogs standing sentinel. Thirty head of mixed-breed cattle stared at us from the feedlot. All one could see of the Titan II site from the Carter farmstead were the blinking light and the tips of assorted antennae. I had an urge to go up to the door and ask the Carters how they felt living in sight of the warhead. Does it bother them to sleep near a Titan II which can be lofted from that hilltop to land on cities 6,000 miles away? We drove on.

On the way home our thoughts were somber. We tried to translate this weapons system into our own experience. The five-megaton warhead could be aimed at Leningrad and hit our Baptist brother Michael Zhidkof and two million of his neighbors. One could misfire and destroy Amsterdam where our son David lives this year. Or it could be aimed at East Berlin where Walter Jantzen and his wife live. Or this warhead might be aimed at Vladivostok, and it might overshoot and hit Hokkaido Island in Japan where our daughter Karen and Steve expect to be next summer. The Potwin missile site is one of 18 Titan II installations circling Wichita. As late as last summer I knew little about this ring of death around the city. In late August at one Titan site south of Wichita 10,000 gallons of toxic chemical accidentally spilled in the lower chambers of the silo. Two crewmen died. Then we began to learn in piecemeal reports of the story of the 18 warheads in our backyard.

Through our minds drifted "Pentagon thoughts." If we were assigned the task of aiming the 18 Titan missiles of the Wichita complex at prime "enemy targets," where would we mark X's on the map? Moscow, with its eight million, of course, and Leningrad with almost four million more. Add Donetsk, Dnepropetrovsk (that would wipe out neighboring Chortitza and Molotschna), Gorki, Kharkov, Kiev, Kirisbyshov, Minsk, Novosibirsk, Odessa, Rostov,

Smolensk, Sverdlovsk, Tashkent, Volgograd, and for good measure–two cities behind the "Iron Curtain": Warsaw and Prague.

They–the enemy–would retaliate instantly, of course. What cities would the enemy destroy in the litany of lethal reciprocity–Wichita, probably, and Chicago and Washington, DC, and...? Surely the enemy is committed to instant reciprocity.

The drizzle had changed to rain. Our thoughts were melancholy. There were periods of silence. After a time Lois declared: "It's all so insane." It is, indeed, so insane this catatonic trust in the nuclear system.

In the dusk a sign bearing this Scripture verse welcomed us to come to Emmaus Mennonite Church: "Believe in the Lord Jesus Christ and Thou Shalt be Saved." We thought of additional relevant Bible verses for church signs in the Potwin area: "Not by might nor by power but by my Spirit sayeth the Lord of Hosts." "Some trust in chariots and some in horses, but we will remember the name of the Lord our God." The insanity of it. Even more the immorality of it. Thinking of the technological brilliance of man's achievement in designing this weapon which can kill 20 million people, the lines of Edwin Markham came to mind:

> Is this the Thing the Lord God made and gave
> To have dominion over sea and land:
> To trace the stars and search the heavens for power;
> To feel the passion of Eternity?
> Is this the dream He dreamed who shaped the suns
> And marked their ways upon the ancient deep?
> Down all the caverns of Hell to their last gulf
> There is no shape more terrible than this....
> More filled with signs and portents for the soul
> More packed with danger to the universe.

An awesome fantasy took possession of my thoughts. In that millisecond after the enemies of this world had all destroyed one another and all their neighbors, I saw ourselves standing before Jesus. He might ask, "Did you have anything to do in helping destroy all my children?" And we would answer, "Well, it's like those concentration camps; we really didn't know about those missiles until very recently. What could we have done? It was all so sophisticated and complex. We were helpless. If you can't trust those in authority, who can you trust?... I suppose we helped pay for that Titan II at Potwin. But you know, we have always believed in giving to Caesar the things which are Caesar's...."

# 1981: Nobody Here But Us Camels

*Printed in* Gospel Herald, *April 7, 1981, and in other publications.*

Verily I say unto you, That a rich man shall hardly enter
into the kingdom of heaven. It is easier for a camel to go
through the eye of a needle, than for a rich man to enter
into the kingdom of God. When his disciples heard it, they
were exceedingly amazed, saying, Who then can be saved?
(Mt. 19:23-25).

Compared to most people in the world we are rich–all of us. I
buy a pair of shoes and the price equals the average per capita
annual income of a person from Upper Volta. We are all camels
and there is that needle's eye through which to crawl.

Our most highly developed gift is the gift of rationalization. We
rich camels have ways of trying to squirm through that needle's
eye. "Of course, it was not a needle but a narrow gate in Old
Jerusalem through which you could squeeze with effort." "The
poor are worse than the rich in their love of money." "How would
we operate our colleges and missions if we did not have generous
rich people?" "God has given some the gift of preaching and others
the gift of making money." "No one needs to be poor; work hard
and save and you can be comfortable like us." "Remember all the
good that Andrew Carnegie did." "Who would elect a poor man as
deacon or college board member?" "We would like to give but who
is going to look out for us in our old age? I don't want to be a
burden to anyone."

There is no escaping all the Bible teachings about money and
possessions. If you were to cut out all the passages about riches,
love of money, hoarding, poverty, and sharing there would be a lot
of blank space in the Bible. Here are only a few of the passages
which could be cited: "If riches increase, set not your heart on
them." "He who trusts in riches will wither." "No servant can serve
two masters." "You cannot serve God and mammon." "Blessed are
you poor." "Woe to you that are rich." "Where your treasure is,
there will your heart be also." "Do not lay up for yourselves
treasures on earth." "Go, sell all that you have, and give to the
poor." "Beware of all covetousness; for a man's life does not consist
in the abundance of his possessions." "Sell your possessions and
give alms." "Give to everyone who begs from you." "Keep your life
free from the love of money, and be content with what you have."
"You desire and do not have; so you kill." "Beware lest you say in
your heart, 'My power and the might of my hand have gotten me
this wealth.'" "Consider the lilies of the field." That avalanche of
biblical teaching ought to slow down the rationalizations of us rich

camels. However, we keep making defensive explanations, because, as we said, we have the gift of rationalization.

I am reluctant to lecture my fellow camels about wealth because I remember those words, "Let him who is without sin cast the first stone." It is not easy to preach sermons on wealth and poverty to a varied group of listeners, each one preoccupied with his or her situation: the widow who lives only on Social Security checks and recently lost much in a fire, a young couple with a second baby and the father just laid off work, the families with two incomes who spend most of what they earn, the one who just came into a large inheritance, those who have a compulsive need to shop, the couple making a costly career change in mid-life, others who are totally absorbed in a growing business, those who are frugal and invest and quietly grow rich. Camels come in many shapes and sizes.

Recognizing that God has a special word for each camel, I would include various elements in a theology of money and wealth. The starting point would be "seek ye first the kingdom of heaven." Then would follow a theology of creation: "the earth is the Lord's, and the fullness thereof"–not only land, but also property, shares of stock, and money. We would look at some uncomfortable world data to remind ourselves that we North Americans are all rich and are using up God's natural resources a hundred times faster than other peoples. We would reflect on the limits of what money can do: "Man does not live by bread [or money] alone." There would be a biblical reminder that we ought not dillydally: "This night thy soul shall be required of thee." Drawing on the Mennonite experience in Russia, China, and elsewhere we would note the ominous warnings of the wrath of the hungry, the poor, and the oppressed.

We would look critically at those not-so-humble explanations as to how we in our shrewdness earned all this money. We would look at covetousness called ambition and hoarding called prudence and ruthlessness called industry. We would discuss money as a resource, not an end.

We must pursue another line to argue that the making of money (saving, investing, planning, managing) can be creative community service. We would suggest that they who save, invest, plan, and manage also serve. Managers and investors can fulfill good public purposes. Such services include restraining present spending for future need, withstanding consumer temptations, husbanding capital funds, anticipating public needs, bringing together money and people and a plan, providing jobs, calculating and taking risks.

After commending the skills and the communal good of the entrepreneur, we would lay on him some biblical admonitions.

Remember the poor. Treat your laborers fairly. Respect God's good earth. Beware of pride. Don't let your treasure pile up. Use it. Give it away. Die poor like you were born. Along with the joy of creating wealth let there be the greater joy of sharing wealth. Let not thy left hand know. Remember the widow's mite. The time is short.

We might end this essay on money and wealth by asking how large was Jesus' estate when His will was probated.

We would reluctantly come back to that needle's eye we must squeeze through. There we stand–all of us camels.

# 1982: Lord God, Go in Front of Us

*Reflections following a mission in April 1982, when Kreider was sent by the Board of Eastern Mennonite Missions to make representation to the Ethiopian government in behalf of the beleaguered Meserete Kristos Church.*

On Easter Sunday afternoon we met with a group of leaders of the Meserete Kristos Church (the Mennonite church in Ethiopia). For ten weeks they had been living under severe restrictions. Church doors had been sealed, bank accounts frozen, church headquarters shut, church programs halted, and leaders imprisoned. They were not disheartened. They were people of hope. They spoke of their church as the Church of the Risen Christ. They were followers of Christ for whom "the stone had been rolled away."

During April three of us went from office to office representing the concerns of our Mennonite people in Ethiopia. Two of us were older men with gray hair one black and one white–and one was a younger man with the agenda, the addresses, the names of persons to see, the driver of the old station wagon. For a time, we thought these efforts were meeting with success. Slowly the possibilities of immediate success ebbed away. Of one thing, however, we were assured: the church was not defeated.

Perhaps adversity brings out the best in a people. I am told that church members in Ethiopia are not unlike Christian people elsewhere. They have their problems, their disputes, their lapses from faithfulness. And yet our Ethiopian brothers and sisters can teach us many lessons.

They can teach us that the church is more than church buildings, institutions and schedules of activities. One brother commented to me: "The church is not closed; they can't close the church; they can't close our hearts." Another expressed it a bit differently: "They came and closed our church. In that moment 40 new churches opened." He went on to explain that now the church meets in small groups in homes. He recalled the story of the first church in Jerusalem: "The disciples were together. They liked each other but they had to split and scatter. And the church grew." He proceeded: "Today some don't understand the church. They think it is a place of meeting."

One of the brothers told me about his small group. He explained that their group meets on Sunday evenings at nine for Bible study, discussion, sharing and prayer. They meet quietly; they sing no hymns. They collect their tithes for the needy. He added that persons in authority "can take away the meeting house but they can't take away the church."

I asked a teacher how he accounts for the calmness and poise with which church members responded to troubles. He answered, "We have had frustrations and anxieties, but once you get over the initial shock you give it over to the Lord. You depend on the Lord. We have a tradition of going around consoling each other and comforting each other. There has been an increase in visiting among us."

One of the questions I often asked was, "What portions of Scripture particularly speak to your needs now?" "Psalms," was the immediate answer given by one. He added, "We should lean on the Lord more than anyone else. David came through troubles like we have to go through." Another listed the following passages which have been especially meaningful to him in these days: II Corinthians 6, Habakkuk 3, Esther 4, Isaiah 40-43, and Psalms 42, 91, and 121.

I said to one of the older leaders, "You as a Christian have experienced much harder times than I." This led to my question, "What sustains you?" To this he responded: "God sustains us. God speaks to us in prayer. He speaks to us in Scripture and in our experience. Through our experiences we can understand the Scripture better." Later he observed that through their experiences they can feel closer to the Christians described in Acts in the first century.

I asked him what prayer means to him. He stated that prayer means much to him. He suggested that he likes short prayers. "The prayer I like to pray is, 'Lord God, go in front of us.' "

He takes the long view. He observed, "As human beings we want to get all the answers from one side—our side. We have to wait. Sometimes we calculate our days in hours and minutes. In God's way a thousand years are as one day." We can learn from their lessons concerning patience.

I wanted to know what was distinctive about their church. In what way are they different as a people? He said this of his M.K.C. people, "They stick at it. They can work in any situation.... They are educators. They have good schools, but it is not only the classroom. It is the way they do things, the way they raise their children. They are reluctant to call themselves 'nonresistant.'" I was not satisfied with this denial of nonresistance and asked, "Aren't you nonresistant in handling the present crisis?" My friend responded, "In this crisis we came under spiritual control. We talked together. We prayed together. We agreed we will do it the Lord's way. The spirit is handling this. We are shaped by Bible teaching."

The above reflections affirm my conviction that this young 30-year-old church in Ethiopia–which at the moment does not have meeting houses, bank accounts, headquarters offices, conference papers–is alive with the Spirit of Christ. They have gifts to give us. They, who were our spiritual pupils, are now our teachers in the faith. They are asking us to pray with them the prayer, "Lord God, go in front of us."

# 1983: Let a Hundred Flowers Bloom

*An excerpt from an article, "'Let a Hundred Flowers Bloom' and 'One Lord, One Faith, One Baptism'" that appeared in the* Mennonite Quarterly Review, July 1983.)

I understand that this is to be a painting with a big brush. Or perhaps this is a reconnaissance mission into unchartered territory before they send in the heavy artillery. For one of our texts we begin with the Apostle Paul's words from Ephesians 4:

> I therefore, the prisoner of the Lord, beseech you... to keep the unity of the Spirit in the bond of peace. There is one body, and one Spirit... One Lord, one faith, one baptism, one God and Father of all, who is above all, and through all, and in you all.

And to symbolize the creeping pluralism in our ranks, we turn to a Marxist text, that of Mao Tse-tung, who in 1956 flirted for a moment with pluralism. Here are Mao's words: "To artists and writers we say, 'Let a hundred flowers bloom.' To scientists we say, 'Let a hundred schools of thought contend.'" Those words were uttered a few months before Nikita Khrushchev delivered his celebrated anti-Stalinist speech.

The world of capitalism, the West, is of course preeminently pluralistic. But in the socialist world–from Tito to Solidarity–there is also a creeping pluralism. Things seem to fall apart. We are posing the question in this conference–"Whither bound Mennonites in an age of pluralism?"–because we too are troubled that things are falling apart with this explosion of choices, this pluralism....

*Pluralism in the Family Experience*

I am convinced that family history, genealogy–once the least of the historical arts–should be tapped as a resource in probing a number of issues central to the Mennonite experience: acculturation, dispersion, boundary keeping, value transmission from generation to generation, group acceptance and rejection, and pluralism in value systems. If we were to open the closet doors on a hundred Mennonite family histories, we might know much more about pluralism in the Mennonite experience. I propose to open four closets in one family history, hopeful that these descriptions are relevant to the issue before us.

The first closet. Our family story derives from the Swiss-South German-Lancaster County, Pennsylvania, stream which deposited the Kreider family on the banks of the Conestoga in the 1710s. For two and a half centuries the family was quietly proud that it was unmixed with Amish blood. After the family moved west to Whiteside County, Illinois, in 1854, it began to exhibit pluralistic symptoms. Grandfather Kreider added farm to farm, one for each child interested in farming. After bearing six children his first wife died and he married his housekeeper, a severely plain Brethren in Christ woman who steadfastly remained River Brethren for the remaining fifty years of her life. There–a touch of pluralism.

His eldest daughter married a Mennonite, who was an indifferent farmer, found spiritual exhilaration in the Assembly of God with their camp meetings. Aunt Tilly and Uncle Abe moved west to Oklahoma for land and freedom. Then came Harry, an aspiring poet whose poems only rarely were accepted by Editor Daniel Kauffman in the *Gospel Herald,* dispossessed of his inheritance by fast-talking salesmen of gold mining stock, happy, serene and plain until the end of his days. Add Abe, who married a Lutheran neighbor girl who died young and left him with a family of six–a loving family, the children faithful Lutherans. Then came Frank, a rough, rebellious youth who married a woman of dubious reputation, took refuge in Oklahoma territory, divorced his wife, returned chastened to marry a Lutheran woman of sterling virtues and to settle down to affluent respectability–the financial counselor to the family. (Because of Frank's marital experience, his brothers shied away from condemnatory comments on divorce and remarriage.) Following were John and Amos who married Mennonites and whose children are still in the fold. Finally, there was half-brother Ben, who grew up in town, who was a soldier for several months in World War I and for the next fifty years was an exuberant leader of the local American Legion, acquisitive in business, a Methodist, with no children, but a man who left handsome legacies for several charities, the care of his horse Rusty, and a Boston Terrier, Frosty.

Here was a Mennonite family–the father honest, generous, sparing in speech, plain of dress, for whom Lancaster County Mennonitism was the distant norm–a kind of Camelot where they did things right, order reigning in the meetinghouses and well-being on the farms. His children reflected diverse life styles, pluralistic values, but they accepted each other's idiosyncrasies. They even loved Uncle Ben, right out of Sinclair Lewis' Sauk Center, Minnesota. They all loved and admired my father–the only one to go to high school or college or seminary–who had pastored the Mennonite congregation in the white meeting house where only two continued to attend. And my father loved them all. Here was an emergent pluralism held together by the glue of family affection.

The second closet: the town of Bluffton, Ohio, in the late 20s and the early 30s. Our family moved from Goshen where my father had taught at Goshen College and pastored the College Church. Ours was a tentative move–my parents keeping their Old Mennonite affiliation for five years. For the first time I attended services in a meeting house which they called "the church" where there were great stained glass windows, a huge pipe organ, plus a piano, women wearing hats, an orchestra for the Sunday School opening, German preaching once a month, and a four- page children's paper from David C. Cook distributed after Sunday School and read during church. My playmates were no longer Yoders, Zooks, Kaufmans and Eigsties, but Reichenbachs, Luginbuhls, Niswanders, Badertschers, Schumachers. Back in Goshen we had known only three kinds of Mennonites: "Old Mennonites" which we were, the plain Reformed Mennonites like Aunt Jenny, and Central Conference Mennonites who had a new church on Eighth Street.

In Bluffton were Reformed Mennonites like our plain-dressing but affluent dentist, Dr. Basinger; Defenseless Mennonites like fourth grade teacher Miss Steiner; those of the break-away Missionary Church like a Sunday School-mate who joined their Gospel Fishing Club. And most of all were the General Conference Mennonites, 95 percent of whose ancestors had come directly from Switzerland, many still speaking *Swietzerdietsch*. The largest Mennonite minority in the community were the Old Mennonite refugees from Goshen: the Byers, Smiths, Hartzlers, Witmers, Smuckers, Lantzes and more–whom Mrs. Mosiman, the president's wife, called "Mennonite Jews," she being displeased with them as a pushy lot.

As a child I needed to make sense of a bewildering range of Mennonite patterns of piety. Across the street from us lived the Schultzes from Mountain Lake, Minnesota–Low Germans, who had prayer at the end of each meal as well as at the beginning, where on Saturdays there was always the aroma of *Zwiebach* in the kitchen, where I first heard *Plautdietsch*. The Schultzes ran an even tighter family ship than did my parents. Next door were the Toshes. Mrs. Tosh was pure Swiss, a Grismore, who had met her husband John Tosh, a non-Mennonite from California, at Moody's or, perhaps, Los Angeles Bible Institute. He was a friendly Fundamentalist who laughed a lot and was leader of our Junior Christian Endeavor. He taught us to say sentence prayers ("Bless the missionaries in foreign fields and help them to win many more souls for thee".... "Be with those who could not be here this Sunday and help them to be here next time"), to memorize Scripture passages, to sing gospel choruses. He also explained how you could be a good Christian and in the army at the same time, like his brother, who never shot anybody and who could have won souls to Christ if he had chosen to. We liked friendly John Tosh but our family nurture led us to hold at arm's length his casuistry on war and nonresistance.

Next door to us was my piano teacher, a staunch Lutheran, totally absorbed with things Lutheran; back across the alley a cultivated, evangelizing Christian Scientist and her atheist or agnostic French husband; across a vacant lot an old couple, the Boehrs, who came from the Palatinate, baked butter cookies, spoke no English, and symbolized an old world piety. Scattered around us were Methodist, Presbyterian and Reformed families and several older people who didn't go to church—which seemed very strange to us because church was central to our lives.

A block away lived S. K. Mosiman, president of the college, a little man with a goatee and a Prince Albert coat, who was married to one of the most imposing women in town. Taller than her husband, she wore flowered hats, had a regal bearing and looked like Queen Mary of England. Born in West Prussia, she came from Beatrice, Nebraska. We knew she was of a higher class than any of us. She punctuated her conversation with phrases I did not hear at home: "dear Jesus," "the Lord provides," "if God wills." An aristocratic pietist she was. Across the alley from the Mosimans was C. Henry Smith, professor, banker, writer of books on Mennonite history, who stood and watched us play football on a vacant lot, wore a Phi Beta Kappa key on a chain. He was a man of means who lived frugally, who once sent me a postcard from Hawaii, and whom we all admired from afar. There were other neighbors: J. E. Hartzler, the great Mennonite platform personage and his wife Mamie of simple and plain tastes; Russel Lantz, choral director, baseball pitcher, who had been imprisoned at Leavenworth for his CO convictions in World War I; the vibrantly alive Boyd Smucker family with their four sons; Professor Berky, who had studied at Woodrow Wilson's Princeton and brought to Bluffton the Honor System; Jacob Quiring, with white tousled hair, who looked a little like Einstein and, when he was asked to pray in church, rose and in a soaring, lyrical voice had conversations with God ("We knew that God was in that holy place"), his daughter my favorite Sunday School teacher. One spring he was asked to leave the college because some said he was "not sound." What that meant, I did not know.

My seventh grade teacher was voluble Wilhelm Amstutz, a master story teller, knowledgeable about every detail in the history of this Swiss community, son of a Mennonite excommunicated for running for county office. Wilhelm had joined the Reformed Church and delighted in telling us stories of Mennonite perversity and pathology in the community. He once asked each member in our class what branch of the service we would join in event of war: army, navy or marines. I remember that occasion–the fear of exposure and the feeling of being put upon by the teacher as he drew closer and closer to me. When my moment of truth came, I mumbled that I didn't choose any service. The crisis passed. I felt better. I had stood up.

In the 1920s four Mennonite refugee families from Russia came to Bluffton, sponsored by the college and local Mennonite churches: the Klassens, Epps, Warkentins, Schmidts. Hearing their stories of war, revolution, famine and flight, we became aware of a suffering church. Our church people gathered old furniture and clothing we didn't need and gave it to them. Some of them didn't seem to be as grateful as some church members thought they should be. Several of the men smoked and that didn't seem right if they were Mennonites and if they were so poor. Two of the men were sick and dying of TB. The wives were strong women and held their families together. I heard some say that they ought to do something about having so many babies. Prof. Klassen, an artist with a fine family, rose to heroic heights in our eyes, when in Allen County Court he declared he would not fight for the United States even under penalty of not receiving U. S. citizenship. I also remember Prof. and Mrs. Peter Epp once making an emotional defense of those Mennonites in Russia who took up arms in the *Selbstschutz* militia. The Epps left the community soon thereafter and disappeared into the anonymity of Ohio State University. One of the refugee families stayed in Bluffton and had boys who were football stars–one going on to coach football at Notre Dame–and a daughter who became a cheerleader married a boy from the Swiss Settlement and baked *Zwiebach* on Saturdays. She had a diary of her mother's trek from Russia, east across Siberia through China to America. That story means much to her and her family where Mennonite convictions now flow deep.

As this child's view of growing up in a Mennonite college town suggests, these college communities have been among the most pluralizing of settings.

A third closet: more like another room. We moved to Kansas in 1935, the year after the great dust storms. A radically different Mennonite world opened up for us. For the first time I heard of Mennonite Brethren and KMBs and Holdeman. I observed at Bethel the bewildering array of ethnic groups. I heard Ed G. Kaufman explain to my father the political intricacies of these differences. All around us were Low Germans. There too were the vigorous Volhynian Swiss in Moundridge and beyond and out at Pretty Prairie; the conference-wise South Germans of Halstead, Deer Creek and Moundridge–sometimes called "Bavarians," who had arrived a generation earlier than the rest and were the architects of the conference union; the staunch and presumed proud West Prussians of Newton, Elbing, Whitewater and distant Beatrice; those of Polish origins of Johannestal and Gnadenberg, more humble, but rich in productivity of leaders; Galicians of Arlington and Hanston; the pure and separatist Swiss of Whitewater; and traces of Hutterian descendants and Pennsylvania Dutch scattered about. In the student body one could feel the divisions: differing dialects still spoken, differing English accents, differing food systems, differing patterns of piety, differing mixes of passivity and aggressiveness, cross-ethnic-line marriages still evoking comment. Are these not intimations of pluralism? What has held this nine-headed ethnic diversity in Kansas together in the General Conference? I have heard three explanations given: hymn singing (the *Gesangbuch mit Noten*), missions beginning in the 1880s with the work among the Cheyenne and Arapahoe in Oklahoma, and in a more tempestuous way, Bethel College.

A fourth closet: Civilian Public Service. At age 22 when I was drafted into CPS Camp No. 5 at Colorado Springs, I had already experienced more pluralism than most. I had just received my master's degree from the University of Chicago, itself a world of choices in an urban setting. For me it was a liberating experience to escape from university studies to live with largely farm fellows of seventeen or more Mennonite varieties–living together in drafty barracks, eating Ma Groening's Low German cooking as we were packed shoulder to shoulder in the dining hall, making friends for the first time with Mennonite Brethren, Amish, Hutterites and Holdeman. Detached from the border-protecting sanctions of home communities and clinging together in awareness of public displeasure with our stance, our pluralism was encompassed by a sense of a new extended family. This family spirit even reached out and embraced John, a Plymouth Brethren; Reuben, the Pentecostal; two Jehovah's Witnesses; George Yamanda, a Nisei CO moved east from coastal California where he imperiled West Coast defenses; Bruce, the restless Methodist; Arlo Sonnenberg, the Evangelical who had a lyrical way with words; but perhaps not the macho Mennonite from Nebraska who left camp after Pearl Harbor to join the army and came back several months later wearing a button: "Jap Killer."

Never in Mennonite history were so many different Mennonites thrown into the same pot and stirred together with Molokans, Christadelphians, Nazarenes, Pilgrim Holiness men, Unitarians, Immanuel Missionary Association members, a sprinkling of atheists and agnostics, and scores more. This enforced acceptance of pluralism had a variety of problems for Mennonites: What adjustments do you make in worship services? Do you use a piano? What books and periodicals are permitted in the camp library? Do you deny John's plea to bring in a Pentecostal pastor to teach Bible class in camp? Who is the brother whose sensitivities are not to be offended? Who are the keepers of the boundaries? What regulations are to be imposed to accommodate the editorial admonitions of the critics of MCC-administered C.P.S.? What kind of leaders will be accepted and can hold these communities of diversity together? Some pastors and favorite college sons pressed into camp leadership lacked the touch. In time leadership emerged primarily from CPS ranks. Camp leaders were principally young, single, college-educated, a few non-Mennonite– a high percentage of whom have since become pastors, college teachers, missionaries and conference leaders in an age of increasing pluralism.

This excursion into one family's experiences is to suggest that Mennonites have had to cope with pluralism–heretofore probably in more manageable portions than is now our lot.

# 1983: Remembrance of Elmer Ediger

*A tribute shared at the memorial service for Elmer Ediger, September
24, 1983. This is selected as one from among some 30 tributes presented
at memorial services and events honoring friends and family members.*

One senses that Elmer Ediger is present with us. He is not gone.
The lives he touched, the careers he nurtured, the institutions he
created, the movements he aided, the family he shaped are all so
full of vitality that they will go on and on. As we contemplate the
unique way in which the love of God was incarnated in Elmer, we
are "persuaded that neither death, nor life, nor angels, nor
principalities, nor powers, nor things present, nor things to come,
nor height, nor depth, nor any other creature, shall be able to
separate us from the love of God, which is in Christ Jesus."
    This evening we are continuing an unfinished conversation with
Elmer, telling one another what he meant to us. Some remember
that first meeting... that last meeting... that occasion when he
invited one to join the staff or a board... that Sunday School
discussion. One is startled into an awareness that there were items
one intended to discuss with Elmer.
    Elmer's life has been full and whole. Born in Greensburg, Kansas,
August 3, 1917, starting school at Meade, he moved with his family
back to a farm near Buhler. The German family Bible lists the
names of father, David J. and mother, Anna Martens, and Elmer as
the seventh of eleven children. One of Elmer's brothers speaks of
Elmer as being the one most like their father–a good man, a sturdy
spirit, a lay preacher, who in the depression saved the family farm
by reluctant sales of pieces of land together with work on PWA
jobs. Poverty, drought, a mother's illness, a tenacity of temper, a
spirit of love welded this family together and shaped the characters
of each of the eleven children and the seventh child, Elmer.
    Elmer married gentle, loving, caring Mildred Gerbrand,
classmate of high school and college, in wartime, October 6, 1943
while he was in Civilian Public Service. To Mildred and Elmer were
born Elaine, Carol and Mark and then five grandchildren–Karen,
Robyn, and Jason to Elaine and Robert Burdette and Christopher
and Eric to Carol and Ron Peters. Elmer loved his family and they
loved him. Mildred was taken from them on June 11, 1974. Then
Elmer and the family received the gift of warm-hearted and
vivacious Tina Block. Elmer and Tina were married September 14,
1975. And now Tina is given the mission–the gift and the grace–to
lead and care for a family that has had a great loss.
    Elmer's gift of leadership is rooted deep in his youth. As
President of the Student Christian Association on this campus one
observed his creativeness and vigor. One remembers the occasion

of his return from a student conference bursting with a hundred new ideas. Fearful that the idealism would wear off, he called together a group of 20 students in a professor's house. They met on successive Sunday evenings to discuss how the values from the conference could be planted on the campus. During those college years Elmer on the side painted and hung paper, probably earning every dollar of his college expenses. One observes Elmer after college–an able teacher, first at Ellis and then at Buhler and at Ellis coaching a basketball team to a league championship. He was always probing: a summer of study at Emporia State–just to see what a state university was like; a summer in an intentional community at Suffern, New York; a summer in an Ashram in the heart of Harlem.

The War came and with it Civilian Public Service. Elmer moved on to a national stage of Peace Churches, government agencies and an exhilarating inter-Mennonite world of Amish and Mennonite Brethren, Holdeman and KMBs, MCs and GCs. Elmer was soon tapped for leadership and, with such men as Orie O. Miller, Henry Fast, and Albert Gaeddert as his mentors, Elmer was soon coordinating the educational programs of several score of MCC alternative service units, with some 2,000 drafted COs. At war's end he was General Director of the whole MCC-CPS program. Those were the Akron, Pennsylvania, years. A colleague then remembers Elmer often at day's end coming "to my door, standing in the doorway and asking what we had accomplished that day." Already those conscious evaluation mechanisms were being etched into his behavior patterns.

We know Elmer as the great innovator. Even then in his 20s Elmer parented and shaped in their infancy two major institutions of the church. He and others launched a variety of voluntary service programs–essentially an alternative education system which has changed the life of the church. VS may be Elmer's most enduring contribution to the church. However, it is overshadowed by the second, the planting, nurturing, and shaping of the Mennonite mental health movement. Elmer was close to the 1,500 CPS men who had served during wartime in mental hospitals and institutions for the retarded–many squalid, crowded, and inhumane. He knew of the hospitals for the mentally ill in the Molotschna, South Russia, from whence his grandparents had migrated. Close to him were loved ones who suffered from emotional illness. In a brilliant memorandum–certainly professionally brash and imprudent–Elmer suggested to Orie O. Miller that a barn and old brick house on an MCC-owned farm in Maryland–land eroded and remote–be converted into a small experimental community for the care of the mentally ill. That was 1946. Out of the seed of that Brooklane Farm has come Kings View, Prairie View, Oaklawn, Kern View, and a variety of psychiatric centers in communities as distant as Asuncion, Paraguay.

There is so much more in the early life of Elmer Ediger: president of the conference young people's union which was fanned into new life under his leadership; seminary study at Bethany and Mennonite Biblical Seminaries in Chicago; the first Executive Secretary of the infant Board of Christian Service; collaboration with brother Albert and others in designing the nationwide Mennonite Disaster Service (another of his innovative contributions.).

Thirty years ago seed was planted which became Prairie View. Of Elmer's administrative gifts, one of his colleagues in the national mental health movement wrote to Elmer

> I feel you could have run anything from the Roman Empire on down. I suppose if you had been in charge of the Roman Empire you would have established satellite centers in Iceland and China, had the Goths and Vandals raising funds, and started community meetings in Crete and the Outer Hebrides....

At lunch two weeks ago I asked a friend of Elmer's, his roommate forty five years ago and in recent years a university professor and administrator: "You knew the young Elmer; what is his secret?" He exploded in a rapid sequence of comments: "Dedication. An administrator who is a teacher. He should be canonized for Prairie View." He went on: "Dedicated people sometimes are insufferable, but Elmer is not insufferable...." "I remember," he said, "Elmer's keen interest in all leaders, all speakers who came to the campus." He was fascinated with leadership and its secret inner grain. We talked of Elmer's creativity. It was not his academic ability–a good student but not a brilliant student. It was not his persuasiveness as a public speaker, nor his ability to communicate in writing. And yet he was a master communicator person to person and in committee. My friend continued, "Elmer's creativity lies in his ability to assimilate ideas and adapt them. Borrowing and adapting, working by analogy–this is Elmer's creative genius. His mind always working."

One searches for the motifs, the themes in Elmer's full and whole life. Dedication, yes. Christ has been the center of his life. In Him and His church he found his vocation. For forty years his only employment has been in the programs of the church. In the church he lived and moved and had his being. Of all the many involvements of Elmer in the life of the church today his deepest satisfactions, one senses, are teaching his Sunday School class–for which he prepared diligently through the week; secondly, his concern for the preparation of pastoral leadership–his work in coordinating a satellite seminary in the Kansas area; and third, attending triennial church conferences–having attended every one from 1941 to the present, perhaps a record.

Returning to the story of Elmer the administrator–Prairie View, church conference, Bethel College, seminary, Paraguay Partners–one is fascinated by the complex patterning of Elmer's ways of leadership and yet the simplicity of the themes:

•the savoring of new ideas–the borrowing and adapting;

•the sense of network, wholeness–how everything is connected with everything else;

•institution as family, as community;

•the leader not in center stage–the art of decreasing as others increase;

•institution as "we" and not as "my";

•seeing decision-making as process, inviting participation;

•a high seriousness–keeping one's eyes on the agenda, calling the committee back to the critical issues;

•pressing the hard questions, dissatisfied with easy answers... dogged, stubborn... tenacious, even vexatious... in the end more options and better answers found;

•an eye for promising staff, strong board members;

•a gift of allowing and encouraging people to work to the fullest with their particular capabilities;

•cultivating a climate of excitement in being on the growing edges of the future... creating models which can be replicated;

•recognizing that honesty (even at the expense of bluntness) bonds community in integrity;

•and much more;

Those who have worked closely with Elmer speak of the exhilaration they have experienced in sharing in those dreams and visions. A secretary wrote to Elmer, "Frequently when those dreams appeared on my desk in your handwriting they looked more like nightmares with arrows, deletions, and insertions. And sometimes it seemed the visions arrived only the night before they were due in Washington."

As is true of each of us, there is about Elmer a complexity, a mystery, the unfinished conversation. There is Elmer in all his high seriousness–mover of institutions, counselor to presidents. There is Elmer who is impish and light hearted, hanging loose from the world–who goes to the office with socks and tie that may not match, who is fascinated in the task of selecting a new car adjustable both to his long legs and to Tina's short legs, who roars with delight to earthy humor told in *Plautdietsch*, who takes his grandchildren out to the pasture to see the ruts of the chuck wagons on the Chisholm trail... who climbs a high ladder to paint the peak of a friend's barn, with brush in hand talking of college and church and projects aborning.

We voice gratitude to Elmer and his colleagues in behalf of the silent ones–all those thousands who through institution and program have been helped to cope with their pain, misery, and loneliness.

We are grateful to Elmer for being a good steward of Jesus Christ who planted the seed. One hears in these lines of Vachel Lindsay a resurrection theme, words which suggest they may have been written of Elmer:

> A hundred white eagles have risen the sons of your sons,
> The zeal in their wings is a zeal that your dreaming began
> The valor that wore out your soul in the service of man.
>
> Sleep softly,... eagle forgotten,... under the stone,
> Time has its way with you there and the clay has its own.
> Sleep on, O brave-hearted, O wise man, that kindled the
>     flame–To live in mankind is far more than to live in a
>     name,
> To live in mankind, far, far more... than to live in a name.

# 1984: Though I Walk Through the Valley of the Shadow of Death

*Presentation at the annual conference of the Central District of the General Conference Mennonite Church, March 30, 1984.*

These are sad stories which I am going to share–sad stories which are also stories of joy and hope. Thirty years ago there were no Mennonites in Central America; today there are as many as 9,000. My message is two-fold: 1. Our kinsmen in these young churches, who were once our children and our pupils, can now be our parents and teachers in the faith. 2. We who have brothers and sisters in Christ in Central America, need not be limited to Pentagon and White House press releases. Members of our Mennonite family can be our eyes and ears. This leads to the words of the Apostle Paul in I Corinthians 1:26-27:

> God has chosen the weak things of the world to confound the things which are mighty; and base things of the world, and things which are despised, hath God chosen... to bring to nought things that are.

The little people, the ordinary people of Central America, bear disproportionately the wounds of violence. They long for peace. They may be wiser than all the powerful generals and brilliant statesmen who are in control. I wish that members of presidential commissions listened to persons like these.

I invite you to listen in on a series of conversations with church people in Central America–much of this taken verbatim from my journal recorded during my travels in Central America last July. As these good and patient people told us their stories of fear, terror, and suffering we sensed that we were walking with them "through the valley of the shadow of death." Psalm 23 came alive for me in Guatemala and El Salvador: "Though I walk thru the valley of the shadow of death, I shall fear no evil...." A feeling of sadness, shame and helplessness lingers. One is frustrated in efforts to penetrate the layers of insensitivity which shield the people of power from the people of suffering. Among many people of power there seems to be a will not to know. We are aware of the complexity which resists quick solutions. We know how easy it is to impose simple theories of Soviet wrong and American right on the tangled stories of these troubled peoples.

*The first of several images.*

We are the impostors who speak the truth, the unknown men who all men know; dying we still live on; disciplined by suffering, we are not done to death; in our sorrows we have always cause for joy; poor ourselves, we bring wealth to many; penniless, we own the world. II Corinthians 6:8-10

We spent a day in a refugee camp in Honduras eight miles from the El Salvador border. Ten thousand El Salvador refugees have fled the terror in their homeland to this camp operated by the UN High Commissioner for Refugees. The Honduran Mennonites and the MCC jointly staff a part of that camp program. Our workers walk the paths along the border, guiding the refugees to safety in the camp. An Italian volunteer, who has led some 2,000 to safety, is called by the refugees "The good shepherd of the hills." We met with nine of the campesino refugees, all simple farmers. We asked each to tell his story. Most began with these words, "Let me tell you what it was like to be a campesino." That oft-repeated line had a haunting quality: "let me tell you what it was like to be a campesino." A centuries-old struggle to survive, a love of the land, a simple integrity. Each one stood to speak, to describe in loving detail the mountain acres he had fled under threat of death. Here are their words:

Three and a half acres of corn, beans, sorghum, with pigs and chickens. We worked the land but we didn't own the land. We worked on large farms to earn money to pay the rent. We had just a piece of roof.... Another: We could not read, as farmers, we did not have enough to eat; we had to flee, left everything.... Another: We had 3 ½ acres of dry land with a house. We had to sell grain low to buy medicines, fertilizer and clothing.... Another: Most of us had to go down to the plains to work on the plantations to earn rent money and fertilizer. On the coffee plantations we received one tortilla for breakfast, two for supper with some beans; water was rationed; at night we slept outside under the coffee trees. Our wages were about $1.50 a day.

Warming to a sense that they could trust these visitors, one declared:

We don't believe in the peace that they talk about. We can hear the guns across the border.... They keep on capturing workers, farmers, students, and teachers. These have been tortured and hung.... We love our country. May you all help so peace may arrive soon.... You can see that we are not enemies of our country. You can see that two thirds of us are children and old people.

As we sat with this circle of campesinos–slight and lean of body, lined and leathery of face, shy and respectful of speech–I had difficulty seeing that here was the enemy that must be destroyed so that we North Americans may enjoy the blessings of freedom, democracy and prosperity.

Later I learned that one of these campesinos was a leader of Bible study groups, "a delegate of the word." He said that hundreds of lay church leaders, "delegates of the word," have been killed in El Salvador. The government back in El Salvador, in their desperate ways, sees anyone who works with the people (organizes a Bible study group, starts a literacy program, forms a cooperative) as the enemy of the government. This delegate of the word, back in his El Salvadoran village, had been one of several village leaders called together by soldiers. He saw his own son hung upside down on a cross and hacked to death with machetes by soldiers–this presumably as a warning to the father. He fled within hours of his son's massacre.

One of the campesinos told of serving on the local election committee which was instructed to prepare on the night before an election a ballot box with an advance tally of election results. This is one of the stories which makes one skeptical of the results of elections.

The Honduran Mennonite, who heads our program at that camp, is a poised, quiet-spoken person, El Salvadoran by birth. He has been a teacher. He always uses the word "we" in describing the work. I asked him why he is engaged in this unpopular, dangerous service for suspected aliens. He, young in the Mennonite church, reached back 400 years in his church memories to speak: "We Mennonites have historically worked with refugees. Our Lord speaks of strangers and taking them in. We are lovers of peace. We share the sufferings of the oppressed here and elsewhere, not just today, not just in Honduras. That gives our ministry of reconciliation credibility. They see what we are and what we say is the same." He was a humble man, but he had a deep sense of assurance and worth.

*A second image.*
Another text, Romans 8, has immediacy of meaning in Central
America:

> What can separate us from the life of Christ? Can affliction
> or hardship? Can persecution, hunger, nakedness, peril or
> the sword? We have been treated like sheep for the
> slaughter–and yet, in spite of all, overwhelming victory is
> ours through him who loves us.

In a friend's home in Guatemala City I met a Methodist pastor
who had just arrived from the highlands where he serves his Indian
peasant people. He sat across the table and spoke quietly, intensely,
an infinite weariness etched deep in the lines of his gaunt face. He
told of how his people in some 40 congregations have been driven
from their mountain homes by army search-and-destroy missions.
They have been herded into militarized towns, "model villages."
The Guatemalan army burns off the fields so that no food will be
available to guerrillas. The army allows no one, he explained, to be
neutral. He described sadly a wasteland of tragedy:

> Some land has been idle for two years. It may look like
> peace but it is all fictitious. Those who move into the
> military-controlled towns do so because of desperate
> hunger. They are forced into civilian patrols, armed with
> machetes and old guns.... Soldiers go out en masse and
> wipe out villages–men, women, and children. The Prince
> of the World is destroying this world.

He told of how 10 leaders in one of the highland congregations
came and said that they could not take communion. They had
blood on their hands; at gun point they had been forced to take
clubs, beat and kill their neighbors who were members of a
Pentecostal church, the Prince of Peace Church. I asked him: "What
do you say to your people if they ask, "How can God, a God of
love, permit this killing?" He looked at me with a penetrating
sadness and said quietly, "They ask that question all the time....
And I ask the same question, too.... And you, too, would ask the
same question if you saw a fellow human being hung up to die."
I inquired what was his hope in this world. He responded:

> It is very difficult to have hope in this world. Those who
> have always had the power in this world–the landowners,
> the rich–still have the power. The problem at its roots is

power.... Poor people have always been deceived. Reformers make offers to the poor but reformers never come through.

He went on:

Many of my people get angry and curse God. That is not right. We need to help our people to believe in God. Often I say to my people: "For me to live is Christ, to die is gain."

We talked of prayer:

Prayer is the best medicine we have.... We get down on our knees. We cry out and spill our needs. We find peace. Many times I have been asked to pray at these burials. Tomorrow may happen to me what happened to that man, that child.... I say to our people that we need both the material and the spiritual in the sharing of the Gospel. We can't just say, "Now we'll pray... and then walk away. We also must say, "We'll buy the casket for your son."

I asked him what his word is for us who live so far away from this suffering. He responded:

You are far away but God is close to you. We need your prayers. We hope you continue to do what your people have done throughout history.... We don't want to think of you as Mennonites or us as Methodists but both as brothers.

As he talked of how he walks each day "through the valley of the shadow of death," he returned to his central theme:

Paul says, "Every day I die." Thus he identified with the suffering. Every day I give thanks for the gift of a new day. I say, "Lord God into thy hands we deliver our lives. Do with us what you want. Thy will be done."

*A third image.*

My imprisonment in Christ's cause has become common knowledge to all at headquarters here, and indeed among the public at large; and it has given confidence to most of our fellow Christians to speak the word of God fearlessly and with extraordinary courage. Philippians 1:13-14.

When we arrived in San Salvador we met first with a Lutheran pastor who only recently had been released from prison and torture, his family not knowing where he was or whether he was dead or alive. One of our MCC workers went to the home of that frightened Salvadoran family to stay with them during those days and nights of fear and terror. This young man only a few years before had been my student–now an MCC worker a part of whose ministry was pastoring the broken hearted. The pastor told of how on the first Sunday after his release he came to preach to his congregation–the church packed and overflowing. He couldn't preach a sermon. He looked at his loving people and was overwhelmed. He found however, that the Apostle Paul had said what he wanted to say. He just read the first chapter of Philippians and wept. They sang and gave thanks and hugged one another and praised God and wept and prayed.

On the edge of San Salvador we visited in the home of a used car salesman, a member of the local Beachy Amish congregation. He had spent six years studying for the Catholic priesthood. He and his wife and children dressed plain: the women wearing cape dresses and prayer coverings. He told of the suffering of a family where recently two sons were killed. He explained:

> The army came looking to kill all of them. They robbed their house of everything. Our congregation helped the family.

Our government plans to increase military aid to that army. He went on:

> Most of those who flee from the mountains seem to have more fear of the army than of the guerrillas. The army often kills those who are fleeing.... In these times just to have life is a special kind of gift. The people want violence to end. They just want to go back to their mountain fields and work.

This Beachy Amish brother described his earlier years in the army and then in land reform work. He spoke of the violence and the oppression:

The army puts guns in people's mouths and blows them up. I can't sleep. When agrarian reform began, a Catholic priest was my teacher. He died because he stood up for the rights of the farmers, encouraging them to get together in co-ops. He was killed by local soldiers controlled by the rich. The animals of the rich were eating better than the workers. When sugar prices rose he urged the workers to ask for higher wages. The soldiers killed him.

I asked him how he as a Christian handles his hatreds. He responded:

I have a goal in my life to let my feelings rest in God's hands. The first desire of a person is revenge. I try to put myself in the position of all who suffer. Only because of God's grace can I overcome my hatred.

This led to a question about what nonresistance means to him. He said that if one follows the Bible,

one must be nonresistant. Different people have different biblical bases for doing things. Some think you should be obedient to the government and kill. They use the Bible any way they want to use it. I am called to be a peacemaker.

I inquired about his vision for his church. He responded:

I am pushing for the church to be more identified with the people–with the people sleeping under the trees. One of the main themes of the church should be to see the needs of the displaced and the refugees as if we were they. In the church are all kinds, including those who want to forget and not to know. Our church is confusing to some because we see the Gospel as faith *and* works.

How often one observes: the sharp distinction between faith and works is a bit of theological cleverness in which only rich Christians can indulge. I asked him what his message was for us in North America. He had a ready answer:

Brothers and sisters in all the world can pray for us here. Speak of what you have seen and heard and not just what you read in the newspapers. Speak of the hope of those who have lost the most. Explain that the poorest have more to fear from the army than from the guerrillas. Almost all the killing is by the civil defense squads.

Here is a voice from a man who came to Christ through the work of the Beachy Amish.

A *fourth image* of a young church in Christ:

> ...they praised God and enjoyed the favor of the whole people. And day by day the Lord added to their number those whom they were saving. Acts 2:47

One Sunday morning we attended a Mennonite Church in Guatemala City. Our minds were full of the stories of scorched earth actions and death squads, torture and fear, the uprooting of a million Indians in the highlands. This was a middle class church full of professionals, most of them young in the faith. That Sunday we listened to one of the most eloquent Mennonite preachers I have ever heard. He did not allow these city professionals to rest in comfort, to insulate themselves from the distant guns. He opened with a challenge that the Christian has a different perspective from the world on defeat and victory, success and failure. He developed the theme:

> God's perspective on defeat and victory is from the vantage point of eternity. If we see God's view of victory and defeat then we have to see the birth of the church as a part of crisis. God's salvation in history moves along in crisis. The church was born in crisis. In the Cross is paradox: to the world–defeat, but to those who believe–victory. There was God with the concept of eternity in the middle of futility producing victory.... It is like the battle of Jericho, no strategy, no planning, just people doing God's will. It all seemed so ridiculous to the world.

He referred to a serious threat that week on the life of the president–then Rios Mont, an evangelical, since deposed. He told of how he was asked to join a prayer chain for the president. He stated:

> I didn't join. I pray for all presidents. I pray all the time. Should we not pray, too, for our enemies? Our attitudes

need to transcend circumstances. That is why I like the Cross. My negativism and pessimism is taken away.... We sit down and pray, "God, oh, change the circumstances." No. You get there and do something. God says get out there and make the Kingdom.

This led him to the triumphant conclusion of his message:

Christ made us more than victors. We have the message of Christ throughout history. We are promoters of peace, peacemakers. Ours is not the peace of the world but a peace that is justice, that comes from the mercy of God. The next time when someone says "We are in a time of crisis" let's say, No. We are in the time of expectancy, the time of birth.

The preacher spoke with gestures and pantomime, whispers and dramatic declarations. He often called for affirmation from the congregation and back came the responses–choruses of "Amens." At the end of the sermon the pastor raised and clasped his hands above his head like a victorious prizefighter accompanied to the amens and applause of the congregation. I was deeply moved. I thought: "Wow, this is a sermon right out of Antioch 50 A.D. or Strasbourg 1528 or Chortitza 1922."

Some weeks before, the President of Guatemala had attended this church, he a born-again Christian. It was his second visit. He was accompanied by bodyguards carrying automatic weapons and Bibles. The congregation had greeted him with more adulation than might be appropriate to an other-worldly Mennonite congregation. The pastor informed the president later that he would be welcome to attend again but that the next time bodyguards should leave their guns outside the place of worship. He was simply to be one of the worshipers. If people wanted to greet him, they should do so outside the place of worship. This Mennonite church was to be the House of the Lord.

These are our brothers and sisters speaking. Do we hear them? Do we hear the words of the Apostle Paul?

God has chosen the weak things of the world to confound the things which are mighty; and base things of the world, and things which are despised, hath God chosen... to bring to nought things that are.

They can now be our parents and teachers in the ways of obedience to Christ. A final word: what can we do? The killing of the innocent ones in Central America is a crisis of conscience today for American Christians, perhaps just as the slaughter of Jews was the test of conscience for the confessing church in Germany.

What can we do? We can listen. We can pray. We can study. We can act–write, speak, phone. We can provide refuge. We can pray: "Father, forgive us…"

I hear the voices of our brothers and sisters in Guatemala, El Salvador, Nicaragua, Honduras. Those voices don't go away. They haunt me. They call me. They comfort me. They lead me to a renewed awareness of Christ in our midst.

Though I walk through the valley of the shadow of death thou art with me.…

# 1985: Child's-eye Views of Nature

*Printed in* Christian Living, *March 1985, based on an audio-visual presentation in convocation at Bethel College.*

The folk hero of the summer of 1982 was a ten-year-old boy, Elliott, a central figure in the film fantasy, ET. A sensitive intelligence lay deep within this slender child. Extraterrestrial wonders were revealed to him which were not disclosed to adult earthlings.

Jesus said that one must be childlike of spirit to be one of his kingdom. It takes the fresh innocence of an Elliott to see the enchanting wonders of anthills, to hear the whisper of grass waving in the breeze, to feel the texture of a lizard's skin, to smell the pungent aroma of a hollow tree. A child's eyes, ears, and nose are closer to the ground where much of the action is.

With pad and pencil in hand, I asked some 20 persons to tell of their childhood and their early memories of wonder and delight in the beauty of God's earth. I asked them to recall those details of discovery as to how the world of nature works. They told their stories of wind and water, leaf and insect, cow in the feed lot and puppy at the back door. One saw these adults as children again along a garden path—touching, tasting, smelling, poking, pinching, stroking, hugging, caressing God's creation.

William Wordsworth suggested that our adult appreciations are shaped in a child's wonder and joy in God's creation:

*My heart leaps up when I behold*
*A rainbow in the sky:*
*So was it when my life began,*
*So is it now I am a man:*
*So be it when I grow old,*
*Or let me die!*

*The child is father of the Man;*
*And I could wish my days to be*
*Bound each to each*
*By natural piety.*

A child has the gift of seeing the little daily miracles of unnoticed beauty that are close at hand, the flower "that dwelt among the untrodden ways"–a violet "half hidden from the eye."

As we hear others speak of their childhood experiences, we are invited to reflect on our early memories. As children what kindled our interest in the outdoors? When did one's heart leap up when beholding a rainbow in the sky, an anthill along the path, a newborn calf in the barn? What were those miracles of daily life we observed as children which quickened in us a sense of awe and love of God's creation?

What follows are the recollections of those I pursued with pad and pencil.

One's attitudes about nature are bound up with place and time—for me, the farmyard, the one-room school. These have a powerful emotional impact which carry over to the present moment....

In Montana is a breed of Bigger Wasps which live on cabbage worms. They dug little holes in the hard dirt path between our house and the outhouse. We watched them by the hour. A Bigger Wasp would capture a cabbage worm and carry it to the hole. They placed a little stone over each hole which they fitted snugly into place with a tiny jackhammer buzzing and vibrating. We called them "zutty bees" because of this vibrating action. With their little jackhammers, they could remove the stone and back down into the hole, thorax first, pulling the cabbage worm into the hole. When they had enough worms, six or seven, they packed the hole tight with dirt.

We once made a one-inch lasso with Mother's thread and pulled it tight around a "zutty bee" when it backed out the hole. We caught him and examined him carefully. Ultimately, we dug up a hole to see what the underground passages looked like. We found six or seven cabbage worms stored away for winter eating.

We studied and played with nature. We had no toys. In town, children might have been less likely to observe nature so inductively. All this was our little secret. Our parents didn't know about these things. They were so busy.

My favorite flower is the dandelion. One of my most satisfying memories I had as a child was to look out our kitchen window in the spring and see a golden lawn of dandelions. We never struggled against what was a weed to our neighbors. Let a thousand dandelions bloom in the spring.

Dad, my brothers, and I built a swinging footbridge of discarded pipes and cable across Big Riley Creek. It wasn't the usual kind of work for a farm family. It was scary, fascinating, standing on the swinging bridge in flood time above the raging current. That is a special place for me because we knew the old farmer who had once lived on the farm and who told us how he remembered as a boy the Shawnee Indians camping nearby on the banks of the creek.

A friend once reminded me how he, when he was eight or nine, came to me, a high school student, for counsel. I had forgotten about this but the memory came back. He asked me shyly that which he was hesitant to ask his father, our pastor: "How are babies born'?" I was wary of saying more than I should. I asked him whether he knew how animals were born. He told me how they had taken their dog to a farm to be bred and then some months later their dog had a litter of puppies. Then I said, "Good. Don't you think it must be much the same for human beings?" He understood. Often when I see him, he retells this story and his first lesson in the mysteries of sex. Now he is a family counselor and consults daily with clients whose sex lives are all tangled up.

My mother disapproved—in fact was horrified at the sight of us playing in mud puddles. She never fully appreciated the educational significance of a puddle or of making mud pies; or the engineering feats of building dams, ponds, terraces, and waterfalls; or of soil analysis in distinguishing among wet gravel, sand, clay, and silt as it oozed between our toes; or of our experimental studies in testing the swimming abilities of different insects. I never could understand why Mother, who was right on so many things, did not appreciate the enchantment of a mud puddle. Sometimes I wonder whether mud and water in the backyard were not as educational as those video games today at the arcade which gobble up quarters.

My earliest thoughts on nature were about running water. I was fascinated how the water from the downspout from our barn ran across the barnyard, into the ditch by the road and down to Little

Riley Creek.... Later I was captivated with how the Little Riley Creek flowed into the Big Riley Creek, into the Blanchard River, into the Auglaize River, into the Ottawa River, into the Maumee River, into Lake Erie, through the Niagara River and over the falls through Lake Ontario, down the St. Lawrence River, into the Gulf of St. Lawrence, and out into the North Atlantic Ocean. I was awed by the inter-connectedness of it all.

I have a love for our particular farm where I was born and where my father homesteaded in 1900. The trees seem to be a part of the family. All were either planted by my parents or by my wife. Before my dad broke prairie there was nothing here but grass, Indian artifacts, and buffalo wallows. Our family has been the only one to live here since the Indians.

I love the challenge of the farm–coping with nature, expecting one thing and getting another, the uncertainty of weather, insects, disease. We intend to leave the land better than we found it–better terraces, the soil richer in humus. You have to love the land. This spring we saw seven wild turkeys, a bald eagle landing on the wheat field, lots of quail, and quite often deer. I love the smell of grass and soil, the earth after a rain, ensilage, the feed lot–especially when the price of cattle is up.

I loved to bundle up after a fresh snow and go outside and follow in the snow the tracks of rabbits, field mice, and once–my greatest delight ever–the tracks of a fox. Snow is a kind of town newspaper in field and woods. Animals and birds report their wanderings. A field mouse visits a neighbor and the bit of gossip is chronicled in the snow. On these mornings not a human being was in sight; the whole white world was mine alone.

They say a dog has a nose that is many times more sensitive than ours. The nose of a human has about five million cells that sense; dogs' noses have up to 300 million cells for smelling and they are much closer to the surface. Even with our dull nostrils, childhood was a wonderland of smells. I loved the aromas of the garden: new peas in the spring, freshly dug potatoes, mint, celery, dill. Then there was the aroma of freshly cut alfalfa, new baled straw, sweet corn pulled from the stalk, wheat bins and hay mows, wood smoke in the autumn air, ensilage, and all those manures–each different in its fragrance–horse manure, cow, chicken, rabbit, even hog. I can smell each one now. I talked with a man who has spent a lifetime sawing timber. He says he knows the smell of every kind of lumber–the most fragrant to him, the lodge-pole pine; and the least pleasant to his nose, the cottonwood.

We once had a frail little baby pig in a box behind the kitchen stove to keep it warm.... The mailman brought cases of little chicks sent by the hatchery. We fed a few sickly ones with oatmeal in zinc fruit jar lids.... In the kitchen there were always seeds being germinated in pans of soil and covered with damp cloth and sitting on top of the hot water heater. We watched them sprout and helped father keep a record of the percentage of germination.

Little things I remember: Studying the patterns of frost on the windowpanes in winter.... Taking a head of wheat and crushing it in my hand to figure out how soon it would be mature.... Looking through the *Burpee Seed Catalog* in wintertime and dreaming about our spring garden.... Watching the shaft of sunshine coming through the front door and seeing the glowing little particles of dust suspended in air. As the light shifted one saw that those glowing particles were everywhere in the air.... Going to the timber on the last day of country school to pick wildflowers and in July getting up before sunrise to go to the timber with milk pails to pick blackberries and coming back with full buckets, our clothing soaked by the dew.

I liked the rhythms of nature.... Throwing a stone into a quiet pond and watching the concentric rings ripple out with receding faintness from the point of the splash. It may have been my first awareness of infinity.... I was intrigued by the rhythmic patterns of horses trotting, horses galloping, horses cantering.... I remember when my father sawed down a 130-year-old dying oak by the barn. He showed me how you could tell the age of a tree by counting the annual rings–wide rings for the years of rain and rapid growth and narrow rings for the drought years. It was like learning a special language.

In the second grade I was entranced with squirrels in the woods. I watched them follow their squirrel runs from branch to branch.

Someone told me that when the first settlers arrived, North America was so heavily forested that a squirrel could travel from branch to branch from Cape Cod to the Mississippi River without touching the ground.

God never made a more calm, quiet, innocent, peaceful recreation than fishing—sitting, waiting, watching, accepting the good days with the bad, patience in good weather and storm. Surely no fisherman can be an evil person. I don't think I ever had more fun fishing than when I cut myself a long pole, bought some fish string for five cents, a lead weight for a penny, a bobber for a nickel, and two hooks for a penny, and went out and caught a four-inch blue gill and a couple of three-inch sunfish. That was living.

Wilderness was so much a part of our life growing up in Zaire. We were aware of the seasons: the caterpillar season, the mango season, the papaya season, dry and wet seasons.... In the dry season we would go out with our Gipende playmates into the bush and build playhouses out of materials of the bush: wood, leaves, grass—our Gipende friends teaching us how to build without hammer and nails.

Our house was always crawling with creatures interesting to watch: lizards on the ceiling catching flies, ants in the sugar, cockroaches in the bathroom, ants in the kitchen, tiny bugs in the flour, scorpions in the bathtub. It was an entomologist's dream world.

Most interesting were the driver ants (army ants) which marched in a phalanx one to two inches wide in one straight direction, wearing a path down into the dirt, and accompanied by scouts on reconnaissance, lieutenants in command, burden-bearers. We were fascinated by the ant lions that sat in a hole poised to catch wandering ordinary ants by throwing up a shower of sand from their hole, which, in turn, created sand avalanches, bringing them into their clutches.

Our pets had a mixture of Zairian and Western names like the dogs, Fino I and II; Fafnir, the antelope; Sigifusz, the rabbit; Dexter, the parrot; Piggy Pugh, a dog that died of a hernia; Big Trudeau, the rabbit; and Goldie, the goldfish.

My father contributed to my awareness of the possibilities and limits of material–in this case, wood. He was a cabinetmaker. The smell of wood is still vivid in my memory. I began to sense the aesthetic dimensions of wood: knots, grain, texture. My father was a demanding craftsman. He valued quality. He joined well. He finished well. He was precise. I remember the smells, especially pine, the wood most frequently used in the shop. I remember the rough boards and running them through the planer, the pockets of pitch and the strong smells. Walnut was a distinguished wood in the shop. It had a commanding presence. When my father was working in walnut I knew it was special. Walnut was precious.

I am sure I was aware of the inductive method long before I heard the term in the classroom. I watched with fascination steam escaping from Mother's teakettle on the stove and sensed some resemblance to clouds, mist, and fog. If the steam caught the sun just right one saw rainbows.

On cold winter mornings I was delighted to see a thin layer of ice on the puddles. I learned that this was first cousin to snowflakes, hailstones, icicles on the tips of twigs, frost on the windowpane. All of this was a form of water. The first chemical formula I learned was $H_2O$. How proud I was of that bit of advanced scientific knowledge.

In early spring we broke off the tips of twigs on sugar maple trees and came back later to break off sweet-tasting icicles of maple sap. An older boy explained to me the miracle of capillary action—how sap climbs the stairs from the roots to the treetop. I understood him and yet I didn't quite understand the marvelous process.

I have difficulty remembering my early moments of artistic awareness—when I began to see differences and patterns. More careful observation leads to awareness. When one says, "You see one redwood, you've seen them all," this is looking without seeing. It is only superficial awareness.

When I was a kid, I did the usual things. Around our town was a lot of undeveloped woodland. One of my friends got a BB gun. To me, this was enticing. My folks wouldn't permit me to have a gun. A BB gun was on the fringes of acceptability. We liked to shoot at moving targets—birds in flight. We went out of town to a favorite woods to shoot.

I should explain that I had forgotten all about this experience, but many years later at a golden wedding anniversary a 90-year-old man came up to me and brought it all back. The old man asked: "Do you know how you got started in bird watching?" Years before be had watched me shoot birds. He had been upset, but I was not aware then of his displeasure.

This old man told me of how he had come over to me with his well-used *Reed's Bird Guide* and gave it to me. He said, "I gave you that book and all your play with BB guns stopped." He was right. I worked on bird identification those early years in grade school and high school without binoculars. It called for careful stalking of birds to identify them properly. Two older friends helped me to discipline myself to observe carefully. Once that pattern was established, the possibilities of making distinctions became more and more refined. The riches of the environment became inexhaustible.

I grew up in a woods along a creek. My sister and I had our own trails along the creek bank which involved crawling under the exposed roots of a sycamore tree. We watched the creek with fascination during the spring floods. The creek overflowed its banks and carried big chunks of ice–some ten to 20 feet across and a foot thick–crashing into trees on the banks, the trees shaking and shuddering under the impact.... I remember walking with Mother, picking spring flowers, but always being sure there were enough left before one picked–and never, never picking trilliums. Mother helped us with the names of flowers and Daddy with trees.... We were always excited to see great blue herons promenading in the shallows of the creek–so special to us, I think, because Daddy was so excited to see them.... I enjoyed seeing a wren family build a nest in the clothespin bag hanging on the carport, the mother wren hatching the eggs, and then watching the little wrens learn to fly.... I liked the sugar maple tree that leaned over the creek and on which we built a tree house platform. We tapped this for maple sap in the spring and boiled it down on the kitchen stove, steaming up the house.... It was thrilling to find an arrowhead on the hillside. After that, we called it "Arrowhead Hill." My sister found a stone fist hatchet in the garden and we found occasional arrowheads in the field next to the house. Daddy told us stories of the Indians who once lived here.... A cat came to live with us one Sunday. We named her "Sunday." She soon gave birth to six kittens whom we named Monday, Tuesday, Wednesday, Thursday, Friday, and Saturday.

I was an Amish child. We knew the seasons–seeding time, hoeing time, harvesting time, resting time. We helped mother plant the garden and knew when to cut up and plant potatoes, sow lettuce, and set out tomato plants. We recognized the little predators, cabbage worms, and potato bugs. We scalded, plucked, and butchered chickens–our first laboratory course in anatomy. At hog-butchering time, we moved on to an advanced course in anatomy. We watched the birth of calves, colts, puppies, and learned something of the beauty and mystery of generation begetting generation.

Almost at the same time that I learned to read, I learned to milk a cow and to know the personal idiosyncrasies of each cow. A little later came the rituals of harnessing a horse. Growing up Amish–some think it was so primitive and backward a world. It was a natural world–full of fun, visual delights, love and surprises, really a progressive schoolroom in barn, garden, pasture, and stream.

I liked finding hiding places and making nests. Under the porch we had a cool hideaway, where we kept the precious treasures of our rock collection. We made intricate tunnels in the hay mow in the barn. Here my sister and I made nests completely in the dark. I remember reading *Alice in Wonderland* and read how Alice fell down a hole. I had a love affair with tunnels, holes, and caves–a lot of fantasizing about curling up in a tunnel with a book.

I was introduced to migratory birds when a pair of mallard ducks landed in our orchard. We had chickens there. They stayed. My father clipped their wings and I felt very sad about that. They no longer could follow the call of the wild.

We moved to Crete, Nebraska. My brother, sister, and I often walked along the creek. We began to feed birds and built a little feeder. We had a purple martin house and they came to our house. We had a vacant lot and a big garden. We got some chicks. We had this one rooster who was continually being pecked by the others. We befriended him and took him on hikes with the three of us–two boys, a girl, and a henpecked rooster. We called him "Tamey." We never butchered him. However, he died a violent accidental death.

Once in Newton, Sand Creek became the center of my activity. This was shared with a friend who later became a horticulturalist. We built houses, shacks out of driftwood. I often hiked on my own along the creek, at least once a week. One of the particular areas to which we hiked was two miles north along the creek to a great big cottonwood. It took five of us to reach around the trunk. We called it the "little Sequoia." Nearby was a little woods, an abandoned woods, which we called "Hermit's Woods."

I remember discovering milkweed pods along the railway which ran through our farm. I stepped on the dry pods and heard them explode and watched the seeds fly away. I was caught up with the shape of the pod and the arrangement of the seeds and how many potential milkweed plants were packed into that pod. I remember taking a pod home and having my dad explain it.

In the world of a child an eroded gully becomes a Grand Canyon; a steep hillside, Yosemite; and a secluded puddle, one's own Walden Pond. Here no adults intrude to supervise "meaningful educational activities."

These are stories from friends and neighbors as they recall their earliest years and their childhood discoveries of the ways of nature, breakthroughs of awareness, warm feelings of delight, awe in the presence of the mystery of God's creation. Here is the childlike spirit: wonder, joy, curiosity, gratitude, reverence, and a buoyant eagerness to tell others. Of such qualities is the kingdom of heaven.

# 1985: The Good War?

*Book review for* Conrad Grebel Review, *July 1, 1985, of Studs Terkel's* An Oral History of World War II *(Pantheon, 1984).*

> We had a ball club there. We played in Manila every weekend.... I'm the only one left out of the whole infield, the only one that came back. p. 97.

> We were ready for a war. We'd had a long depression. People needed a change, and a war promised to make things different.... That was the most popular war we ever had. p. 166.

An admiral's reflections on World War II triggered this book's title, *The Good War*: "We see things in terms of that war, which in a sense was a good war. But the twisted memory of it encourages the men of my generation to be willing, almost eager, to use military force anywhere in the world." p. 193.

This is the fifth, and perhaps the best, of Studs Terkel's oral histories, two of the most widely known being *Working* and *Hard Times*. Terkel is a lawyer, journalist and Chicago TV personality with an insatiable curiosity.

Terkel's interviews with 125 persons, some famous like John Kenneth Galbraith, but most ordinary persons, are drawn from experiences in every theater of World War II. Terkel will be faulted for violating established guidelines of proper oral history gathering: failure to cite time and place of interview, failure to use ellipses to identify portions of interviews excised, failure to identify where the tapes or transcripts are deposited, and more.

This, however, is insightful, intriguing, fast paced storytelling. It suggests a method of historical data gathering which is within the grasp of non-scholars. One senses that in this oral history gathering are hundreds of hours of good therapy for those who were interviewed. One is made aware of the wealth of wisdom which comes out of the mouths of ordinary people who for a brief time lived intensely.

For many of us–whether we were soldiers, civilians or conscientious objectors–World War II was *our war*. We followed the news hour by hour. Etched in our minds are the images of war as appeared in pages of *Life*. We may have dissented, yet we identified. Terkel's interviews bring back a thousand memories. For many it was "the most exciting span of time" they ever experienced. "When I came back, I felt there wasn't anything I couldn't do." p. 308. One remembers: "When I was eighteen, I was gung ho, completely a creature of my country's propaganda machine." p. 215. Many concede, "It was a war that had to be fought." p. 185. Another ponders, "I think everybody still felt good about the war in '47, '48, '49. One wonders, could Truman have unilaterally committed American troops to Korea unless there had been a lingering romance of the Second World War?" p. 68

In these interviews one finds blacks, women, and ethnic minorities for whom this was a "good war." A. Philip Randolph threatened a march on Washington and "scared the government half to death." Franklin D. Roosevelt in 1941 issued Executive Order 8802, "the first real executive blow for civil rights. It was the war that caused it." p. 338. Many women found meaningful jobs outside of the home for the first time. A black reported that he learned to read at twenty-seven: "The G. I. Bill. It paid my tuition and that made the difference. If anything came out of the war, that was it." p. 158. An Italian of a working class family tells of being lifted out of the inner city into a middle class life in the suburbs, "The war obliterated our culture and made us Americans." p.143.

One is moved by the wisdom of those who lived through World War II. Here is a man who lied about his age to get into the Marines at sixteen: "The Marine Corps taught us... that the Japs are lousy, sneaky, treacherous–watch out for them.... Who's brainwashin' you on all this? I've been married for twenty-four years to Satsuko.... She's the best thing ever happened to me." p. 178. A mountain woman comments: "No bombs were ever dropped on us. I can't help but believe the cold war started because we were untouched. I don't know how chaplains can call themselves men of God and prepare boys to go into battle. If the Bible says, Thou shalt not kill, it doesn't say, Except in time of war.... The more people they kill, the more medals they pin on 'em." p. 113.

One observes clarity of conscience embedded in ordinary people. A nurse reflects: "I've always had the theory that they made us [nurses] officers... to keep us away from the hordes and keep us for the officers. Oh, there was a terrible class feeling." A veteran of the Battle of the Bulge speaks: "The reason you storm the beaches is not patriotism or bravery. It's that sense of not wanting to fail your buddies." p. 39. Another who fought his way into Germany states: "We were passing the Germans we killed. Looking at the individual German dead, each took on a personality.... These were boys like us. It has the flavor of murder, doesn't it?" p. 44. A Jewish medic confesses: "I started looking at them at first as Germans and Nazis. Then I started looking at them as victims.... Why shouldn't I take care of a sixteen-year old German kid that's been shot to pieces?" p. 287.

A subterranean stream of pacifism wells up in many who once found excitement and romance in the prospect of war. A soldier who was in continuous combat for eleven months in Europe reflected: "There's something in some men that will seek power and the rest of us will follow. There are a few dissenters, too few. If there is another war, there will be no winner. It is madness." p. 263. An army nurse whose fiancé died at Pearl Harbor asks: "We did it for what? Korea? Vietnam? We're still at war. Looking back it didn't work.... And my oldest son I'm happy to say, was a conscientious objector." p. 134. Another reflects the changing mood: "I think a lot of fellows in World War II gave their children silent permission to say no to the army." p. 521.

This is a powerful book emerging out of the memory of a people who once saw in World War II a "good war," but many of whom now look back in sadness.

# 1985: Loner for the Lord

*Book review of John Hersey's* The Call *(Knopf, 1985), printed in* The Mennonite, *December 2, 1985.*

This is an absorbing novel of an American missionary (YMCA), David Treadup, 1879-1950, who served in China from 1905 through the emergence in 1949 of the People's Republic of China.

David Treadup, a big man on the Syracuse University campus, heard the call from leaders of the Student Volunteer Movement "to evangelize the world in this generation." One follows in this 700-page novel this driving, courageous, self-willed, naive, engaging, mistake-prone man through a life of intense activity devoted to mission service in China. A persistent, old-fashioned activist, he rallies after every setback to start afresh. In the end he fails, is rejected and drifts into the melancholia of agnosticism. But did he fail and was he ultimately rejected?

*The Call* led me to reread Langdon Gilkey's *Shantung Compound* with its account of another man's internment. In it victory and hope emerge from the pathology of prison life. I wish Hersey had read Gilkey. It might have led him to a more hopeful conclusion. I wish Hersey had met James Liu, our 81-year-old Chinese brother who has visited among us and has recounted for us his story from the bitter years, a story of failure, imprisonment, harassment, rejection. Now James Liu appears among us serene of spirit, loving, forgiving and joyous in the Christ who dwells within him. He has hope for the church in the new China.

John Hersey, the distinguished author of *Hiroshima, The Wall* and *A Bell for Adano,* writes knowledgeably of China. He was born in China and grew up in the home of missionary parents.

Hersey tells his story of David Treadup against the backdrop of a half-century of turbulent Chinese history. He uses letters, a journal and an end-of-career memoir to give the novel the feel of documented authenticity.

In this captivating novel, I found a major parable. Treadup was a can-do, modern Christian individualist without a church base, no sense of a comforting and caring congregation, no correcting and encouraging community of discernment. He was a loner for the Lord. That is a contradiction of terms. The message is there for all: fundamentalist loners, humanist loners or just ordinary Christian loners.

To be faithful and to survive in our world we need brothers and sisters and the enveloping arms of the church.

# 1986: A Conservative's Case for Peace

*Printed in* Wichita Eagle, *May 18, 1986, and reprinted in several other publications.*

My first years were spent just 10 miles across the fields from Dixon, Ill., where Ronald Reagan grew up. My father was a corn and hog farmer. He cared for his land with affection. He was dutiful to his family, a careful steward of his land, respectful of the natural patterns of order, cautious in buying new equipment, slow to borrow money, appreciative of traditional values, calm in crisis, and a person of self-reliance. His neighbors might have called him a conservative.

The term "conservative" is a big tent which covers a wide range of persuasions. Cultural conservatism defies definition, but is associated with certain values such as order, discipline, deference to authority, a respect for the natural environment, a commitment to decency in private and public behavior, a respect for other peoples in the world, a disquietude about the excesses of materialism and technology, a distrust of outbursts of passion, and a preference for restraint and moderation in political conduct.

Mr. Reagan may not have all the attributes of this profile. In fact, he probably is not a classic conservative. The above characteristics, however, do describe an authentic conservatism which provides the base for these reflections on a conservative's assessment of the American military complex. The conservative sees the military as the servant of national policy and priorities, not the master. The conservative places a restraining hand on outbursts of national indignation. The conservative, in contrast to a radical or an ideologue, is cautious and skeptical, deliberate and level-headed. Above all a conservative is prudent.

Conservatives since the days of the Old Testament judge Samuel to the Roman farmer Cincinnatus and to our own John Adams have preferred rule by civilian leaders to rule by professional military men. We have school boards because we have known that education is too important to entrust it all to professional educators. We have lay church councils, sessions and synods because we know church life is too important to entrust all authority to preachers and priests. It follows that national security is too important to yield all decisions to the professionals of the Pentagon and the arms industry. A conservative knows the self-aggrandizing drives of persons and institutions.

Conservatives since the days of Adam Smith have insisted that the burden of proof rests on those who argue for more government and larger public expenditure. Less government is presumed to be preferable unless there are persuasive reasons to the contrary.

One is acting in a traditionally conservative way when one resists an escalating military budget. A conservative asks, "Isn't there a less expensive way of doing this? Isn't the old model still quite adequate for your needs?" A conservative, hostile to all imperialism–communist or capitalist–questions whether the U.S. border really should embrace the capital of Nicaragua or extend to the Persian Gulf or to the streets of Tripoli. Conservatives are naturally suspicious of overextended commitments. This is not isolationism, but common sense. Conservatives love their country but cannot be religious nationalists.

Conservatives since the days of the prophet Elijah and the English public servant Thomas More believed that a universal moral order exists to which even rulers must answer. Conservatives, thus, are instinctively uncomfortable with the use of dirty tricks, bribes, subterfuge and payoffs to hit men, planned political assassinations and arguments that "our good cause justifies the use of any means." A conservative is wary of spy systems above the law, whether they be Russian or U.S. Of them they say, "A plague on both their houses."

Conservatives know the limitations of power. They know one cannot readily resolve conflicts by throwing money at problems. Billions sent to despotic rulers in South Korea, the Philippines or South Vietnam do not buy democracy and peace. Billions spent on stockpiles of bombs is as unwise as a farm implement dealer overloading his inventory with acres of new tractors and combines–even when his rival is so foolish to make the same mistake. Conservatives know that many problems around the world are too tangled in ancient injustice and too complex to buy quick solutions with money or military strikes.

Conservatives know that in the marketplace one can do business with people one does not like. One can work out transactions with difficult people. Businessmen know that the buyer and seller both have to win something to make a deal. If one side insists on winning everything, no deal can occur. Conservatives and businessmen know that both parties have to trust each other if one is to do business. Businessmen are experienced in the ways of "live-and-let live" and "let's-sit-down-and-talk-business." Marketplace savvy is applicable to the superpowers doing business with each other.

Conservatives appreciate the creativity of inventors and engineers, but they also have long memories and know that new technology does not bring instant solutions. They know that new technology often has unexpected disastrous side effects. Conservatives remember that the introduction of gunpowder and muskets did not halt warfare; warfare soon moved to a new level of intensity and destructiveness. The introduction of tanks on the western front in 1918 did not offer a quick end to war. Tanks begat tanks.

The bombs of Hiroshima and Nagasaki did not usher in a new era of nuclear deterrence and peace. The bomb spurred competitive bomb production. A conservative will doubt whether the Strategic Defense Initiative (SDI) can provide a quick fix for peace. Conservatives caution that prudence, diplomacy and patience are more to be trusted than new military gadgets.

Although conservatives respect duty, order and patterns of authority, they also respect the rights of people to their freedoms. They don't like to see the big and powerful pushing helpless people around. Hence, the rights of Baptist dissenters in the Soviet Union, Korean non-citizens in Japan, uprooted farmers in El Salvador, and harassed Palestinian peasants on the West Bank are a concern to conservatives even when their own government might choose to ignore the violation of these human rights.

Conservatives have a streak of frugality. A dollar saved is a dollar earned. The prudent cost-conscious citizen does not abandon responsibility to the Pentagon spenders and the privileged military contractors. A conservative businessman knows that his business can go under if he piles up too big an inventory. If a country has enough warheads to destroy Moscow 10 times, it appears foolish to a fiscal conservative to buy enough warheads to destroy Moscow 1,000 times or 2,000 times.

Conservatives know that what makes a country strong is not "horses and chariots" but a healthy, united, happy, productive society. A conservative sees a nation's strength measured not primarily in stockpiles of nuclear warheads and the proud data of per capita military expenditure. A conservative sees a nation's strength measured by the vigor of its agriculture, the productivity of its industries, the creativity and energy of its work force, the viability of its infrastructures and the quality of its educational systems.

Conservatives realistically assess human limitations. It must have been a conservative who said, "Don't bite off more than you can chew." Conservatives know that when people presume to play God they are apt to develop inflated and obnoxious egos. Hence, they are skeptical and even critical of governments which try to lord it over other governments. Conservatives caution their government not to bully or violate the territorial integrity of other countries: Afghanistan or Grenada, Kampuchea or Libya, Poland or Nicaragua.

Conservatives shy away from using bumper stickers, marching in demonstrations or joining political causes. This, however, may be the time for conservatives to declare that they do not rubber-stamp every Pentagon request or presidential impulse to push the panic button. Conservatives wish to be people of peace because they are cautious, rational, parsimonious and prudent.

# 1986: The Recovery of the Academic Vision

*Printed in* Faculty Dialogue: Journal of the Institute for Christian Leadership, *Spring-Summer 1986. A paper presented at the Second National Conference on Faith and Learning, Bethel College, North Newton, Kansas.*

The title of this presentation, "Recovery of the Academic Vision," is triggered by the 1943 presidential address given by the late Harold S. Bender at the American Society of Church History: "The Recovery of the Anabaptist Vision!" As a youth who looked forward to graduate study after the war, I saw in that address the heavenly vision of scholarship. Bender became one of my mentors. Although I learned in time that there is no "recovery" of a past golden age, the memory of an exhilarating intellectual discovery lingers. It was like John Keats' "On First Looking into Chapman's Homer".

Fifty years ago last fall I enrolled as a sixteen-year-old freshman here at Bethel College. Only the administration and science buildings remain from that era. Things have changed, including the whole world of higher education. In a recent issue of *The New York Review of Books*, Andrew Hacker reviewed twelve contemporary books on higher education. The following excerpts from the article reveal an academic revolution:

> Between 1960 and 1983 undergraduate enrollments trebled, growing from three million to almost ten million.
> During the same period the enrollments at private colleges fell from 40 to 21 percent.
> In 1963, 25 percent of graduates majored in education, now only ten percent. Now almost 25 percent major in business. Health majors have increased 131 percent.
> Vocational programs require students to do as much as 80 percent of their work within their specialties.
> With the exception of psychology, which has 56 percent more majors than 20 years ago, all arts and sciences have declined in the percentage of degrees awarded: English down 72 percent, mathematics 67 percent, philosophy 60 percent, foreign languages 58 percent, physical sciences 40 percent, social science and history down 38 percent.
> Eighty-five percent of all enrollments in the humanities take place during the freshman or sophomore years

228 Looking Back into the Future

with remedial composition accounting for much of
this total.
In 1968, 85 percent hoped college would help them to
"develop a philosophy of life"; today only 44 percent
have that expectation.
Women now receive 32 percent of the academic doctorates
compared with 11 percent 25 years ago.
Fifty-one percent of full-time students supported Ronald
Reagan's reelection.[1]

We see in the above randomly selected data evidence of a radical
diminution in the strength of private liberal arts colleges. They are
an endangered species. Often, however, danger and crisis bring out
the best in an institution. In weakness one may find strength. One
hears those lyrical words of Isaiah: "He gives power to the faint;
and to them that have no might he increaseth strength.... But they
that wait upon the Lord shall renew their strength; they shall
mount up with wings as eagles; they shall run, and not be weary;
and they shall walk and not faint." Since the private liberal arts
college no longer carries much of society's higher education load,
it should be liberated now to pursue a more precisely targeted
vocation. Perhaps we can now be that which we should always
have been.

In this conference each of us views the issue of faith and learning
through the windows of particular institutions. My thoughts focus
on the Christian liberal arts college. I am convinced that no one can
formulate for this kind of institution a universally acceptable
academic vision, no *Summa Theologia* everyone will embrace. Mao
Tse Tung often observed that there is no such thing as Marxism,
only Yugoslav Marxism, Italian Marxism, Chinese Marxism. So,
too, Christian higher education finds incarnation in a set of givens
of a certain people and college, the givens of a particular history
and place with its embedded values, and the givens of educational
tasks peculiar to a particular community.

Among Christian liberal arts colleges are motifs which suggest
common strengths–both real or potential:

Communities, each with a story;

---

[1]Andrew Hacker, 'The Decline of Higher Learning:' *New York Review of Books*,
February 13, 1986, pp. 35-41.

Communities of human scale where all can observe in differing disciplines quality scholarship and contemplate the connectedness of all knowledge;

Campuses where frequently all can be together in one place to sing, to laugh, to listen, to pray, and simply to see one another and be reminded of who are one's academic kinfolk;

Communities each with a corpus of shared values where the faculty just might be able to agree on a core curriculum;

Campuses of size, spirit and commitment where the decision-making process is agile and sensitive in consensus responses to pain and crisis, needs and visions;

Communities of compassion where one cannot readily isolate oneself as an island of anonymity or alienation;

Communities where the Jesus perspective might break through in unexpected ways;

Communities where student and teacher can be friends and colleagues;

Communities where one accepts limitations, analogous to the poet who, in writing a sonnet, is limited to only fourteen lines.

In a moment I shall elaborate on these motifs–the germinal power of the tiny mustard seeds of higher education.

But first, would you help me understand that which appears to be some unacceptable foolishness in the Gospel? Do the following biblical words apply to institutions, even Christian institutions? "Many that are first shall be last." "He hath exalted them of low degree." "Who among you is wise or clever? Let his right conduct give practical proof of it, with the modesty that comes of wisdom." Could there be secret strength in the very weakness of the small Christian liberal arts college–a college not obsessively driven, but relaxed, yielded, with a lilt of wit, a touch of God's amusement in observing the comical posturing of competitive academics–that is, a college which "does not think of itself more highly than it ought to think"? Implicit in amusement with ourselves is confession and in confession is the beginning of wisdom. Simone Weil, the French author, has a haunting comment in her book, *The Need for Roots:* "The essential fact about the Christian virtues, what lends them a special savor of their own, is humility, the freely accepted movement toward the bottom."[2] Biblical truth, of course, comes in pairs: humility and self-assurance, modesty and confidence. The question remains: can a good college have this most essential of the virtues, humility?

And so we proceed further into a humble inquiry into the recovery of the academic vision. As I prepared for this address I assumed that wise things will already have been said about the stages of faith, quality education, the ingredients of learning, and the art and grace of integration.

I want to reflect on five distinctives of the small Christian liberal arts college as it seeks in a particular way to integrate faith and learning: (1) the telling of the story, (2) a certain kind of community, (3) a particular quality of scholarship, (4) a sense of vocation, and (5) the awe of the *kairos* moment.

*First, telling the story.* Everything begins with a story. Colleges are keepers of the memory, the stories sacred and secular passed on from generation to generation. The Christian college is the keeper of a particular story, at once the universal and central story of all human experience, recorded in the Old Testament and continued in the New Testament, a story of God acting in history and calling forth his community, a story that is fulfilled in the good news of the birth, life, death and resurrection of Jesus Christ. In a Christian college are told stories scientific and humanistic, stories old and new, but here one story is told which every person must hear, know and ponder. It is the story of Yahweh, the stumbling pilgrimage of his people, the calling out of a new people of Christ, and the beckoning vision of the Peaceable Kingdom. Biblical metaphors become a part of the language of the community. This concern then lays powerful claims on the general education curriculum of colleges identified as "church" or "Christian!"

A college is the keeper of other stories rooted in particular value-laden memories. These must be told and retold, dramatized, and formed into visual images. One may, one must, share one's college story unapologetically and one should call forth parallel stories and radically different stories. Last year in teaching a course on the Anabaptist-Mennonite experience, I invited to the first class one of Free Methodist background and another of Catholic background, each to tell of growing-up years. The interplay of Wesleyan, Catholic, and Anabaptist memory lifted all to new levels of self-

---

[2]Simone Weil, *The Need for Roots, The Simone Weil Reader,* ed. George A. Panichas (New York: David McKay, 1977), p. 184.

awareness. As the late poet John Ciardi once observed, "Meaning begins in analogy."

One may observe that natural science does not fit the story form. However, as one remembers the process in solving scientific problems, certainly there is story: standing on the shoulders of the past, retracing steps, identifying blind alleys, recalling breakthroughs.

I am captivated by novels which grow out of the Jewish and Catholic experiences: *The Chosen* and *The Promise, The Name of the Rose* and *Clowns of God.* They help me to understand my own identity. So also does Garrison Keillor when he describes his hometown, at once our hometown, of Lake Wobegon. We know his feelings of marginality as a reluctant member of the tiny "exclusive" Brethren and his sneaking admiration for those uninhibited Catholics of the Church of Our Lady of Perpetual Responsibility who celebrate in regal fashion the Feast Day of St. Francis and the Blessing of the Animals.

Last year I interviewed thirty-one of our faculty, asking each two questions: What led you into your particular discipline? Second, what drew you to Bethel? They told their stories, many of which are highly instructive as to how faith and learning are intertwined. Two faculty members speak:

> We had a little pump organ in Zaire. Mother and my older sister played it. I wanted to learn. When we returned to the States for a year of furlough my third grade teacher knew how badly I wanted to learn to play the piano. She made arrangements for me to take lessons. Later I learned she paid for my lessons. My piano teacher was quick to note strengths and to work with weaknesses. Her challenges were always within one's reach.

> My world fell apart the summer I graduated from high school. My dad left my mother. Something inside me told me that maybe our church college would understand what I had gone through. They'd understand. Church was important to me. I think I tried to make choices as to where I could get the best treatment. The college was a basically honest college, a community. I didn't get mothering, smothering. In time I told my story to my faculty adviser. He listened and then said, "I know how you feel. I've gone through it. When I was a boy my father left my mother!" I got the feeling he cared. I could keep on living.

*This interview had two parts. My informant was to meet a student and so we arranged to meet again in an hour. I waited, perhaps an additional thirty minutes before she returned. She resumed her story:*

The girl who came to my office wanted to drop a course. I asked, "Why?" She said that her parents had just told her that they were going through with a divorce. The girl was crying. I told her my story. She decided to stay. I even put my arms around students sometimes.

A small Christian liberal arts college, thus, can be a place where significant stories can be told and attentively received. It is a place where the biblical story can and must be told. The first distinctive is: the telling of the story.

*Second, a certain kind of community.* We continue with faculty stories:

I took three courses in literature from her. She gave me encouragement. Standards. Integrity. Absolute love and commitment to the student. All courses she taught were exciting. We read Macbeth. She helped us understand the color words in that drama: "Golden net over silver!" She made images powerful. She helped me to an understanding of the romantic movement, the romantic vision—Wordsworth, Keats, Shelly—all of whom are still my favorites. She provided a critique of the romantic vision. I don't know how she did it. If one knew her secrets, one would know the mysteries of great teaching.

When did philosophy break into my consciousness? The roots are many, but there was the first sprout. The time I became hooked, enslaved was in Introduction to Philosophy. I had a running dialogue with a student friend, a psychology major; his name at the moment I cannot remember. He was taken up with the idea that all ideas were rationalizations after the fact. I found it difficult to rebut that. I think that was the most important event in committing me to the philosophic quest: "What is truth?"

I want to believe that the Christian liberal arts college holds an academic bias that all knowledge is interconnected, interdisciplinary, an intricate web of linkages and bondings: prairie ecology and the vision of the peaceable kingdom... the grace of the fast break in basketball and the artistry of "Swan Lake"... the final scenes of *Color Purple* and resurrection themes.... I want to believe that a Christian scholar is thorough and brings to the academic altar quality gifts.

Quality education is communal. The teacher is more than a brilliant hit-and-run lecturer to a throng of note takers seated in the outer reaches of an auditorium. The academic camaraderie of the natural science laboratory models a way for the rest of the campus: students and faculty clad in those egalitarian white coats, peering through microscopes and beckoning to colleagues to "come see," graphing data on neat charts and exclaiming for all to hear–"beautiful, just beautiful," sharing together the communion cup of coffee brewed over a Bunsen burner. Creative solitude is essential, but most of learning is communal. More evidences of the community context of learning:

> One weekend a teacher takes a group of students on a carefully planned field trip to three cities. On Monday morning she finds on her office desk a yellow rose with a note of gratitude.

> A group of students, many who had studied in the Urban Life Center in Chicago, work for several weeks in planning a convocation on racism on the campus. Some thirty students are involved: black, Hispanic, international, and others. They take on all the prickly questions with an open, candid, fast-paced program of slides, taped campus interviews, videotapes, panel discussion, roving mike interviews of persons spotted in the audience. It did more to raise campus consciousness on race than the most eloquent high-profile authority ever could have done.

> A student with a brilliant athletic record comes to college to play basketball but discovers choral music, chemistry, religious studies, and Norwegian literature. The choir displaces varsity basketball. The highlight of the college year for him is the homecoming concert to a packed audience on the choir's return from spring tour.

> After the final curtain on the last night of the production, "JB," the cast gathered in a lounge to discuss their perceptions of the experience, including how good people cope with inexplicable tragedy. They were joined by alumni members of the first production of JB twenty-five

years before, plus parents and friends. The discussion revealed multilayered perceptions: each actor's reflections, alumni actors' perceptions filtered through twenty-five years of tragedy and joy, way back there Job's perceptions, those of the audience, and somewhere God listening in. Surely He was in that holy place.

The foundational prayer of the Christian academic community and of the Christian faith is the natural, human, and agonizing prayer: "I believe, help thou my unbelief!" The mind and spirit of the scholar of faith are caught in the words, "Now we see through a glass, darkly; but then face to face: now I know in part; but then shall I know even as also I am known!" Here one should be able to question, doubt, and even deny and be accepted. One simply asks of the student that the story and the community be taken seriously.

The community is shaped by a sense of place and time. Listen to the words of Wendell Berry in his *Recollected Essays*:

> The approach of a man's life out of the past is history, and the approach of time out of the future is mystery. Their meeting is the present, and it is consciousness.... The endless wonder of this meeting is what causes the mind, in its inward liberty of a frozen morning, to turn back and question and remember. The world is full of places. Why is it that I am here? What has interested me in telling the history of [this place] is the possibility of showing how a place and a person can come to belong to each other–or, rather, how a person can come to belong to a place.[3]

A college green, a campus clearing in the forest, the human scale and design of buildings–all these shape the feel of community, are silent carriers of values, and are to be savored with gratitude. This place with all its linkages of memory calls for imaginative and joyous celebration of community in festivals, worship, services of gratitude, intramurals, learning fairs, homecomings, anniversaries, convocations, forums, film and drama weeks, tree-planting days, campus work days, dinners and barbecues, frolic, song and play–some ritualized and some spontaneous. Recently a college assembly addressed by Garrison Keillor burst into the long and complex Lowell Mason choral hymn, "Praise God from Whom All

---

[3]Wendell Berry, *Recollected Essays, 1965-1980* (San Francisco: North Point Press, 1981), p. 45.

Blessings Flow!" Deeply moved, he asked the students the next day to sing it again. Song unites congregations, causes and campuses.

The Christian academic community accepts persons at different stages of faith development. Although it is not the church, this caring college offers intimations, images, anticipations of what the church might be just as the church offers anticipations of what the Kingdom of God, the peaceable kingdom, might be. "Meaning begins in analogy."

But a disclaimer. We must confess that even in a small college we faculty members know so little about the interests and career longings of each of our colleagues. So often I have heard the cry of loneliness: "Nobody knows what I am trying to do in my classes!" We ought to provide opportunities for faculty to teach faculty.

*Third, a particular quality of scholarship.* That special quality is encapsulated in the phrase, "to have the mind of Christ." We have seen evidences of distinctives in small Christian colleges–clearly not their exclusive possession: a bias toward connectedness and wholeness, the firm insistence by friendly mentors on quality in studies, the infectious inquisitiveness of peers, a curricular common ground in general education, protective cover for the skeptic and the prophet, the helping hand for the faltering and the disheartened, the naturalness of cross-disciplinary dialogue, and people talking with others about the books they are reading. Two brief stories from the interviews:

> I remember a book read by seniors for the senior orals: C.P. Snow's *Two Cultures.* I read this as a junior when it was being widely read by faculty and seniors. I was intrigued. I had always hoped that I could bring things together between two cultures. The debates we now have over the Capstone course for seniors relates to a residual unhappiness with the loss of senior orals.

> The real turning point in my life was the decision in college not to specialize. I wanted to do everything. I was a freshman; my one confidant was a senior. As a freshman I took a course in religion in which we were to choose a book to read. I chose *Sickness Unto Death.* The instructor advised against this treatise as too difficult: guilt, sin, forgiveness, the dialectical. I set my mind to it. It was difficult, but I enjoyed it. I could do it.

David Stockman in his recent book, *The Triumph of Politics,* asserts that the circle of leaders close to the president do not read. "They watch the tube," he wrote. "Reality happened once a day on the evening news!"[4] Surely, a small liberal arts college can nurture a love of reading and can expect competency in writing and speaking. Foundational to learning and the keepers of the biblical memory is reading, writing, and speaking.

The image of having "the mind of Christ" suggests a high view of inquiry. "The Spirit searcheth all things, yea, the deep things of God!" "When he comes who is the Spirit of truth, he will guide you into all the truth!" In this metaphor of "the mind of Christ" is a suggestion of the meeting place of faith and learning.

*Fourth, a sense of vocation.* The Christian college carries in its bosom all those biblical themes which suggest that meaningful knowledge is for action, for transformation, talents to be used, called to obedience, invited to be a servant, ministers of reconciliation, the Word made flesh, coming down from the mountain to Capernaum. Writ large in the Christian world view is the vision of the people of faith sent as a pilgrim community with a sense of calling, vocation, mission. The unique dimension to Christian college career counseling is the encouragement to seek places of service where one joins others in a faith community which supports, nurtures, and provides fellowship and resources of discernment. The biblical image is of sending out the seventy two by two. I sense we equip students inadequately with the tools and the will to go forth as agents of transformation in society, especially to work in and from the base community of the church.

Encompassed by the sanctions of conformity in our society, I hope our graduates might be liberated from these conformist claims of success and status. The gospel in its foolishness asks disciples to serve with distinction in the margins, the cracks, the shadows, and along the less traveled road. How does one market those concerns in attractive three-color admission brochures? Stated in other terms, the function of the Christian college is to prepare students for servanthood leadership.

In the two thousand years of history of the Christian church, the residential liberal arts college has existed for only a tenth of that period. If collegial wholeness must yield to professional autonomies and if Christian colleges become indentured to society's market preferences, it behooves the church to think of additional options by which it could be served in the tasks of people-nurturing and leadership equipping.

---

[4]David A. Stockman, *The Triumph of Politics* (New York: Harper and Row, 1986).

*Fifth, the* kairos *moment*–"the spirit of the Lord is upon me...," this unique and awesome period in time, signs of great changes, a sense of impending crisis. Jesus asks: "Can ye not discern the signs of the times?" One observes signs: The slow death of the family farm. The sprawling power of multinational corporations. The bureaucratization of health care. The cultic appeal of sports spectaculars. The escapism on TV of carefully choreographed cheap grace. A self-congratulatory national religion with a presidential high priest serving as the amiable liturgist. And the Great Terrorism of nuclear annihilation.... The writer of Chronicles records: "The children of Issachar... were men that had understanding of the times, to know what Israel ought to do" (I Chronicles 12:32).

The Christian college at this moment of history just might be less entrapped in the conventional and doomed wisdom of this world. In the high voltage and precarious wiring of faith and learning may be circuits of wisdom for reading the signs of the times. Among the signs, I call attention to two:

David Stockman's confessional in *The Triumph of Politics* of a small group of ideologues at the national controls, economic illiteracy in high places, sloppy decision making, leadership preoccupied with optimistic images of certitude. All this and anxious thoughts as to those who control the button of Armageddon.

William Broad's description in the recent book, *Starwarriors*, of those "best and brightest" young scientists at the Livermore National Laboratory, devoid of liberal arts perspectives, with little trace of transcendent sensitivities, driving relentlessly to design a new generation of weaponry which they acknowledge won't work. The death of learning. The militarization of science.[5]

A recovery of the academic vision? It is time to retell the story of the Suffering God, who calls a people to obedience, whose son died for our sins on a cross and who rose again and invites us to follow him as bearers of his cross.

Our vision?

To tell the story.

To be a community.

To find joy in the community of scholarship.

To go forth with a vocation to transform.

To be aware that the hour is late.

---

[5]William J. Broad, *Starwarriors* (New York: Simon and Schuster, 1985).

I love this two-line notice which appeared in our *Daily Announcements* on March 24, just after the Senate vote on Contra aid:

> PEACE CLUB MEMBERS: We will meet tonight at 8:00 p.m. to collect our wits and carry on. Let loose and have some fun!! See you there!

In these little pieces of the blithe spirit is hope for the Christian college.

# 1988: The Pile of Debris at Jackson and Vine

*Printed in* Bluffton News, *January 1988.*

Leaping out at me from the January 5 issue of *The Bluffton News* was a six-column-wide photo of a mountain of splintered debris, the distant Bluffton Town Hall visible in the upper right hand corner. Below was a caption: "The house at the corner of Jackson Street and Vine Street was torn down.... The lot will be used for an addition to the elementary school building."

This was not just a heap of debris, not just a house; that once was our house. For four years, 1931 to 1935, my parents, Amos and Stella Kreider, my brother Gerald and I lived there. In that wreckage lie many memories. That was once the First Mennonite parsonage, the gift of Peter Thut, who also gave the farm, now the Nature Center, to Bluffton College.

The memories of other families lie in that rubble at Jackson and Vine. There lived the Samuel M. Musselmans and their children Dwight, Vivienne, Frances and George; after us the H.T. Unruhs and Earl and Mildred; the Jesse Smuckers and David, Leonard, Mary Ann and Joe; the Alvin Beachy family; undoubtedly others.

That sprawling house at Jackson and Vine, wrapped with a big front porch, built T-shaped in Midwestern Gothic, had character and lots of space. Gerald and I delighted in the rambling series of rooms. Although church volunteers had just laid new hardwood floors in three downstairs rooms, Mother, I remember, wept as she first contemplated the task of properly furnishing the house and working in a kitchen with no running water.

In the back yard grew a large highly-productive sugar pear tree and a garden which produced abundantly. Especially do I remember the aroma in September of Dad's banked-up rows of celery. Back by the alley was a chicken coop where the Musselmans raised rabbits and which Gerald and his friends converted into a club house. In the chicken yard I planted black walnuts given by Scoutmaster Bob Schaublin, which soon grew into a thicket of young trees, one of which today is a mature tree in the backyard of Howard Raid.

The sidewalk in front of the house on Jackson Street was made of cut slabs of the smoothest sandstone, perfect for roller skating. Along Vine was a brick sidewalk overgrown with grass which we mowed.

When Dad took on the First Mennonite pastorate in the late summer of 1931 we moved from a neighborhood on Lawn Avenue immediately surrounded by the families of Adams, Fenten,

Longsdorf, Tosh, Schultz, Steingraver and more. On Jackson Street we acquired a new interesting set of neighbors. Between us and the Grade School lived the Dillmans in a stucco bungalow with daughters Dora and Marilyn Holmden, who diligently practiced her xylophone a few feet from our bedroom window. Mr. Dillman operated the cigar-newsstand on Main Street across from the Town Hall. Across Vine were the lively Stonehills with children John, Joanne, Elmer and Caroline. Sundays after church we headed for the Stonehills to read the Sunday comics. Nailed to the side of the red barn back of their house was a basketball hoop where we practiced our two-hand set shots. On occasion Mr. Stonehill took us along on his milk route stopping in farmyards to pick up their full milk cans. We regarded Mr. Stonehill as the strongest man in town. Across Jackson lived the Alspaughs, who had a dry-cleaning shop. From afar we admired son "Swatty" as a great athlete; his older sister, a teacher, often crossed the street to visit with Mother. Separated by a vacant lot from Alspaughs and next to the Methodist church was the Methodist parsonage, which seemed to have a change of residents each year in August.

Behind us across the alley on Lawn Avenue were the Ed Goods and son Dale. Gerald spent many hours in Ed Good's machine shop on the alley watching Ed make tools and fittings on his lathes, grinders, drill presses. The squeaking of swings, teeter-totters and merry-go-rounds and the continuing babble of children's voices from the playground reminded us that the playground was a noisy neighbor.

Only a block away were all the costly delights of Main Street. In Bigler's Meat Market we picked up free scraps for our dog Scotty. Often we sprinted to Ed Reichenbach's Grocery or the A. and P. to get an item needed by Mother for dinner. Occasionally in winter we would be sent to Hankishes to get a quart of fresh oysters for stew. The only time our family would go out for a meal was to one of those 15 cents-a-person jitney suppers served at the Methodist Church, just across the street from our First Mennonite.

Those years, 1931-1935, were Depression years. The intelligence network of the tramps had data on that house at Jackson and Vine and often two or three times a week Mother served tramps at our back door. Mother had a round blue tray and a special set of dishes for her tramp guests. Often they asked for odd jobs. I admired Dad's gift to draw them out in conversation.

There at the corner of Jackson and Vine the world of politics and war broke into my consciousness: FDR's flight to Chicago to accept the nomination, the exciting 1932 election, Father Coughlin's radio addresses, Mussolini's invasion of Ethiopia, Hitler's rapid rise to power in Germany, the grim news filtering out of Russia and all those New Deal names–CCC, CIO, NRA, WPA....

The Depression was a great leveler in our neighborhood at Jackson and Vine. Many families got along with no car. Our family car was a 1928 Model A Ford two-door sedan, which was not replaced until the summer of 1935, then with a Ford V-8. Congregation members, lean of cash, were generous in providing us with fresh produce, which Mother stored away in the partial basement: rows of canned fruit, vegetables and meats, potatoes in a bin, eggs immersed in a brine-filled crock, dried apples and pears, bushels of apples, a huge crock of sauerkraut. No recreation room in basements in those years. Down there in the dark basement with the food reserves was the softwater cistern, the coal furnace and coal bins.

There are other memories from that house on the corner of Jackson and Vine. Somewhere under that pile of debris was the place where we pitched in summertime our family umbrella tent and slept outside with our friends. People sat on their front porches in those days. Always there was someone swinging on the Stonehill's front porch swing. Along Jackson would march bands and school classes in the annual Harmon Field Day Parade. In summer we waited for the ice truck and when it stopped in front of our house we would leap on the back end and reach under the cool heavy canvas to snatch slivers of ice.

That parsonage at Jackson and Vine was a nerve center of the congregation. Members called to report births, deaths, illnesses, accidents, trips to the hospital, a suicide. Ashen-faced people came to the door to talk in private with Dad; all we knew was that some were having problems. Couples–sometimes shy, sometimes bubbling–came to see Dad; we easily guessed their purpose. Many words of anguish and joy were once heard within those now demolished walls. Early we sensed that with certain information there were confidences to be kept.

Those heaps of rubble trigger other memories.... Gerald's dash out of the house when he heard Mr. Potee ring the last school bell.... Those flute lessons with Helen Hartzler coming to the house.... Christmas presents hidden under the sofa in Dad's study.... All that woodwork and furniture we dusted imperfectly as a part of Saturday morning chores.... Scrubbing the coal soot from that big front porch.... That stream of house guests received into our home.... That first date, to a Leap Year Party sponsored by the Girl Reserves, with Hanna Wilkins, who lived just down the street, stopping to pick me up.... Ruth Yoder, the school religious education teacher, boarding with us.... Ollie Diller, studying for his doctorate in forestry at Ohio State, coming to visit his fiancee Eunice Conrad, who came to our house on weekends.... Ollie helping me with my forestry merit badge for Scouts.... Weekly meetings in our house of the Fighting Tiger Patrol.... J. Winfield Fretz coming to speak to me about attending Bluffton College.... And in the spring of 1931 before we moved to the parsonage, walking to Rev. Musselman's house and telling him that I wished to join the church.... Memories in the rubble.

That was not just a pile of rubble at Jackson and Vine. That was our house. Memories linger there which no bulldozer can remove.

# 1988: Three Days in the Life of James Liu

*An article in the* Mennonite Weekly Review, *July 14, 1988. This is one of several articles written about Robert and Lois Kreider's visit to China in April 1988.*

We were standing on the first floor of the house in Hengyang where James Liu, his wife, Hazel, and son Timothy had lived for 26 years, now the residence of a family that makes funeral wreaths. James pointed to the ground, "Here during the Cultural Revolution we buried our knives and forks. They are probably still there under the concrete slab."

He pointed to the garden, "There we burned our Bibles, hymnbooks, photographs, and papers. I prayed to God for forgiveness." In those days of terror Red Guards broke in and ransacked houses looking for evidence of people's foreign connections.

On a Friday in early March we first sighted 84-year-old James Liu, standing on the railway platform of Hengyang with son Timothy and grandson Paul. The three smiling persons were a little island of welcome and friendliness set against the background of hundreds of blue-gray clad passengers rushing for the exit. Twelve years before I had passed through Hengyang on the train, not knowing then that James and Hazel were still alive and residents in the city. "It would not have been appropriate then for you to have visited us," James commented. "It would have created problems for us, but that has changed." Hengyang, an industrial city of 600,000 is still off the tourist path. During the three days of our visit we saw not one foreigner.

My wife, Lois, and I had come to Hengyang to present James Liu with copies of the book, just off the press, which he had helped write and which I had edited: *James Liu and Stephen Wang: Christians True in China* (Faith and Life Press, 1988). He received the book gratefully as a benediction on his life in which joy and sorrow have intermingled. His first comment on receiving the book was, "I want to translate this into Chinese."

James' life reaches back to the last days of the Manchu dynasty when he was born into the home of a poor peasant Confucian family. Mennonite missionaries befriended the family. James studied in the Mennonite schools at Kaizhou (Puyang), attended college with Stephen Wang at Bluffton and Bethel colleges, returned to serve his church in China, was caught in the maelstrom of invasion, famine, civil war, and revolution. After World War II he served with the Mennonite Central Committee, taught public school after Liberation in 1949, was harassed and imprisoned during the Cultural Revolution, and then restored to his former status with a pension. Through it all, including the lingering illness and death in 1984 of his wife, Hazel, he has carried on, cheerful, radiant, friendly—never a word of complaint, always grateful and forgiving.

James lives with his son Timothy, daughter-in-law Edna, and grandsons Paul and John. On arrival we were driven to their home in a car provided by the factory where Timothy works. The factory also provides a small cottage where they live at the end of the top lane on a hillside. When James and family first came to Hengyang forty years ago, this area was in rice paddies. The sidewalk lane on which they live is quiet and clean with potted plants and friendly neighbors, with family living spilling out all along the communal sidewalk.

We were ushered into their living room, which is also James' bedroom. Here is his desk, photographs of Hazel and the family mementos, four shelves of books, a small TV, storage boxes and cupboards, James' bed, and several chairs. In this room Timothy set up a folding table and Edna served us a twelve-course dinner. Timothy, who had been denied opportunity as a youth to attend university because of his father's foreign connections, is an electrician at a nearby factory. Edna teaches Chinese in a school. Paul recently graduated from high school, and John is a student in the No. 1 Middle School where James once taught.

While we were finishing our dinner, a lean, leather-faced, smiling man with missing teeth appeared in the doorway: Xiao Gung Sung. Wearing a padded brown Mao jacket and fur hat, he was accompanied by his wife. He was the first of ten orphans we would meet from the MCC home for 250 orphans which James and Hazel had directed from 1948 to 1951. I asked this man, who had once been a beggar child picked up on city streets, what he remembers of the orphanage. "Oh," he answered, "the singing. I loved to sing hymns." Each day he would appear somewhere to join us on our visits about the city.

That afternoon James, who walks with a cane but never shows a touch of weariness, took us through crowded, grimy streets to a factory apartment house, up four and then five flights of stairs to the apartments of more "MCC orphans." One was deaf and around whom swirled a conversation in sign language. Another was the little lame girl, now a mother and retired, whom forty years ago James carried to safety when they with orphans fled the besieged city. James is for these orphans their genial, loving foster father.

On Saturday morning James took us to an oil extracting factory on the banks of the Xiang River which long ago had been an elegant family temple of the wealthy family Shen. From 1948 to

1951 it had been an MCC home for 250 orphans. The plant manager gave us the run of his factory. James reconstructed for us among the machinery, stacks of bricks, and bags of oil seeds the memory of an orphanage: "Here we had daily chapel. There the playground and beyond the gardens. Here classes. There the boys' dormitory and here the girls' dormitory. Aaron Herr slept here, and that was Wilbert Lind's room...."

Standing on the banks of the river, he pointed to the place where he and Hazel filled twelve scows with orphans and fled upstream, around the bend, and up the smaller Zheng River, artillery fire alerting them that the city was under siege. Several of the orphans we met those days acknowledged that they are alive today because of James and Hazel and their MCC colleagues.

James took us to the No. 1 Middle School, where he had taught English and Russian language. He pointed to the site of the second classroom where during the Cultural Revolution he had been held prisoner for three years. Here his job was to clean toilets and carry out the night soil. He and other teachers were subjected to public grilling and were paraded barefoot in ridicule through the streets. Now twenty years later he is received back as a beloved elder teacher and friend. As we walked the grounds, the friendly entourage of principal, vice-principal, former teachers, and staff colleagues grew to 14 or more. From James comes not a murmur of bitterness about those earlier years of rejection. When we asked James, "Do you meet persons who mistreated you during the Cultural Revolution?" he answered, "Oh yes, all the time. But–I understand. They wanted to be good Chinese."

After church on Sunday as we were seated on the bed of our host awaiting dinner, James sang for us hymns he once learned from missionaries P. J. Boehr and E. G. and Hazel Kaufman: "Bringing in the Sheaves," "I Need Thee Every Hour," "Joy to the World," "Come Thou Almighty King," "Low in the Grave He Lay," and many more.

I asked him about his favorite books of the Bible. From the Old Testament he mentioned in order: Joshua, Psalms, Proverbs, I and II Samuel, Genesis, Jonah, and Job. He added, "I read these books often." His favorites from the New Testament are Romans, 1 and 2 Timothy ("good for young people"), 1 and 2 Corinthians, 1 and 2 Peter, the Gospel of John, Revelation ("I have read that several times but it is hard to understand.").

Earlier I had inquired about the church in the six counties around Kaizhou and Daming, a thousand miles to the north, where once the General Conference Mennonites had a flourishing mission of 2,500 members. He was prepared for this question. He unfolded a page of notes in Chinese characters. He reported as many as 20,000 worshipers in several registered congregations and scores of house churches. In Daming four graduates of the earlier Mennonite Bible School are caring for the church. In Qing Feng the government has returned a Mennonite church building to the local congregation which is registered with the government. In addition, Christians meet in seven house churches. In Dong Ming a congregation of 100 members contributes funds to rent a house for worship.

The church in Chang Yan is registered and has some 10,000 attending services in 27 house churches in city and countryside, with about 4,000 baptized members. In Kaizhou (Puyang) the church is growing rapidly with many from the local oil fields attending one of the ten house churches. They have two pastors, four less active pastors in their 80s, and ten house church lay leaders. The congregation is planning to send students to one of the seminaries which have opened. James, who is a layman, is like the first-century Paul, a pastor-counselor who writes and receives many letters from the churches which were planted in his youth.

This frail man exhibits incredible energy. We estimated that on a Sunday we walked five miles along crowded streets. Several times he turned to us and inquired, "Are you tired?" Of course, we were tired, but we were reluctant to acknowledge it, observing his tireless spirit. He walks a half hour in the morning and in the evening, takes an afternoon nap, reads, writes many letters, visits and entertains friends, listens to the evening news. I was impressed with his fund of knowledge about current political events. He tells of an old teacher friend who visits him regularly and together they study the Bible. Wherever we walked in the city curious people gathered around us. James always took time to explain patiently to them who were these strange, tall, foreign people.

Surely James is one of God's saints on earth: full of grace, a friend of all. "Friendship," he says, "is so important. I try to keep friends, not just here, but in other countries as well. That is what makes for peace."

The Monday morning we took leave of James and his family we were in the train station, swept along, buffeted by hundreds of people struggling to get on the express train to Changsha. We became separated from James. When we next saw him we were standing in the aisle inside the train packed in with 240 others in one car. Just as on arrival, outside the window of the car were the three smiling faces of James, Timothy, and Paul. James' last words: "This is the way to learn about the common people." He smiled and waved as our train pulled away.

# 1989: The Years of the Dragon, 1976 and 1988

*Printed in* Bamboo Leaves: a China Reader, *China Educational Exchange, 1989.*

The first time I visited China was in 1976, the Year of the Dragon. Twelve years later, this March, my wife Lois and I again visited China, also the Year of the Dragon. In Chinese legend the fierce, fire-breathing imaginary beast, full of power and grandeur, traces back 4,000 years. The dragon symbolizes the Chinese nation, China's ancient culture, and the majesty of imperial tradition.

The year 1976 had all the awesome attributes of the dragon. That year the Great Proletarian Cultural Revolution, a convulsive decade (1966-1976) of self-destruction, was staggering to an end. The year began with the death of the most beloved of the founders of the Communist Chinese state, Zhou Enlai; it ended with the fall of the hated Gang of Four. That year the great general of the Long March, Zhu De, died. And on September 9 died the dragon leader himself, Chairman Mao Zedong.

Six weeks earlier I, and millions of Chinese, had a premonition of Chairman Mao's death. Late Tuesday evening, July 27, our tour group arrived in Beijing. In my room on the sixth floor of the Peking Hotel I looked down on Tienanmen Square and beyond to the Forbidden City. A few hours later, Wednesday morning, July 28, at 2:45, I was awakened by a moaning roar, a great shaking, the sound of breaking glass, creaking furniture, falling plaster. I looked down on the Forbidden City and the court where Mao lived. All was darkness and pouring rain. Flashes of lightning illuminated the walled city. No electricity. Immediately I thought of the Mandate of Heaven, that ancient sign of calamitous events and the fall of emperors. Much later we learned that it had been an earthquake, 9.2 on the Richter Scale, with its epicenter a hundred miles away in Tangshan. The Chinese authorities waited thirty hours to acknowledge to the world what had happened. Much has changed since that Year of the Dragon, 1976–the last year of Chairman Mao. In 1976 every railway station, airport, classroom hotel lobby and office displayed a picture of Chairman Mao. Not only Mao, at the rear of every classroom were pictures of those whom I recorded in my journal as "the big four": Marx, Engels, Lenin, and Stalin. In 1988 Mao's image is gone. Not until the end of our third week in China did we see a picture or statue of Mao. Finally in Beijing, one picture at the gate to the Forbidden City, a statue in front of the library at Beijing University, and Mao's embalmed body in the mausoleum on Tienanmen Square. Gone, too, from public billboards and walls of public buildings are the Mao slogans: "Serve the People," "Study Hard and Make Progress Every Day," "Long Live the Great Solidarity of the Peoples Throughout the World," "Friendship First, Competition Second," and dozens more. In 1976 hardly a paragraph was spoken without reference to Mao. In 1988 we heard no one speak of Chairman Mao. When we asked questions about him, we seemed to touch a discomforting nerve ending. The Chinese prefer to move on to other topics for conversation.

In 1976 on our visits to every factory, commune, school or hospital, our hosts seated us in a reception room, served tea, and subjected us to a thirty-minute political briefing on the illustrious leadership of Chairman Mao, the bitter years before the 1949 liberation and the glories of socialist struggle. In my 1976 journal notes appear often-repeated comments: "Our task is always to wage class war.... Enemies must be destroyed: landlords, bourgeois, merchants, and intellectuals.... Chairman Mao's great contribution is to emphasize the role of peasants, the vast countryside, need to mobilize peasants and workers to wage together ideological warfare. The party is the vanguard of the proletariat...." On and on, over and over again. In 1988 we heard not one political sermon. We found it difficult to pry out of our informants any Marxist explanations.

In 1976 I prepared a list of more than one hundred Chinese "no-no's" as we heard or observed: no lipstick, no neckties, no film celebrities, no lawyers, no dogs, no Coca Cola or 7-Up, no beauty parlors, no churches, no golf courses, no fast food chains.... In 1988 much has changed. In sight of Mao's tomb a Kentucky Fried Chicken franchise is thriving. People with money play golf on the greens near the Ming Tombs and cases of Coca Cola are stacked high at the Great Wall. The no-no's are eroding away under the ravages of modernization.

In the Year of the Dragon 1976 political posters were everywhere. Many featured Mao: the peasant Mao in fields of grain, the worker Mao wearing a hard hat in a steel mill, the teacher Mao surrounded by adoring children, the visionary Mao standing on a mountain top gazing off into the distant future. Posters of smiling, energetic youth building the new China conveyed a message that here was one big, happy, productive family. In 1976 on Nanjing Road in Shanghai I bought more than sixty of these propaganda posters preserved now as collector's items from the Cultural Revolution. In 1988 I returned to the same bookstore to find none of those ideological posters. In their place were a few posters of plump babies, silky kittens and sheep grazing in meadows. Gone were all the images of revolutionary fervor. And as an item of dubious modernity, a poster of the American film star, Brooke Shields.

In 1976 at Wuhan on the Yangtse we spent a day at a university administered by a revolutionary committee where the vice chancellor was a factory worker. For three hours that afternoon a series of professors confessed to us their past capitalist and elitist sins and described their conversion to Mao's revolutionary teaching that all of society is a university. That day, although we met students and faculty in these revolutionary testimonial meetings, we saw no one in class, no one studying in the library, no laboratories in operation. We suspected that the university was really not functioning as an academic institution but as a retreat center to kindle the fires of revolutionary passion. Now in 1988, guided about the campus of Beijing University by Stephen Wang's grandson Guo Xu, a graduate student in international law, we observed a campus teeming with students. In the library they sat elbow to elbow in a large reading room. Obviously, the university had returned to academic pursuits after the ten year wasteland of the Great Cultural Revolution, which many now call "the Great Mistake."

In the Year of the Dragon 1976 we heard in Beijing that somewhere in that great city Christians were again meeting for public worship. But then came the earthquake and our evacuation from Beijing which prevented our checking into this rare phenomena. Later that week in Shanghai I visited what had once been a Methodist Church and where in the 1940s the Mennonite Central Committee had offices. In 1976 I had seen no evidence of church life, only what appeared to be a school or rooming house. Early in the morning on Good Friday, April 1, 1988, Lois, our daughter Karen and I visited the church. Mary Jane Dal, the pastor, met us and told us of a communion service the evening before and a Good Friday service that afternoon. She took us on tour of the church. In an upper room we saw a large painting with an inscription from the second chapter of the Song of Songs: "The winter is past... the spring has come." On Sunday in every city we visited we found a Protestant church where we could worship.

In the Year of the Dragon 1976 we had no opportunity to visit in Chinese homes. One had to be careful. In that year our tour group traveled through Hengyang by train. Then I did not know that an old friend, James Liu, was living in the city. Hengyang, however, was then off-limits to foreign visitors. James now says it would have been ill-advised, probably politically injurious, for him, had we tried to contact him in 1976. Three years later we learned that James and his wife Hazel were still alive and living in Hengyang.

Now in 1988 Lois and I spent three days with James and his son Timothy, daughter-in-law Edna and their two sons. Today a visit to Hengyang requires no special permission. Similarly, we visited Stephen and Margaret Wang and their family in Jinan, Shangdong Province, simply assuming we could go where we wanted to in China.

Many contrasts come to mind. The few grim, cavernous Soviet-style hotels of 1976 and in 1988 many modern hotels, even Holiday Inns. In 1976 the intense fear of an imminent war with the Soviet Union and in the 1988 of Gorbachev and Deng Xiaoping the relaxation of those fears. In 1976 the continuing hymns of praise to the Great Proletarian Cultural Revolution and in 1988 the general acknowledgment that that decade had been a tragic mistake, an enormous waste of human resources. In 1976 the idealization of the commune as a model for a decentralized, rural-based socialist society and in 1988 silence on that experiment. In 1988 everywhere multiplying free markets and private enterprises. In 1976 much talk of self-reliance and in 1988 of an "open door" to the West.

Two Years of the Dragon: 1976 and 1988. One reflects on the wrenching changes in the Chinese national experience. One remembers the millennia of continuity in the patterns of Chinese living. The words of the biblical writer, now inscribed in that upper room in Shanghai, come to mind: "the winter is past... the spring has come."

*Kreider with Stephen Wang, 92, and grandson Guo Xu, Changchun, China, 1998.*

# 1989: Ten Modest Proposals

*Printed in* The Mennonite, *March 28, 1989. Kreider was speaking to the emerging possibility of the integration of the Mennonite Church and the General Conference Mennonite Church.*

I am pleased to see the two conferences moving toward closer fellowship and integration. The five recommendations (Jan. 10 issue) appear to focus on the task of clarifying basic ideas. This is suggested by the use of such words as "rationale," "conjoint confession," "polity statement," "models," "structures."

Mennonite peoplehood is served by rightly formulated tenets and structures, but even more it is served by cultivating loving, sensitive, understanding relationships. The most fruitful result of statement preparation may be the new friendships formed in the process. One phrase of particular significance among the five recommendations is this: "the deepening of mutual understanding...."

To help weave the fabric of mutual understanding, I offer for consideration 10 modest proposals:

1. Secure commitments from 1,000 General Conference members to subscribe to the *Gospel Herald* and commitments from 1,000 Mennonite Church members to subscribe to *The Mennonite.*
2. Combine and publish jointly the GC *Handbook of Information* and the MC *Mennonite Yearbook.*
3. Have each congregation invite at least one speaker annually from the other conference.
4. Have each district conference invite one speaker from the other group to its annual conference.
5. Have each conference send a fraternal visitor to the annual meetings of each board and commission of the other group.
6. Agree that for the next several years each group will establish new committees or task forces only as joint endeavors.
7. Integrate provisionally several closely related committees or programs and set a time to review whether the move is mutually beneficial.
8. Taking a cue from the Kansas Relief Sale, arrange in a number of Mennonite communities, where there are both MC and GC congregations, for a Fellowship Sunday when GC families entertain in their homes MC families, and MC families entertain GC families. Each guest would contribute, say, $10 to a joint GC-MC fund such as for

church planting. If this is a satisfying experience, repeat it annually.

9. In several dozen Mennonite communities arrange for a Saturday GC-MC teach-in with a GC telling the story of the Mennonite Church and an MC telling the story of the General Conference.

10. Revise Recommendation 5 by removing the 1995 deadline and call for annual joint progress reports. Let the process be unhurried and relaxed. Theology and polity flow from shared experience. Similarly integration probably flows most naturally from lots of little shared experiences: eating at the same table, sleeping under the same roof, singing, working, playing, listening, visiting, worshiping, studying and praying together. Of such there needs to be more.

# 1989: Camelot at Sharp's Chapel, 1937

*An article in the* Mennonite Weekly Review, *May 25, 1989,*
*describing a reunion of volunteers in a Quaker work camp at Sharp's*
*Chapel, Tennessee, the summer of 1937. Among the roots of Mennonite*
*Voluntary Service is the experience of young Mennonites serving in the*
*1930s in Quaker-administered summer work camps.*

Recently at Pendle Hill, a Quaker retreat center near
Philadelphia, we opened a 52-year-old time capsule.

I was 18 in the summer of 1937. The U.S. population was only 125
million–half what it is today. Despite bold programs in President
Roosevelt's New Deal, the Great Depression lingered in the land.
Few rural families had electricity. In East Tennessee annual per
capita income was less than $100. In Michigan auto workers were
staging sit-down strikes. Hitler, Mussolini, Franco and Japanese
generals were launched on a militant, threatening course. New
British Prime Minister Neville Chamberlain was talking
appeasement. Japan occupied much of China.

In those "best of times, worst of times" the crown jewel of the
New Deal was the Tennessee Valley Authority, or TVA, which
historian Henry Steele Commager heralded as "the greatest
peacetime achievement of 20th century America."

That summer of 1937 I was one of 38 college students (27 men, 11
women) who spent two months in an American Friends Service
Committee (Quaker) work camp at Sharp's Chapel in the TVA
region of Tennessee. Recently 18 of us, plus spouses, met at Pendle
Hill for our first reunion in 52 years. Seven of our number had
died. Despite diligent efforts, nine could not be located. Of the 22
remaining campers, 18 came to the reunion. Then in our
youth–now in our 70s and retired–this was a Rip Van Winkle
experience.

To recover a sense of place of a most memorable summer, I had
returned earlier in the month to Clairborne County, Tenn. I went
first to TVA headquarters in Norris to obtain topographical maps
of the Sharp's Chapel area. Three TVA officials heard my story and
offered to spend the day helping me find the site of cherished
memory.

They had wanted to inspect an old grist mill dam on Lost Creek,
now a historic site. It turned out to be one we had attempted to
rebuild and salvage as a fish-rearing pond. We found our way to
the site of the abandoned barracks of CCC Camp 13 where we had
lived, now a barren hillside. I talked with a middle-aged man in a
wheelchair on the front porch of a dilapidated house on the site. A
couple of goats were grazing at the front steps. He was too young
to remember our camp.

Below the camp we located a small concrete dam, which then leaked because of underground caverns and which we sought to repair. For a month we drilled with jackhammers a hole 20 feet down into the bedrock to block off the cavern. We failed. Today the dam is one-third full of water. I remembered a water-powered grist mill then in operation. It was gone–the only remains were some foundation stones and evidences of the head race and tail race. On an isolated peninsula of Norris Lake we located the 50-acre virgin beech forest to which we had walked for a Fourth of July picnic.

Near the camp, boarded up and with an abandoned gas pump in front, was Stiner's general store. The aged proprietor, the keeper of community memories, had died. Some miles away was the tiny store and post office of Sharp's Chapel where we talked with Mr. Brewer, the old postmaster, who still remembers the CCC Camp.

The hill country has not changed much. The lush forested hills garlanded with flowering dogwood are beautiful in early May. Gone are the patches of corn, tobacco and truck gardens–then the evidence of subsistence farming–replaced by green meadows in the valleys with grazing cattle. The shabby farmsteads littered with abandoned cars and farm implements are still there, but well-built residences also dot the landscape. Straightened-out hard-top roads have replaced many of the winding gravel and dirt roads. But now there are so few people and farm animals–an emptiness, the people off to work in Oak Ridge, Toledo or Detroit. I thought of Goldsmith's poem "Deserted Village."

I was in awe of my peers at the Quaker camp: three-fourths of them attending select Eastern colleges and universities–Princeton, Yale, Vassar, Swarthmore. Ten of the 38 were members of the Society of Friends, a sufficient number to establish a Quaker spirit in the camp community. Burns and Elizabeth Scattergood Chalmers, both sensitive and caring, gifted in the art of consensual leadership, contributed much to the sense of community. Years later in reading the story of Andre and Magda Trocme in *Lest Innocent Blood Be Shed*, I was delighted to learn of Burns' key role in aiding Jewish refugees in wartime Vichy France.

An Oberlin graduate said he had passed up his 50th class reunion to attend. Max Adenauer, retired city manager of Cologne and son of Konrad Adenauer, Chancellor of West Germany from 1948 to 1967, had flown from West Germany. Five came from the West Coast. Nigel Bicknell, retired member of the British Foreign Service, came from Dorset, England. Nigel asked what tug had brought us together. What had that summer experience 52 years ago meant to us? Then we were all single. Most of us were undecided on vocations and had years more of study.

And abruptly across our path cut the wide swath of war. One was killed in combat in Europe. Max Adenauer was struck by a British bullet in 1943 which, he says, was his salvation because otherwise he would have been sent to the Stalingrad front. Another was commissioned an officer and fought from the Normandy invasion, through the Battle of the Bulge, to the River Elbe and the meeting of Russian troops. Nigel, who considered himself a conscientious objector, chose photography and the Royal Air Force. He made two forced landings, one in the North Sea. Two of us served as COs for more than four years in Civilian Public Service, as did husbands of two of the women.

Twenty-two survived the war, have married (one divorce), become grandparents, earned doctorates, practiced law, held professorships, written books, entered government service, been ordained to the ministry, held administrative posts, changed their religious affiliation (four to Quaker, one from Episcopal to Judaism). Six have served with the AFSC or Mennonite Central Committee. We were at ease, I think, in picking up the conversation after 52 years.

We sensed back in 1937 that reticent Max Adenauer opposed Hitler's Third Reich. Then we felt it inappropriate to expose him with questions. He agreed: "I felt uneasy. Nazis were everywhere. In New York I saw German children goose-stepping in Nazi organizations. It would have meant problems for my family and especially my father to have spoken my feelings. It was very dangerous." He said coming to the reunion was for him an emotional thing.

"In 1938 the times were very dark for my family," he said. "Here I came to see freedom. I never expected to see you again." Denied an extension of his U.S. visa, he returned to six years of military service in Germany. He spoke appreciatively of his father and his principles: his commitment to human dignity, democracy, Christianity (which for him was "strong but not dogmatic"), and the Atlantic Alliance. When asked, "What sustained you during those difficult years?" his immediate response was, "My family."

Nigel Bicknell, who radiated international charm and exuberance in 1937, has not lost it. The Sharp's Chapel experience was "satisfying, inspiring, encouraging," he said. "Then we were at the height of our idealism. I thought then that I was a pacifist. It is sad to see the slow erosion of our idealism, to see how I have lowered my principles to fit in." He said he had come "to see what you look like and whether you have improved any." He triggered an hour of discussion by saying, "I came to hear what Sharp's Chapel did for us."

The comments flowed: "I was impressed by the doctrine of passive resistance, a new idea for me"... "This was the ultimate democratic experience"... "I had great hopes then that we would be able to bring about lasting social betterment, but I guess I have grown more skeptical or pessimistic"... "Of all the groups of age-peers with whom I've associated, the friends at the Friends camp were the most significant."

Many of us were drawn to the camp at Sharp's Chapel to learn more about the TVA experiment, a kind of Camelot in its day. We were captivated by TVA chairman Arthur Morgan's idealism, his decentralist philosophy, his commitment to cooperatives and his concern for self-reliant farming communities. A year later we were shocked to learn of his dismissal from the TVA chairmanship, followed by the rapid ascension of David Lilienthal, with his focus on electric power production, which led later to nuclear power.

As TVA gained a monopoly of all electric power production in the region, it built a number of coal-fired steam-generator plants at mine heads. The TVA, once the symbol of ecological idealism, became the largest consumer in the nation of high-sulphur, strip-mined, non-union coal, which left land bare for the ravages of erosion. It went from benevolent idealism to acquisitive pragmatism in one generation.

The two fish-rearing ponds at Sharp's Chapel never held water and never could be used. In fact, they were not needed. A whole summer of labor was for naught. Fish experts back in 1937 thought fish would not breed in the big new Norris Lake, but fish did not read planning studies. They pursued their primeval instincts and stocked the lake abundantly.

Those two months in the summer of 1937 are strewn with parables, if we but have the eyes to see. The Quaker camp: how do you create community–a product of work or a gift of grace? What makes for stimulating learning environments? How can one best pass on particular values?

The TVA: Do institutions born in a fanfare of idealism inevitably become pragmatic, acquisitive and ethically insensitive? How can one reconcile rapid economic development with good stewardship of natural resources? What are the possibilities and limits of planning in a complex society?

Development: What are the possibilities and limits of outsiders (northerners, college students) doing good? What are the possibilities and limits of outsiders entering a different culture and becoming agents of change? These, of course, were not the questions of a youth of 18. But they are now the ponderings of a man of 70.

# 1989: Ten Days That Shook My World

*Written October 24, 1989, after returning home from the hospital for heart surgery, a writing shared with family and friends.*

Mine was not an unusual experience. Two weeks ago today I had quadruple coronary bypass surgery at St. Francis Hospital in Wichita, KS. Eight days later I returned home. Not long ago this particular surgery was rare–a daring, ultimate procedure in medical science. Now it is routine, an estimated 170,000 Americans annually undergoing this surgery. I understand that some controversy surrounds the question of whether surgery is to be the preferred procedure in so many cases.

Having only rarely been hospitalized my mind is now flooded with many thoughts about this intersecting of two worlds: the complex and amazing world of medical science and the embracing community of family, friends and church.

Fourteen hours after I lost consciousness prior to the operation, the first reassuring words I heard came from a nurse whom I could not see. "It's three in the morning. All went well. You are doing fine. Your wife and daughter have gone home." Beautiful words, "your wife and daughter." Immediately I thought: " 'Your daughter'–that must be Joan, our daughter who is an obstetrician-gynecologist in Minneapolis." I had not known that she was coming to be with my wife Lois and me. How thoughtful. I slipped into a peaceful sleep.

In the morning appeared Lois and Joan. With them came the news that daughter Esther from Evansville, Indiana, and daughter Karen and son Luke from San Francisco would soon be on their way to Wichita. I could not talk, tubes in my mouth and nose, but I could see them, and they could touch me. I sensed how presence can be even more eloquent than words. Just to know that they were there.

From the words of the nurse at three in the morning and each who followed, I was impressed with all the nurses, aides and attendants–their cheerful spirits, words of encouragement and affirmations of my progress. Their words and touch and attentiveness were a healing presence.

Still hooked up with tubes, wires and monitors, I was moved from the intensive care to a semi-private room. Cards and messages arrived and a few visitors were permitted. In reading the cards and hearing the messages, I sensed that my life was being carried on the "eagles' wings" of prayer. That simple awareness has the quality of the awesome.

Among the cards were messages from persons who have shared my experience–heart surgery, heart problems–some much more perilous than mine. Several cheerfully welcomed me to "the club." There is a "fellowship of those who have gone the way of the bypass." This may not be unlike the fellowship among those who have had cancer. I remembered again the death of our first child and our awareness then of all those others who had also lost their first child. Welling up in me is a resolve hereafter to reach out to others who are going this way.

Three days ago I received a phone call from a doctor friend, who knew of my case and was himself going to have heart surgery. I sensed that even doctors, who may have more apprehension about these things than the rest of us, have need to be reassured.

I had not realized what a joy it is to have one's doctors enter the room: the anesthetist, the cardiologist and the surgeon. Each came radiating an assurance of my well being, that all was well, that they were pleased with my progress. Again I thought, their words were important, but even more their presence—standing beside the bed, even sitting on the edge of the bed, touching, explaining, answering questions. One doctor, substituting on the rounds, dropped into a chair on the far side of the room, flipped noisily through my big book of charts and talked of my problems from twelve feet away. His was not a therapeutic presence.

I was struck how a patient must—for the best results—be completely yielded (*Gelassenheit*) to those in whom one's care rests. I could hide nothing. Every part of my body was exposed to their eye and touch. Here I, a grown man accustomed to administering programs and the schedules of others, was called to be a child again.

In the hospital I was called to a reversal of roles. I, the parent—who had held in my arms Joan, Esther, and Karen, who had changed their diapers and lifted them up and hugged them when they grieved—was now their child, for whom they had come home to care. To be a child again, here was an intimation of the Kingdom of Heaven.

When I went two weeks ago to the hospital to have tests, expecting to return home within hours, I had no thoughts of my life in danger. With many unfinished projects, my thoughts were focused on the future. But now I was beginning to sense that I was edging closer to that border region between life and death. Instantly priorities change. Some goals don't seem so important any more. The line of the Psalmist kept running through my mind: "Though I walk through the valley of death I shall fear no evil." I am grateful in these past days for a sense of assurance of the goodness and support of family, friends, church members, medical profession and God's encompassing presence.

Several days after surgery when I attended instruction with a group of other heart patients, I was shocked to look about me at my peers: some helpless, ashen faced, grey-blue of pallor, many hooked up to tubes and tanks. It was looking about me into mirrors of we the living dead. Is this how I looked? I was amused and yet that group image was sobering. I better take seriously each step in the way of recovery.

From surgery until the day of my release from the hospital, I was wired to a monitor box. Across the hall from my room sat two persons, their eyes constantly watching on the monitor screens for evidences of irregularity. When I could move about in the corridors, I stopped to ask the big black man, whose eyes were glued to the monitor screens with the zig-zagging lines, which one was my record. He pointed out the pulsating graph–my own particular heart-beat story. This big man came into focus in my mind as Almighty Jehovah looking down on each of his children, seeing every hair on every child's head, every sparrow that falls.

I will always associate my hospitalization with the San Francisco earthquake, 5:04 p.m. PT, October 17, 1989. With millions of others I was watching on television the prelude to the third game of the World Series. Again it abruptly put many things in perspective. My health problem is a trifle in comparison to the burdens of many.

Some seem awkward in coping with another's illness. A few appear embarrassed, shy as they grope for appropriate words to say. It is difficult to acknowledge the fact of trauma in another. A few fill the anxious spaces with a rush of talk, such as reporting on similar health problems of others. It must be even more difficult to know what to say to the ill whose prognosis is reported not to be encouraging.

There may be something good being confronted with a great big STOP sign in one's life. Now I take naps without a sense of guilt that I must be up and at it. I have yielded myself to a dietary plan which means avoidance of certain foods, more limited intake and a slow, deliberate savoring of each bite. I delight in the regular walks through the autumn leaves during these lovely Indian summer days. I am writing postcards to friends–no carbon copies to file–a time to think of others. I am reading books just for the fun of it, with less sense of obligation that each must relate to the current project at hand. A time to read the current revised edition of the *New English Bible* just off the press. A time to talk with visitors, with no fleeting diverting thoughts of telephone calls to make, letters to finish for the evening mail.

Those quaint words from Proverbs keep running through my mind: "a virtuous woman is a crown to her husband"… "her price is far above rubies." Lois' instincts were so immediate and sure. When on Monday I proposed to take the pickup and run down to Wichita for the test, she said, "No, we'll go together." Following that test, I did not return home but remained for surgery. Lois is the one that Monday evening who phoned our five children to report developments. Lois is the one who rearranged her responsibilities to spend much time with me each day at the hospital. Lois is the one who has read all the instructions and is helping me to be attentive to the steps required for recovery. This is a time to count one's blessings, and especially Lois.

This is an expensive and time-consuming way to learn some lessons, but these are good lessons.

*Kreider with "Mirror of the Martyrs" exhibit, ca. 1993.*

# 1990: An Invitation to the Martyrs' Mirror

*An article that appeared in the September 1990 issue of* Mennonite Life.

"Robert, I have just learned that the Luyken plates are available for sale." This was the excited voice of Amos Hoover, Old Order Mennonite historian and friend, phoning from Denver, Pennsylvania, in late May 1988. He was reporting that the lost twenty-three copper plates of Jan Luyken, used to illustrate the 1685 *Martyrs' Mirror*, had reappeared. Hoover and I had been pursuing the twenty-three plates since 1977, when he and friends had purchased seven of the known thirty surviving plates. Unfortunately the remaining twenty-three had slipped into the hands of a non-communicative art collector near Cologne, Germany. One hundred and four of Luyken's copper etchings had been used to illustrate Thieleman van Braght's second edition of the Martyrs' Mirror. Some of the plates were seen in 1930 but were thought to have been destroyed in World War II. Thirty plates had briefly reappeared in 1975.

On a Saturday morning market day in early April 1989 in a bakery-cafe in Grünstadt, Palatinate, each of the copper plates–300-year-old artistic treasure–was carefully unwrapped and laid before us on the white linen table cloth. The aroma of coffee and freshly baked pastry enveloped this ritual of the unveiling. Here in our hands were Luyken etchings last used in printing the German edition of the *Martyrs' Mirror* at Pirmasens in 1780. A sense of awe.

On the flight back to the States I cradled in my lap the package of twenty-three plates. In the name of a group of patrons, The Martyrs' Mirror Trust, we had taken possession of the plates, but I did not realize how these plates and the *Martyrs' Mirror* would soon take possession of us. I can now understand an academic friend who recently commented that he had almost decided to devote the rest of his scholarly life to the study of the *Martyrs' Mirror*.

Long ago I had purchased a 1950 English edition but through the years I only dipped into it occasionally to harvest illustrations. Often I had brought it to a class or lecture and placed it alongside the Bible, the *Ausbund* and Menno Simons' *Fundament Buch*, and then pointed to the four as foundational to our Anabaptist-Mennonite faith. I admired the *Martyrs' Mirror*, praised it but neglected to read it systematically. Like most Mennonites, I viewed it with respect but from afar.

In the months since the acquisition of the plates we have been preparing an exhibit, "Mirror of the Martyrs," to feature the Luyken plates and to tell the story of Anabaptist martyrdom. This exhibit opens September 21, 1990, at the Kauffman Museum, North Newton, Kansas, and then moves on in May 1991 to Goshen College, Goshen, Indiana. The exhibit is designed to be readily transportable to other Mennonite centers in North America, even overseas, and to university, church and art centers elsewhere.

Since the receipt of that phone call in May 1988, our planning has been shaped by three concerns. First, the surviving Luyken plates should be kept together, neither the prideful possession of one institution nor scattered among many owners. The collection is to be held as an inter-Mennonite trust. Second, these Luyken etchings should be viewed as more than intriguing, aging artifacts to be savored by the few. They can be carriers of a collective memory. The plates offer an opportunity to tell in innovative ways the dramatic story of faithfulness under test. Third, these old plates carry not a parochial tale but a universal story. Anabaptist martyrs are kin to a host of martyrs past and present. Today more prisoners of conscience languish in cells than in the 1500s. The age of the martyrs is not ancient history.

John S. Oyer of Goshen College and I have worked with Robert Regier and the Kauffman Museum staff in the preparation of the exhibit and with Merle and Phyllis Good of Good Books in the publication of a catalog-storybook. In this research and writing we have been drawn into intriguing avenues of inquiry. I wish now to reflect on what could be a lifetime agenda for the study of the *Martyrs' Mirror*–an agenda calling for research papers and even doctoral dissertations.

*The Martyrs–Follow Their Example*

John Foxe's *Book of Martyrs* is said to have been, next to the Bible, the most widely read and influential book in seventeenth century England. The *Martyrs' Mirror* in particular periods and places has influenced Mennonites and their spiritual associates in similar ways. We need to assess the impact of the *Martyrs' Mirror* on the life and faith of the church. Has it shaped and changed lives? Among us are those who have been profoundly affected by this book with its high call to discipleship. A leading peacemaker tells of how his father on Sunday afternoons gathered his children and read to them stories from the *Martyrs' Mirror*. An industrialist friend recounts how he took this big unread book with him on a trip to South America and soon was so captivated that he seized spare moments to read the book in its entirety. A Mennonite historian relates how an older cousin told him stories from the *Martyrs' Mirror* and kindled in him a lifelong fascination with his

Anabaptist heritage. A Central American brother declares: "These stories in the *Martyrs' Mirror* are our stories, El Salvadoran stories." One wonders how many Mennonite pastors have drawn from the *Martyrs' Mirror* in their preaching. In Christian education in our churches have these stories been used and with what effect? Are they remote, inspirational epic tales or do they have a true-to-life contemporary bite? We need to know more how Old Order peoples, with their deep and continuing affection for the book, have used the martyr memories in Christian nurture. It would be interesting to survey new congregational members of non-Mennonite backgrounds to learn whether these martyr memories are repulsive or invitational.

Thieleman van Braght, editor of the 1660 first edition, saw the *Martyrs' Mirror* as his contribution to help his people, softened by affluence and neglectful of their heritage, to recover a virile, biblical faith. "Read it again and again," he wrote. "Above all, fix your eyes upon the martyrs themselves and follow their example." The story is told how he gave a copy of the *Martyrs' Mirror* to his seven-year-old niece who was beginning to read. We want to know whether the telling of martyr stories really helps in passing on and renewing the faith.

Those who have pressed for the republication of the *Martyrs' Mirror* have invariably been motivated by concerns for renewal and recovery of a nonresistant commitment: in the 1740s the Pennsylvania Mennonites anticipating colonial conflicts on the frontier and in the 1770s Palatine Mennonites sensing imminent warfare among the great powers. Certainly renewal is one of our expectations in this recovery of the Luyken plates and in the telling of their story. Deep within us we long to find the purity of a movement at its source. Van Braght and Luyken can help us in that quest because they are closer to the source.

*The Martyrs' Mirror Compared*

Mennonites have viewed Thieleman van Braght's *Martyrs' Mirror* as a unique work of a unique people. It, however, is a member of an extended family. Its ancestry dates back to writers of the early church–Eusebius, Tertullian and Origen–and the many medieval chroniclers. It has immediate parentage in *Het Offer des Herren* and accompanying hymnbook (*Lietboecxken*) of 1562 and Hans de Ries' *History of the Martyrs* of 1615. Van Braght's *Martyrs' Mirror* relates to the sister volumes, *Ausbund* of 1564 and the *Hutterian Chronicle*. Beyond these are martyrologies of other traditions: Rabus (1552), Crespin (1554), Haemstede (1559), Foxe (1559) and many more.

Comparative studies of van Braght's volume in the context of other martyrologies would shed light on Anabaptist perspectives.

*Thieleman van Braght the Historian, 1625-1664*

In the catalog for the exhibit, *Mirror of the Martyrs*, John S. Oyer examines twenty-nine of the martyr stories told by van Braght and illustrated by Luyken. This account by account review of supporting data, context and plausibility could be extended to the remaining stories. It would provide a basis for evaluating van Braght's historical care and judgment. We must ask how van Braght's selection and exclusion of martyrs shaped subsequent perceptions of the normative Anabaptist. Although van Braght as historian has had his critics, measured by seventeenth century criteria, he can probably be judged a credible and superior historian. He must be compared to other martyrologists, observing in each levels of historical skill, archival diligence, interpretive gifts and the propensity for embellishment. Such studies could lead to a reassessment of van Braght as a third or fourth generation communicator of the Anabaptist legacy.

*Jan Luyken the Printmaker, 1649-1712*

Clearly Jan Luyken was gifted as a printmaker with superb technical skill. He designed more than 3,000 copper plates to illustrate histories, Bibles and his eleven books of religious verse. When he was commissioned to illustrate the 1685 edition of the *Martyrs' Mirror*, he had already illustrated more than ninety books. As one studies the 104 etchings in the *Martyrs' Mirror*, one marvels at his sensitivity to detail and his portrayal of the serenity of martyrs on the threshold of death. His artistic works have been neglected by keepers of artistic taste. Now we encounter a gifted artist whose time for study and recognition has again come. A first step would be to publish an annotated edition of the best of his more than 300 etchings of biblical scenes.

*A State-of-the-Art Publication*

The prospering Mennonites of Amsterdam and Haarlem published in 1685 a two-volume *Martyrs' Mirror* which may be considered a state-of-the-art work in seventeenth century printing: quality of paper, care in printing, typographical style, use of etchings, craftsmanship in bookbinding. Amsterdam was then a distinguished center of printing. If one were to compare the 1685 edition with other illustrated books published in The Netherlands in the 1680s one could test the above affirmation: "a state-of-the-art publication." Of particular interest is this early Mennonite use of image to amplify the power of text. Here is evidence of Mennonites embracing modernity.

*On the Wings of Song*

First was the martyr event. Then came the telling of the story, passed on from person to person, congregation to congregation. Some stories were early recorded in broadsides and distributed widely, these martyr tales were even embraced by the wider Protestant community. From the very beginning the martyr stories were carried on the wings of song. Prisoners composed martyr ballads of their trials and faith. The *Ausbund* is a collection of martyr hymns. Entries of a martyr's death in the *Hutterian Chronicle* often carry a notation such as this, "A song was written about him, which is still sung by us." In song the Anabaptists made their "good witness."

This role of song as a bridge between the event and the oral, between the oral and the written is analogous to the springtime of other movements: American slaves and the Negro spiritual, the Civil Rights Movement and "We Shall Overcome," the protest movements of the Sixties and ballads. Today we may gain better insight into a people's theology by listening to the hymns they sing than by reading their creeds. Those who select the hymns shape theology. Anabaptist studies would be enriched by a comprehensive examination of martyr hymns in their genesis, content, circulation and influence.

*Execution as Theater*

Authorities staged the execution of Anabaptists as a ritual of civil religion and public drama. A spectacle-hungry citizenry was offered entertainment and a morality play: God's wrath and warning visited on Anabaptist dissenters thought to be destroying the unity of the churchly community. Van Braght named his book, "Bloody Theatre." In staging the execution of a martyr the rulers offered all the elements of high drama: stage, script, director, cast, stage hands, props, choreographed movements, spectators and reporters. Petrus Spierenburg in the *Spectacle of Suffering*[1] and

---

[1]Petrus Spierenburg, *The Spectacle of Suffering* (Cambridge University Press, 1984).

Michel Foucault in *Discipline and Punish*[2] describe the role of ritual and spectacle in early modern European patterns of punishment. The intransigence of Anabaptists under torture and their joyful acceptance of death subverted the climax of the morality play. In time, torture and public execution became counterproductive. A thorough study of Anabaptist martyrdom in the context of sixteenth century penology could provide insight on the effectiveness and limitations of persecution today. We would also probably find a trail of influence from martyr steadfastness under torture to modern legal protections against self-incrimination.

*Quest for Respectability*

We have observed in efforts to recover the martyr memory a desire for renewal and a concern for faith transmission. The strands of people's motivation in the distant past elude the historian. And yet I am haunted by a suspicion that the elegantly printed and illustrated 1685 edition of the *Martyrs' Mirror* was offered to the public by the affluent Amsterdam and Haarlem Mennonite patrons as evidence of their eminently respectable Dutch character.

Dutch identity had been shaped in the eighty-year struggle against Spanish domination. Dutch historians celebrated the liberation movement in biblical terms as the chosen Israelites escaping Egyptian tyranny. The conflict produced its martyr heroes–Egmont, Hoorn and William of Orange–and an arch villain, the Duke of Alva. The stories of the Council of Blood, the Spanish Fury at Antwerp and the Siege of Leiden were told and retold in picture and word. The Dutch story was a glorious account of good pitted against evil. Then in 1685 the Mennonites, living on the margins of Dutch respectability but increasingly prosperous and well-positioned, came forward with the 1685 volume, perhaps intimating that they, too, had a glorious story of a liberation struggle against oppression. In their cultivated modesty the Mennonites were not so brash as to assert such intentions. This hypothesis could be tested by comparing the depiction of the Dutch liberation experience with that of the Dutch Anabaptist martyrs.

---

[2]Michel Foucault, *Discipline and Punish–the Birth of the Prison* (New York: Vintage Books, 1979).

*A Search for Meaning*

Many excellent articles have been written about biblical and theological motifs in the *Martyrs' Mirror*. One finds here a rich lode of themes: God's lordship of history, the meaning of salvation, Christology, discipleship, the two kingdoms, hermeneutics, eschatology, the church under the Cross, the nurturing community, apologetics under pressure and many more. Scholars have been plucking out significant single themes for study. Now a composite theological picture needs to be sketched from the martyr books, including the *Ausbund* and the *Hutterian Chronicle*.

The *Martyrs' Mirror* may be at its best as a sourcebook of case studies in Christian ethics. What beliefs are worth dying for? Do any persons have the right to abuse another's body? Why do good people torture and kill? Why do modern governments torture and kill? Why do the powerful fear the weak? What would you do if?... And then there are those haunting stories to ponder such as Dirk Willems rescuing his pursuer.

If we would understand the *Martyrs' Mirror*, we must read it antiphonally: a *Martyrs' Mirror* story and a contemporary story of martyrdom: El Salvador, the Gulag, Robben Island, West Bank, Chile, Uganda, Cambodia, Leavenworth 1918.... The *Martyrs' Mirror* is as current as the annual report of Amnesty International. The age of the martyrs is not past.

# 1992: An Invitation to Unconventional Wisdom

*From commencement address at Bethel College, May 24, 1992; condensed version appeared in* Mennonite Weekly Review *and* Bethel College Bulletin.

Society sees you graduating seniors as educated persons. You know that is only partially true. The test of an educated person is whether you are still a learner when no course requirements hang over you.

Let us start with books. Do you realize that you may be in the twilight years of the Gutenberg era when the educated person and the book-reading person were one? Book communication–with its beginning and end, its unfolding storyline and its reasoned progression of thought–is challenged today by radically different patterns of communication.

A current movie such as *JFK*–with its 2,500 cuts, flashbacks and flash-forwards–is a three-hour assault on the subconscious. This is post-Gutenberg communication: visceral, subconscious, seductive. You–educated in the reflective, deliberate, analytical ways of the mind and the book–need to make sense out of this new communicative bombardment of rapidly flashing, pulsating, high-intensity images.

This leads to *unconventional wisdom advice number one: don't discard the book–just yet.* As graduates you now have opportunity to read books when no one requires you to read them. Expressed theologically, you no longer live under a state of law, but under a state of free will and grace.

Remember, a book in the pocket is worth two on the shelf. I suggest that you keep several books going at the same time to fit your varied moods of mind and spirit. Now may be the time for a fresh reading of biblical classics: the Psalms or the prophet Amos or Matthew–or Dosteyevski's *Brothers Karamazov*.

I offer this *second word of unconventional wisdom: your contribution to society may be less in your answers than in your questions.* Of all the gifts of learning, the queen of gifts is curiosity. The resolution of a problem begins with a penetrating question. All about us is information to be uncovered with questions. Locked in each person is a fascinating story, lodes of informational ore.

Accumulated trivia, organized, becomes treasure. And so–with a few questions–the waitress, the backhoe operator, the watch repairman become your teachers. When Jesus urged us to be childlike he had in mind that we should ask questions as do little children. One naive question is worth a dozen half-right answers.

Some say our age has no heroes–only throw-away Kleenex heroes, momentarily useful but soon discarded. Recognizing this pervasive cynicism, I offer as *the third word of unconventional wisdom that we do need models.* From this we cannot escape. Stated theologically, God incarnates, that is, wraps truth in persons. Maybe this is the time for you to pass on a word of thanks to those who inspired you, nudged you, even scolded you into shaping up. You, too, have been role models, mentors to others–teachers unawares: showing interest, encouraging, listening, helping, challenging. No matter what your vocation, you all are called to be teachers–to pass on the joy of learning, the better life.

Reflecting on the role of master mentors, I invite you to a fresh receptivity to the person of the Master Teacher, Jesus, whose life, teachings and person are an inexhaustible spring of renewal and guidance for life's journey.

Despite your best-laid plans, your future will be buffeted by blows to your self-esteem–some devastating. Few of us can handle these hurts alone. Few of us can reach our full potential as loners. *The fourth word of unconventional wisdom is that to reach your full potential you need to be a part of what Central American Christians call "a base community."* The best support communities encompass diversity, not just a group of mirror-image friends.

God created congregations to help us cope with tough problems in a tough world, to celebrate, to help us together pass on values and faith, to caution us from making foolish decisions, to encourage us to take risks, to have fun together, to be a place where you can say, "I blew it; forgive me."

For fulfillment, don't try doing it alone. Each of us needs an embracing fellowship, a support community, a base community, one of God's congregations.

I hope you have caught a vision of a better world, a more humane society, alternatives to human conflict, appreciation for communities that care about hurts, loneliness and suffering of others. Glimpses of hope.

If the conventional wisdom is that the establishment out there has to clean up the mess, and of this you only despair, I urge that there is hope and it begins with you and me.

*The final word of unconventional wisdom: embrace several causes that will leave this a better world when you depart.* The real action in society may be in the cracks–freezing and thawing in the tiny fissures. Action that is patient and persistent. Action with people who are a bit unconventional, that is, creatively out of step.

You have arrived for such a time as this. God bless you and make you a blessing.

# 1992: A Boy from Am Trakt and a Boy from Altona

*A presentation at a Christmas dinner attended by Mennonite Central Committee staff and families at Ephrata, Pennsylvania, December 4, 1992, where Peter J. Dyck on his 78th birthday and William T. Snyder on his 75th birthday were honored.*

A long time ago during what we have come to know as World War I–and which may come to be known as the beginning of the 70 Years War–two boys, Peter and William, were born in distant places off the beaten path. In course of time emerged two world class Mennonites, both of whom have profoundly shaped the direction of Mennonite peoplehood in the 20th century.

*Peter*–one of three sons and six daughters was born to a prosperous landed Mennonite family in the village of Lysanderhöh in the Am Trakt on the upper reaches of the Volga River that flows south to the Caspian sea. The decade before 1914 had been the golden era of the Russian Mennonites–a people confident, growing–100,000 and more, with aspiring industrialists and professionals, substantial numbers affluent, a people of destiny. Little Peter's first years were nestled in a neatly defined world in which there were only three kinds of people: *Mennoniten, Colonisten* (that is, neighboring German Lutherans), and *Russen*, lots of the latter and all servants. His was a wholesome, warm, cohesive community of family, faith and land. But on the horizon–ominous clouds.

Those were the last years of the Romanov monarchy, Czar Nicholas II on the throne, four years later he and his family murdered. Two thousand miles to the East in Zurich another Nicholas–Nikolai Lenin–dreamed and planned an alternative future for Russia: the first Marxist state.

Czarist armies in 1914 marched confidently to do battle with German, Austrian and Turkish foes, only to be abruptly hurled back at Tannenberg. Mennonite kinsmen from Prussia, who had abandoned their nonresistance, were marching with German troops deep into France–within artillery-sound of Paris. The Czarist military ordered Peter's father to service. He, a conscientious objector, chose alternative service in forestry. Little Peter's carefully structured world was slowly crumbling.

*William*–far away in the grimy railroad town of Altoona in the Pennsylvania hill country, was born into another Mennonite family who had only recently left a rural Old Mennonite community to identify with a struggling General Conference Mennonite city mission. The Snyders–grandfather Abram and uncles Jacob and

Herman–were lay Mennonite preachers who had planted four little mission churches–Altoona, Roaring Springs, East Freedom and Napier–known as the Snyder churches. The three Snyder preachers continued to dress plain even after leaving the Old Mennonite fold.

Parents of little William and his two sisters were William Sr., a foreman in the Pennsylvania Railroad shops, and Susan Gorman of a Scotch-Irish family, hill people of indistinct church commitment. William had a brother he scarcely knew, fifteen years his senior, who left home to be a trucker and died at twenty one. None of William's playmates were Mennonite. They were Irish Catholics who went to mass at St. Leo's, Polish Catholics to St. Stanislov, Jews to Synagogue Beth Emmanuel, Russian Orthodox and more. Within a block or two of the Snyder house on the corner at 1830 Twelfth Avenue was a tavern, a Jewish delicatessen where William bought bagels–arriving each morning on a New York Baker's truck, McCormick's corner grocery, Butch's barber shop, the Palace movie theater–where Bill attended on occasion–being discrete, of course, in his selection, Abel Vetter's barber shop, Ollie Orbason's cigar store and newspaper stand. On the side Ollie was the neighborhood bootlegger, for whom Bill's father once posted bail, much to the displeasure and chagrin of his mother. Where Peter's father had welcomed Alexander Kerensky, the Social Democrat, as a liberating Russian political spirit, William's father voted Republican–Harding, Coolidge, Hoover–but who in the New Deal era yielded to an appreciation of FDR.

The year of William's birth the United States entered the war–an ally of the Russians, the British and the French. Neither for the Snyders nor for the Dycks was this their war. Later young William would remember vividly the war's aftermath incarnate in the ravaged bodies of two young men, his father their legal guardian, both men gassed in the trenches of France and confined to veterans hospitals.

From 1917 to 1927 as young William was learning to read and write English, play baseball and was memorizing the lineup of the Pittsburgh Pirates and Connie Mack's Philadelphia Athletics, Peter in the village beyond the Volga was learning to read and write German and Russian and to cope with the techniques of survival: the Bolshevik Revolution that erupted in Petrograd and spread to far-off Lysanderhöh, pillaging the village, those terrifying house searches, the tortuous Bolshevik bureaucracy, a father risking his life on a many-day trek south toward the Caspian Sea in search of food, Peter's near death from typhus. Then the arrival of the long-awaited relief food and clothing from MCC, a Fordson tractor (the first MCC venture into agricultural development), and the burst of hope with the New Economic Policy (NEP) with its relaxation of collectivization and confiscation–but then the death of Lenin, the emergence of the hardliner, the Marxist man of steel, Stalin. The abandonment of hope. The family's flight from the once peaceable kingdom beyond the Volga to a new home on the Saskatchewan prairie.

In August 1920–William almost three and Peter almost six–in Elkhart, Indiana, at the Prairie Street Mennonite Church a group of Mennonites from a half dozen American Mennonite groups–mostly strangers to each other–met to create a temporary agency to send food and clothing to kinsmen in Russia suffering from hunger and want. Some twenty years later Peter from Am Trakt and William from Altoona would find their way into the program of the still youthful MCC and would rise rapidly in MCC servanthood ranks

Was it a calculated plan that brought William and Peter together in 1947 and 1948 to launch the exodus and resettlement of thousands of Mennonite refugees on the *Volendam*, the *Charleton Monarch*, the *Stuart Heintzelman*? Was it accident? Chance? Or was it providence? I lean toward providence but providence clothed in mystery and a sense of awe at the ways of God with his children.

Peter and William were boys during the Great Depression–William in Altoona with thousands unemployed from the shops and mines, Peter on the Saskatchewan prairie of an immigrant family, poor, with quaint ways–the Dyck children arriving at school, not with sandwiches as real Canadians did. They brought a bucket of borscht and a loaf of bread. The humiliation of being taunted and not able to defend themselves in the strange English language. The Canadian/American depression was for Mennonites the great leveler–a war experience in which they like their neighbors fought and survived–buddies all in the struggle. Peter and William, to this day both frugal and eminently prudent, must be understood as being sons of the Great Depression. Perhaps those far off childhood days have helped them to empathize in a special way with the children of hunger in Somalia, Sudan and Haiti.

What is it that gives some families a special edge of faithfulness? Families that carry the embers of commitment from generation to generation? Peter and Elfrieda, Bill and Lucille–who have given lifetimes of service to the church and then their daughters, Ruth and Rebecca serving in Malawi and Lesotho and Sharon and Margaret serving in Kenya, the Philippines, France and India. I am fascinated by the Snyder family, who lived in downtown Altoona. Surrounded by the world: a father who used his railway pass to take his son to Pittsburgh to see the Pirates play in old Forbes Field, the immortal Honus Wagner still around knocking out flies; William delivering the *Altoona Tribune*, the city's democratic daily, a route that took him to a customer in the red light district on Ninth Street. And then to note how the Snyders, devoted to their Altoona Memorial Mission Church, provided rooms for two mission workers, Martha Franz from Berne, Indiana, and Elizabeth Foth from Kansas. The family kept the faith in a polyglot, blue-collar city.

The immigrant Dyck family of eleven particularly intrigues me: after several years in their first farm home in southern Saskatchewan the family moved north to be a part of the Tiefengrund congregation where the family could draw upon the nurturing ministries of the church. There is the image of Elder Regier, usually in swallow tail coat, stopping at the door as he entered the place of worship and saying in German, "The peace of God be with you." As would the writer of Hebrews, one could recount the stories of family faithfulness of not only Peter but also John and C. J. and Elise and Renata and Clara and more. What is the chemistry of commitment in a family? The elusive art of passing on the faith? Raising a family may be like the skill of dribbling a football–you can't be sure which way the ball will bounce. A good family: is it careful nurture? Grace? Certainly the mystery of God's ways with his children.

When Peter went off to study at the University of Saskatchewan in 1937, taking with him a one hundred pound sack of oatmeal–following, as he did, a recommendation of Mahatma Gandhi–and surviving on a three-times a day diet of oatmeal porridge–he was one of the early ones of the 1920s immigrants to go off to college and then to return to serve the church. Peter and William were part of a new wave of college-educated men and women who appeared in the post World War II period and stood poised to serve the church. William was the first of his extended family to attend college. He came close, however, to choosing a neighboring Brethren college, Juniata. J. Winfield Fretz and Arthur Rosenberger from the Mennonite college at Bluffton leaned on him and he chose his church college where in due course he met Lucille Steiner of a pure Swiss Mennonite line. Again: Accident? Chance? Or was it providence? At Bluffton a new world opened to him: he a city youth with city friends now found friends of kindred mind and spirit. Responsibilities gravitated to him: manager of the college bookstore, catcher on the varsity baseball team. Stimulating teachers: the Mennonite historian C. Henry Smith who wrote books; Russell Lantz who had been imprisoned at Leavenworth for his CO convictions; J. P. Klassen–the artist and a refugee from the

Chortitza who had known war, revolution and hunger and had survived with a winsome Franciscan-like spirit; Kathryn Moyer who taught literature, her teaching of Thompson's poem, "The Hound of Heaven," still lingering in his mind. Later there would be an invitation to return to Bluffton to serve as business manager. By then, however, he was committed to a life with MCC.

Peter came to Akron in 1941 and William in 1943–Peter on his way to England, William up from the CPS camp at Luray, Virginia, to help in the administration of the CPS program for COs. That Akron of 1942, the one I first knew–I can see it now: the meandering trip from the Lancaster railway station on the Ephrata trolley, at first one MCC phone and that on a party line, offices and dining room and some sleeping quarters all in the big main house on the corner of Main and 11th, daily chapel in the living room–each one taking his or her turn leading and the singing from *Life Songs*, many of us providing our own typewriters, my typewriter stand an orange crate.... Needing multiple copies? Eight sheets of onion skin and seven carbons.... Eating elbow to elbow in the crowded dining room. Mrs. Byler hovering over her brood.... Each one taking a turn doing the laundry–even Bill hanging out the wash.... When Peter left for England the summer of 1941 he went to New York City, put up at the YMCA near the Battery, spent a month going from shipping office to shipping office until he found passage and then on a converted whaling ship, the *Hektoria*, followed by a 28-day trip in convoy to Liverpool. Now a seven-hour jet flight from New York City to London.... In 1942 no MTS or word processors or FAX machines or photocopying machines. Then we all cut stencils and operated a messy mimeograph. And each one's business was everyone's business. In those days we all read all the incoming and outgoing telegrams and cablegrams. One big happy, nosy, impertinent family. One thing can be said: the staff today has improved its social graces.

Peter and William have ridden the wave of a technological revolution. Peter was one of the first persons I know who took movies–we, who only a few years before did not dare see movies. MCC, the instrument of shocking modernity.

World War II is the great divide in Mennonite institutionalism. Before 1945 at war's end few of our groups had conference headquarters–just unpaid board executives with stuffed brief cases and no secretarial help.... Few or no church camps, homes for the aged, retreat centers, museums. Few overseas mission programs. No church planting strategies. No mental hospitals. No MDS. No MEDA. No VS. No relief sales. No MCC shops. Many congregations on the prairies were still worshiping in original pioneer one room meeting houses. With World War II came a sense of empowerment to Mennonites as they successfully raised funds and administered camps for 5000 CPS men, as across Canada immigrants paid off their travel debts, as young lay leadership was thrust to the fore in the war years, and not the least–as Mennonites prospered in war time. These are the conditions out of which exploded the postwar era of a broad spectrum of new church institutions and programs. We became an increasingly busy people, our piety incarnate in our multiplicity of activities. William and Peter have directed traffic in this congestion of institutional programs.

We must acknowledge that the MCC record has not always been a glowing story of upward and onward from one success to the next. All of us in MCC–Peter and William, too–have taken our lumps. Powers and principalities and dark forces, our own mistakes and stupidities, plus God's all-wise over-ride of our presumptuousness has often prevented us from realizing some of the fondest of our dreams.

I think of Peter working so hard to encourage European Mennonites to form their own European MCC. The nodding heads and affirmations but then the murmurings of doubt and the dragging of feet. The unvoiced "no".... This may lend sympathy and insight into the arduous and prolonged task of creating a European Economic Community, a Common Market, a Council of Europe, a common currency.

I think of William and the Vietnam quagmire. MCC ready to accept the risks of enveloping battlefields and the vexatious ways of the military to be able to do some good. Add to this the frustrations of seeking to put together an ecumenical consortium of aid in the context of perplexing ethical issues where every proposed solution was flawed.

This is both the glory and the agony of the MCC–we who were once from the Am Trakts and the Altoonas, the Goessels and the Blooming Glens being thrust into a complex ethical world of shades of grey, a tangle of puzzling choices. But in this confusion the Bills and the Peters and all of us draw on the shaping moral memories and the empowerment of nurturing congregations: Altoona Memorial Mission and Tiefengrund Mennonite Church.

Time is slipping by with so much yet to tell: Bill in CPS, Peter and Elfrieda in wartime England and postwar Holland, William and the miracle of Paraguayan development, Peter and the MCC friendship with the Orthodox of Greece, William and Orie with their vision of service in Africa and Asia, Peter and Bill going to and fro over the face of the earth–seeing more of this world than Marco Polo.

Tonight I think of the midnight hours of January 30-31, 1947, at Lichterfelde West railway station in Berlin and the Berlin Exodus–no story in the Mennonite experience in the 20th century more captivating than this. I can see it now: a bitterly cold night, army trucks laden with silent refugees rolling from the Ringstrasse to the station, a stream of 1200 refugees climbing into railway box cars, the floor of each car covered with straw, each car equipped with a stove and with a stovepipe protruding from a slightly open door. A mood of anxiety and expectancy, apprehension and hope. Out there in the night lay the Russian zone: dark, menacing. A big hug from Elfrieda when I arrived with a quick assignment of tasks. My phone calls from an MP post to Helmstedt, the checkpoint on the British-Russian zonal border, to locate Peter speeding eastward out there on the Autobahn. Peter's arrival at the last moment. The long train slipping out into the night. Back to the Ringstrasse–going from house to house–the deathly emptiness and stillness of that once refugee community of 1200.

I think of that boy from Am Trakt who that week had met with General Lucius Clay, who in turn had conferred with Marshal Sokolofsky of the Soviets. Meetings in the presence of Robert Murphy, the de facto American ambassador. The temerity of this Peter, thirty-two years old, speaking truth to power.

I think of another youth, this one from Altoona, William, twenty-nine years old, who across the Atlantic had been working tirelessly, going back and forth from Akron to Washington to New York–the original shuttle diplomacy–knocking on doors, making phone calls, submitting briefs, proposing options–to prepare the way for the Berlin Exodus. Similarly was C. F. Klassen, Elfrieda's older brother, moving back and forth from Amsterdam to London to Geneva. In the records of William a litany of names come to recall: George Warren of the State Department and Meyer Cohen of the IRO, a General Wood and a Colonel D. C. Frost, Oliver Stone and Ugo Carusi, William Hallan Tuck and Sir Arthur Rucker. William worked the corridors of power as Peter had done in Frankfurt and Berlin.

Tonight we recognize appreciatively two men of faith to whom we as a people owe so much.

Again as I ponder the ways of God with his children, I ask: what brought Peter from Am Trakt and William from Altoona to the MCC? Was it accident? Chance? Or was it providence? I believe it was providence clothed in mystery with a sense of awe and gratitude.

# 1993: The Amish: Tradition and Transition

*Printed in* Tradition and Transition: An Amish Mennonite Heritage of Obedience 1693-1993, *ed. V. Gordon Oyer, Illinois Mennonite Historical and Genealogical Society, Metamora, Illinois, 1993.*

We came to Metamora with varied expectations (1) as descendants of the Amish probing the tributaries of family history; (2) as scholars searching for leads, tips to solve the puzzle of the Amish phenomena; (3) as the curious intrigued by Amish living museums scattered across our land; (4) as the lonely longing for a lost homeland, a yearning for an idyllic past; (5) as Anabaptist-minded seeking reconciliation and renewal.

Those of us here are mostly Mennonites. Once we were ashamed of our quaint Old Order Amish cousins, but now we appear eager and proud to embrace them. But they are not here to be hugged–the hook-and-eye-wearing, Ausbund-singing, horse-and-buggy-riding, ban-using Old Order Amish. As was proposed Thursday evening, we have come to celebrate a schism–that is, a church split, a conflict, the Amish division of 1693. Here we are the backsliders from the high moral ground of Jakob Ammann of 1693–all of us to be counted as "out of fellowship." When in all our history have we celebrated a church split, a family quarrel? When will we celebrate the Lambist Wars of the Dutch Mennonites, the Herr division of 1812, the Oberholtzer schism of the 1850s, the Brueder Gemeinde division of 1860, the Indiana-Michigan Conference ruptures of the 1920s, the Holdeman purges of the 1970s? Something to ponder: the celebration of a church division.

This meeting is so different from academic conferences I attend. Yesterday we had scholarly papers but also a drama in a barn, an emotion-generating simulation, an evening with a poet. We have observed here scholarly integrity, yes, but also fellowship. There has been no need here to tiptoe gingerly in our conversations–at first a careful reconnoitering in banal pleasantries. As both old and new friends we could plunge at once into critical issues which often touched concerns of the heart. We have observed here scholarly detachment, yes, but we have been grabbed by the existential embrace of 1693 issues which are at once 1993 issues.

We have been invited to internalize the issues: What does this Amish story mean for me? We feel the tug of polar purposes that must be reconciled: tradition and transition, the givenness of the past and the drivenness of change, preservation and renewal. We are caught between the order "not to remove the ancient landmarks," "not to cut down the sacred forests," but also "to make all things new."

I wish to share a series of motifs I have discerned in this conference and that will continue to intrigue me. I shall review rapidly these musings, foregoing the scriptural references that might suggest a complementary biblical linkage:

1.  The haunting thought that things did not have to happen the way they did. There might have been alternatives, even better alternatives. The essence of conflict resolution is the expectation that there are good alternatives that are not violent, not coercive; that conflict need not result in win-lose solutions but can be resolved as win-win. In times of transition with traditionalists resisting change and progressives calling for change there is need for large-hearted pastoral persons, firmly planted in tradition, who can listen, counsel, affirm, admonish the young rebels. These pastoral persons can say to their fellows of the establishment, "These are our boys. Remember when we were young. They love the church. We must find ways of keeping them in the fold with their energy, vision, and affection for the church."

2.  A sense of awe and admiration in the presence of people who take religion seriously–for whom, in the words of the woman in the drama, a follower in 1693 of Jakob Ammann, "the truth is too important to sacrifice." I have been reading Stephen Carter's book, *The Culture of Disbelief*, in which he describes today's secular elite as ones who view religion as a kind of hobby, like building model airplanes, irrelevant, marginal, acceptable if you do not take it too seriously, good for children and old people. Among the Amish, religious convictions are a matter of life and death.

3.  Jakob Ammann is a captivating personality, a Harper's Ferry John Brown–the John Brown of Anabaptism. Is there a role for extremists, those given to hyperbole and exaggeration, overstatement? They are provocative, stimulating. They shake up the complacent. We who choose to be circuitous and nondirective may need in the church the Jakob Ammanns, but, please, not too many.

4.  The elusiveness of humility and the power of the weak. One remembers the drama, *The Terrible Meek*. Simone Weil speaks of humility as the servant of all the virtues. It undergirds all the qualities of character. But humility is so fragile, like a snowflake held in the palm of a warm hand. Seek to examine it in the light and it melts. A shadow of uneasiness crosses the mind when male authority figures

admonish their people to be humble, submissive, and obedient. Humility, like faith, must take wing as free response.

5. The Amish biblicism. The Amish live, move, and have their being in Scripture. They are neither fundamentalist nor modernist. They transcend or are indifferent to the wars of biblical interpretation. In their approach to Scripture one observes a common sense selectivity, a Christo-centric reading.

6. The Amish art and grace of passing on the faith, and without benefit of all the educational and institutional aids provided for us. The child and the youth is enveloped in a nurturing environment of family and community. It is like the gentle dew of heaven, almost imperceptible, and yet if one is in it long enough one is drenched–baptism by immersion.

7. The Amish are a liturgical people. Note the formula statements of humility, the rituals of worship, the lectionary of Scripture readings, the kneeling for prayer, the dipping of knees at the name of Jesus, the formulas of greeting of guests. These liturgical patterns or rituals are lubricants for community well-being. In the Amish one sees a high church liturgical people. One ponders the importance of liturgical patterns in the life of the church.

8. The Amish and their reluctance in discussions of faith to use many words. A concrete faithfulness rather than words in sharing the faith. One does not hear from them an enumeration of "the four basic principles" or "the ten steps to the abundant life." In a sense they sing their faith. Faith is made incarnate in field, garden, dinner table, and quilt. Because the Amish are not rushing to verbalize about their way of life, perhaps the Mennonites as first cousins of the Old Order Amish are called to the role of being understanding interpreters of the Old Order Amish to the wider community.

9. The pragmatic but puzzling way the Amish respond to modernity–that enveloping menace but also that liberating friend. Modernity is a mix of change, choice, specialization, mobility, anonymity, individualism, technology. Feeling the push of modernity the Amish have cultivated the art and grace of dragging their feet and sometimes yielding. As one Amishman expressed it, "We try to keep the brakes on social change, you know," and then he added after a pause, "a little bit." Those who have children know that

parenting involves the art of holding the line and then knowing when and how to give in. The Amish are not just hold-the-line people but have been resourceful in the techniques of selective resistance and selective yielding. Tradition and transition.

10.  Mennonite intellectuals have been bemoaning entrapment in a Schleitheim ethical dualism: God's pure people called out from a godless world of neighbors and enemies. One hears a call for a theology and ethics for Christians making their way amidst a perplexing world of gray rather than black and white, a world of ambiguity, of half-goods and half-bads, a world of the lesser-of-two-evils, a call for intermediate options, tentative, adaptive, flexible. One glimpses in the Amish ethical system an alternative to a normative Anabaptist ethic. Appearances to the contrary, the Amish may look less to ethical norms than to the discerning, correcting, empowering role of the congregation. With a focus of authority in the base community, the Amish adroitly walk through the perilous mine field of modernity.

11.  In yesterday's fascinating simulation we tried to jump out of our cultural skins and to empathize with the thoughts and feelings of Amish brethren 130 years ago in a barn in Wayne County, Ohio. We experienced the impossible-possibility of seeking to identify with another culture in another time. A cross-cultural experience. We have in our Old Order Amish first cousins a nearby resource for us as we seek to develop the gifts of empathy in a land of diversity. They are so radically different, but they are our cousins. Of them we need no longer be ashamed.

12   An awareness of the significant influence of the Amish on wider Mennonite peoplehood. With at least half of present-day members of the Mennonite Church of Amish ancestry, we acknowledge how the church is continuously being renewed from its right flank.

Finally a note of gratitude:

• That the Old Order Amish have preserved themselves to make their gift of presence and witness now in the twentieth century.

• That they are our spiritual cousins from whom we can learn lessons of faithfulness and can be warned of pitfalls.

• That hovering over the Amish story is a mist of mystery; that we do not understand in full; that though we play the games of a

*Diener Versammlung* of 1865, there is so much that continues to elude us.

• That we are in the presence of God's children whom God loves and whom God has covered with his wings for a purpose, a purpose we may only dimly perceive.

For our homeward journeys we have thoughts to think and prayers of gratitude to pray. We thank those who brought us together for this *Diener Versammlung* 1993.

Recently I learned that the martyr memory lingers in the liturgy of the Old Order Amish and the Old Order Mennonites as they open a worship service. It is appropriate to close this service with the formula of the Old Order people: "We are grateful that we can gather here to worship the Lord unmolested and undisturbed" or "We thank you Father that we can come to worship you with open doors and open windows."

# 1994: Agents of Change Unawares

*Foreword to Alex Sareyan's book,* The Turning Point, *subtitled "How Persons of Conscience Brought About Major Change in the Care of America's Mentally Ill" (Herald Press, 1994).*

This is the story of 3,000 men, conscientious objectors in World War II, who helped change the world of mental health care in the United States. They were agents of change unawares. One fourth of all the 12,000 conscripted COs in the United States volunteered to work in 61 state mental hospitals and training schools for the mentally retarded. The men were joined by hundreds of women COs–wives, friends and summer volunteers.

These conscientious objectors served primarily as attendants on the wards–the bottom rung of the hospital staff hierarchy. Rarely given formal orientation, they were handed keys and often deposited on wards with instructions to look after a hundred patients. Wartime was the "snake pit" era of institutional care: aging buildings, overcrowding, depleted staffs, cramped budgets, and penal-custodial attitudes toward the patients, often called "inmates." Alex Sareyan, the author–himself a CO in the front trenches of this service–is one of scores of COs whose concerns were sensitized in wartime alternative service and have devoted lifetimes to the cause of improved care and understanding for the mentally ill.

In the first chapters of *The Turning Point* Sareyan has gathered the stories of the CO experience in mental hospitals and training schools. One can hear it now: the clank of iron doors, the rattle of attendants' keys, the hissing of steam pipes, the babble of hundreds of voices, the angry bark of weary employees. One can smell it now: the urine-soaked clothing and bedding, the odor of herded-together bodies, the fetid air of toilets with clogged drains. One can see it now: cots row on row, disheveled patients on benches against the walls, wet slippery floors, nondescript globs of food dumped on metal plates. Sareyan brings to vivid memory the ugly side of the American institutional experience. All is not pathology in this study. The author reports of those in the system who had a vision, who were committed to radical change in patient care and who welcomed the COs as collaborators in institutional renewal.

The conscientious objectors, who entered this institutional world as amateurs, learned fast and developed concerns. This was a crash program in consciousness-raising. Sareyan weaves together the stories of how COs almost stumbled into roles as agents of change. *The Turning Point* is a source book on how in a variety of ways little people, the powerless, can affect radical social change.

The major contribution of the COs in producing change in this complex and formidable environment was simply their dependable quality service: thoughtful, sensitive, gentle, caring. They viewed the patients as persons in whom there was hope for recovery–intimations here of a new kind of therapeutic community. COs affected change by telling the truth. The author relates how many attendants not only worked on the wards but observed carefully and reported sensitively what they saw. It was not a pretty picture that was exposed at Cleveland State Hospital, Eastern State Hospital in Virginia, Hudson Valley State Hospital and in other institutions. These allegations led to headline articles in the press, formal investigations, several shakeups in hospital administrations, and heightened public awareness. They did not point fingers of accusation so much as they recorded sadly the problems that plagued the system.

In particular hospitals COs brought a breath of hope that an old institution could reform itself. Sareyan draws on his experience at Connecticut State Hospital where he and his CO colleagues innovated programs to encourage communication among staff and, most importantly the patients. In addition they launched a varied statewide program to enlighten the public toward fresh, positive understandings of mental illness.

An amazing story of creativeness and coalition-building is told in the chapter, "The Turning Point." At Philadelphia State Hospital (Byberry) four bright and energetic COs launched a movement to improve health care at the basement level–on the wards. They published the *Attendant* (later to be *The Psychiatric Aide*), focused on raising sights and empowering the attendants who were in hourly contact with patients. Soon it had a national circulation. They established a data-gathering center that provided an information bank for journalists writing articles for *Life* and *Readers Digest* and for the publication of the influential book, *Out of Sight, Out of Mind*. COs with training in law worked with the American Bar Association to prepare model legal codes to protect the rights of the mentally ill. Step by step they put together a coalition of psychiatrists, hospital administrators, politicians and public spirited citizens that became the National Mental Health Association that expressed a new era of understanding of the mentally ill.

Meanwhile, the Mennonites, led by COs motivated by wartime hospital experience, established across the country a series of psychiatric centers that modeled the new wave of community-based care for the mentally ill.

*The Turning Point* is a celebration of how a few little people–considered by some to be politically marginal–can profoundly affect change in the grim, grey institutions of our society. This is a voice of hope. Further, this volume is an informative grassroots treatise on the art and delights of building coalitions of diverse and kindred people to achieve change in flawed public institutions.

# 1995: Coming to Kansas Sixty Years Ago

*Printed in the* Mennonite Weekly Review, *September 21, 1995.*

Sixty years ago this August our family moved to Kansas. My father, Amos E. Kreider, who had been pastor of the First Mennonite Church, Bluffton, Ohio, had accepted a position as professor of Bible and director of religious life at Bethel College. For Mother, my brother Gerald and me this was our first trip to Kansas.

Dad did not come with us. He was attending the triennial General Conference in Upland, California, that closed on August 9. It was a special trip for me because I was permitted to do most of the driving from Ohio–in our new Ford V-8 that had replaced a 1928 Model A Ford. We drove west on U.S. 50 along the Santa Fe tracks, through Emporia, Cottonwood Falls, the Flint Hills, little towns with elevators. And all around us limitless space, wide horizons, big sky country. This to us was, wow, the West. We approached Newton (no North Newton then) with high expectations. I was 16 and just graduated from high school. I would be enrolling as a freshman at Bethel College.

I had studied carefully the illustrated brochures published by Bethel College. The campus promised to be a garden spot. Ed and Hazel Kaufman, good friends of my parents, had talked up the college: renovations, new faculty, innovative programs, expanding student body. After a crisis of survival in the early 30s, the time of the Great Depression, the college was on the make. We were eager to see our new home and the campus. We arrived in Newton about the same time Dad came back from California on the Santa Fe.

But no garden spot did we find. The campus was dry, brown, dusty, and hot. Temperatures soared into the upper 90s, no rain for weeks. Only one paved street, College Avenue, on the campus. People were still talking of the dust storms of that spring and Black Sunday, April 14, when the sky was dark like the night. Some feared a repetition. The campus had a look of improvisation, tentative, with renovation projects on many sites, ditches and raw earth, and box cars and old interurban cars waiting to be installed. Our house on 27th Street, like some other residences, had just been moved to the campus–no work yet done on grading and landscaping. The block across the street toward 24th street was a vacant lot with clumps of cactus growing in spots. And yet we liked it.

We delighted in this place that was throbbing with energy. Immediately we received invitations for meals from the J. F. Moyers, the Kaufmans, the Harshbargers and more. Our neighbors were the Paul Baumgartners, the P. S. Goertzes, the Davey Richerts, the Walter Hohmanns. On the corner lived J. W. Kliewer, early president of the college, who had roots in college beginnings 50 years before. Within a few days I had a job helping dig a ditch from the Administration Building north to the newly-built college barn and next to it a residence, Green Gables. It was another house that had been moved from Newton. There I met President Kaufman in a new role–de facto supervisor of buildings and grounds. He stepped into the trench to show us how to step up our productivity with pick and shovel. For the first time I heard murmuring in the ranks about the administration.

The Kaufmans had been good friends of my parents for two years at Bluffton. My parents were pleased to renew an old friendship. I listened in on the adult conversations, fascinated when Kaufman described all the different kinds of Mennonites living in the area: the Swiss, South Germans, West Prussians, Polish, Galicians, Volhynian Swiss, Pennsylvania Dutch. Here was a Mennonite diversity that we had not known in Ohio, Indiana, or Illinois: different dialects, food systems, church customs. The talk sometimes turned to church politics, which sounded as intriguing as the affairs of the New Deal. Kaufman commented freely on the power brokers among the Mennonites. This was heady talk for a 16-year-old.

I was intrigued by the up-beat vitality of the campus. Everywhere renovations: Science Hall basement converted into classrooms, offices and space for a printing press; improvements in Goerz Hall, Elm Cottage, and the Administration Building. We were told that a half dozen of the frame buildings had been moved across the prairie from Halstead 40 years before. People talked enthusiastically about the college choir that was just returning from a sweeping tour to the West Coast, including a concert before 2,000 at the Upland conference. Along with the everywhere-present, energetic president, I was dazzled by the young Willis Rich–assistant to the president, man with a hundred ideas and surging with enthusiasm. Arriving on the campus that fall was another bright young faculty member, Benny Bargen, he, too, bursting with ideas and energy.

That September Bethel's enrollment hit a new high: 314. We had 136 in our freshman class–the biggest freshman class ever. We elected Walter Claassen, later a Newton banker, president of our class, and to the Student Council, Margaret Regier (Rich) and Billy Thompson, later to be Stated Clerk of the Presbyterian Church in the United States. The president informed us that we now had a number of new Ph.D.s on the faculty–enough to place Bethel in the top ten percent of colleges.

I was a bit intimidated by all the student talent around me. Everyone looked so smart and, especially, so mature. Many of my freshman classmates were in their 20s, their college studies having been deferred in those depression years for lack of funds. Some had been teaching one-room school for several years on one- and two-year certificates. From their minimal wardrobes, I sensed an equity of poverty among fellow students. They seemed to be so much more wise than I in the ways of the world. I was only 16 and needed to shave, maybe, once a week, or every two weeks. And so in my timidity, I dug in, hit the books, and sought to be a scholar.

Along with other academic innovations, Bethel had introduced general education. One was a dubiously contrived course combining psychology and composition. The best part of that was that I wrote three major papers, one on Leo Tolstoy and another on the poet Edwin Markham, who was a campus speaker and guest in our home. The single most important course in my college career came that first semester: History of Civilization, taught by a master teacher, E. L. Harshbarger. For the first time I was liberated from the confines of one textbook; he gave us an outline and pointed us to the library. With his sweeping portrait of the past, I was instantly hooked on history. Other vocational dreams–architecture, forestry, journalism–quickly slipped away.

I had known my father as a pastor and now I observed him as a teacher and as campus pastor. Although I kept my distance from taking Bible courses from him until my junior year, I observed him with renewed respect. I was pleased how students found their way to the house to talk with Dad. I was also impressed how Dad and Mother, although newcomers, were drawn into the community.

Mother was soon teaching a Sunday School class for young married women. That October she was invited to give an address at the Western District Women's Mission Conference. At Upland, Dad was elected to a nine-year term on the Foreign Mission Board–that, just four years after he and Mother had moved their church membership from the Mennonite Church to the General Conference. He seemed to be out almost every Sunday preaching in area churches, one being the ordination service at the First Mennonite Church in Newton for missionary S. F. Pannabecker. Dad and Mother appeared to be warmly accepted in this new community and they were happy.

With Dad serving on the Mission Board, a frequent visitor at our house was P. H. Richert, the dour-looking pastor of the Tabor Mennonite Church, who was also secretary of the board. The General Conference had no headquarters in those days. Richert appeared to keep the mission files in a brief case that he brought with him on his visits.

On several occasions I went with Dad when he spoke in churches. I recall how I was struck by the Old World appearance of the elderly in the congregations–simple black dresses and black suits–"plain people," even without rules about plain dress. Although Dad always spoke in English, one saw evidence of German in worship services. When we came to Newton, I began reading the *Mennonite Weekly Review*, then a four-page paper, 25 cents for a six month subscription. I was intrigued in reading the obituary notices to find so many were listed as having been born in West Prussia, Poland or Russia. We had moved into a community where memories of an immigrant past were still fresh. A touch of Willa Cather's *O Pioneers*.

The Bluffton of the early 30s where we had lived was a town of 2,000 where we walked to everything: store, church, school. Living a mile outside Newton one needed a car. I found it exciting to live on the edge of Newton, a city of more than 15,000–a division point on the Santa Fe with 30 passenger trains a day going east and west, all stopping at Newton. I heard a lot of railroad talk, such as debates as to the threatened displacement of steam locomotives by diesels. The number one topic of conversation in Newton, especially with the approach of November, was high school basketball. Year after year the Newton Railroaders were in the state tournaments, often the state champions. Everyone knew the names of the high school greats: Coach Frank Lindley, Frosty Cox, and others. Not far away was the nationally famous McPherson Oilers; a semi-pro basketball team before the advent of the NBA. James Naismith, inventor of the game, came that fall or the next from Lawrence to the campus to tell of the peach baskets and the beginnings of basketball at Springfield College in Massachusetts.

Still operating in 1935 was an interurban line connecting Newton with Halstead, Sedgwick and Wichita, making connections beyond. We were told that once a spur came all the way to the Bethel campus. The Newton airport was then on the northern edge of Newton, bounded on the north by old U.S. 81 (now the area of the Northview School, Alco, and Faith Mennonite Church). I think it was that fall that I had my first airplane ride, a loop over Newton in a Ford Tri-motor, the price, 50 cents.

Just off the east corner of the airport on Main Street Henry Unruh had a gas station where he sold eight gallons for a dollar. Another good buy in Newton could be found at Young's Lunch, next door to the north of the Methodist Church. There one could buy six hamburgers for a quarter. At Young's Lunch I was introduced for the first time to chili, Mexican cuisine beginning to make inroads.

I was taken aback by the fact that Newton showed evidences of the old Confederacy. Although there was a black community of 500 in Newton, Jim Crow patterns prevailed. Blacks were confined to a Jim Crow section in the theater and were denied access to restaurants, the swimming pool, barber shops and to the varsity high school basketball team where black skin would touch white skin.

To refresh my memory of those distant times, I turned to the August and September 1935 issues of the *Evening Kansan Republican* and the *Mennonite Weekly Review*. Wheat in Central Kansas that drought year averaged 10.1 bushels to the acre and was selling for 86 cents. The big news was the air crash and death in Alaska of aviator Wiley Post and humorist Will Rogers. Satchel Page pitched a Bismarck, North Dakota, baseball team (a rare mixed Negro-white team) to a national semi-pro championship. Shirley Temple could be seen in "Curly Top" at the Regent theater. In August in Washington Roosevelt signed the Social Security bill. A half million young men were in Civilian Conservation Corps. The U.S. military budget had risen to $806 million–$6.35 per man, woman and child. Mussolini was poised to invade Ethiopia.

The week we arrived in Newton Mrs. J. C. Mack, editor of the *Kansan*, wrote a blistering attack on President Roosevelt and the New Deal, using such words as these: "revengeful penalties upon wealth," "economic quackeries," "brazen contempt for the Constitution," "impudent dictatorial rule," "national bankruptcy and political chaos." This was strange talk to me who cheered many of the innovations of the New Deal.

The move to Kansas was for our family what we would call a "cross cultural experience." Exhilarating.

# 1995: Christmas Letter in Our Fiftieth Anniversary Year

*Letter sent to friends in December 1995, the 50th anniversary of the wedding of Lois Sommer and Robert Kreider at Pekin, Illinois, December 30, 1945.*

In the 25th chapter of Leviticus the words of the Lord to Moses are recorded: "...you shall hallow the fiftieth year and you shall proclaim liberty throughout the land to all its inhabitants. It shall be a jubilee for you: you shall return, every one of you, to your property and every one of you to your family it shall be holy to you."

This is our jubilee year. On a wintry Sunday afternoon, December 30, 1945, in the little white frame country church, Lois' home church, at Pekin, Illinois, we were married–Robert's father A. E. Kreider, the pastor. We had met seven months before in a committee meeting in Chicago. Lois was then studying for a master's degree at Columbia University. Robert had just been released from four and a half years of alternative service as a conscientious objector in Civilian Public Service.

We reflect back with gratitude on our life together these 50 years: postwar Mennonite Central Committee (MCC) relief work in Germany and... Robert's three years of doctoral study at the University of Chicago... the birth and death of our first child... Esther's birth in 1952, Joan's in 1953... the first position, the first car, the first income tax–Bluffton College, Bluffton, Ohio, building a house in the woods on the bank of the Riley... Robert's appointment as academic dean of Bluffton... Karen's birth in 1956, David in 1959, and Ruth in 1961... our year at Akron, Pennsylvania, with Robert off to Africa, developing the Teacher Abroad Program... Lois' 15 years of leadership in Girl Scouting... buying a farm at Bluffton... in 1964 Robert elected president of Bluffton... Lois engaged in much entertaining... with others the purchase of wilderness land and later building a cabin in the Sangre de Cristo of Colorado... in 1970-71, Robert's sabbatical half year, a family trip "circumnavigating the Mediterranean"–a VW van, 22 countries, a classroom on wheels... Lois helps start the first MCC international crafts-thrift shop in the U.S.–now more than 120 in the U. S. and Canada... in 1972-74 Robert on a roving assignment conducting a self study for the MCC... Lois and Robert on a four month round-the-world trip visiting MCC areas of service in Africa and Asia... and then the move in 1975 to North Newton, Kansas.

In our jubilee year that which may lay claim to an entry in the Guinness book of records is the birth of four grandsons: Noah

Kreider Carlson, October 13, St. Paul, Minnesota; Mark Regier Kreider, February 26, Gainesville, Florida; Levi John Yoder, June 23, San Francisco, California; and Matthew Ulrich Kreider, October 8, Munich, Germany. The four cousins will meet for the first time December 28-January 1 when all twenty-three of us are together at Newton for our Christmas and 50th anniversary celebration.

A busy year. We have violated the Leviticus instructions not to sow, reap or harvest in our jubilee year. Lois flew to Gainesville, San Francisco, and Munich to provide grandmotherly services. Robert had conferences at Fresno, California, Waterloo, Ontario, and Millersville, Pennsylvania. In May Lois attended at Bluffton College the 50th anniversary of her graduation, the same week that Robert spoke at the Kauffman Museum on the opening of the exhibit, "MCC–the Gift of Hope," which he curated. We hosted Lois' Sommer family for a reunion on the 4th of July weekend. Robert prepared a *Map / Guide to Mennonite Communities of South Central Kansas* and the two of us led tours of the region for the large Wichita '95 conference. In August we joined Ruth and Uli in London for a two-week bed and breakfast tour of northern England and Scotland and the Orkney Islands. In October Robert gave the commissioning address at the inauguration of Douglas Penner as President of Bethel College. In November we joined Lois' two brothers and spouses for an Elderhostel visit to the Mayan world of the Yucatan.... This year our family spread out to more time zones. Karen and Steve and boys moved from San Francisco to Tokyo, where Steve is now bureau chief for the *Wall Street Journal*. They arrived on the 50th anniversary of the Japanese surrender.

We are planning a simple reception on Sunday, December 31, from 2 to 4 in the afternoon at the Red Coach Inn, Newton, KS. We would be pleased to have you join us and meet the family. It is always good to hear from you. We wish you a blessed Christmas season and the best in the New Year.

*Do not be afraid; for see—I am bringing you good news*
*of great joy for all the people; to you is born this day in the city of David*
*a Savior, who is the Messiah, the Lord.* Luke 2:10-11

Robert & Lois Kreider

# 1996: Coming to Bluffton, Ohio, Seventy Years Ago

*Printed in* The Bluffton News, *October 3, 1996, seventy years after the arrival in Bluffton, Ohio, of the A. E. Kreider family, August 1926.*

My father, Amos E. Kreider, for three years had been commuting from Goshen to teach at Witmarsum Theological Seminary, which was located at the corner of College Avenue and Spring Street.

Our house was a bungalow built that spring and summer by Ed Amstutz, who operated a sawmill across the Nickel Plate tracks on College Avenue. Now the residence of John and Sally Sommer, for many years this house had been the home of Wilbur and Elfriede Howe.

Our family was the first renter of this house built of hardwood recently cut from local woodland. The move to Bluffton brought our family together after those three years of Dad's commuting. On weekends he had made the trip by public transportation: interurban (rural trolley) from Goshen to Warsaw, Indiana; Pennsylvania Railroad from Warsaw to Lima; interurban again from Lima to Bluffton.

The exciting thing for my brother Gerald, six, and me was the abundance of vacant lots surrounding our house. Behind us was our wilderness–Little Riley Creek. We lived next door to the I. B. Beeshy family, who occupied a big stucco house set far back from the street–to our eyes, a palatial setting. On the other side of the Beeshys were vacant lots extending to the home of Prof. H. W. Berky and family on College Avenue. To the "east" (we soon learned that this town was laid out on an angle along an old Indian trail) were four vacant lots stretching all the way to the red brick house of the Lewises, who had a barn in the rear and kept a cow that grazed in the creek bottom. Across the street toward town were vacant lots from Franklin Street to the alley where the large Kohli family lived in a small frame house.

Someone living on Lawn Avenue pastured a cow in a fenced area across the street (about where Howard Raid lives today). Gerald and I grew up viewing vacant lots as a community asset. Here we could do our own thing–free of parental supervision. We toiled for days–maybe a few hours–to hollow out a cave in a gravel bank. We failed; the top kept caving in. Here on vacant lots Garfield Steiner taught us the rudiments of a game heretofore unknown to us: football.

The most enticing area was at the lower end of our lot: Little Riley Creek, for us a wilderness area of trees, thickets, muskrat holes, a mighty river flowing over limestone. On three successive

Sundays that first autumn Gerald fell into the creek, this leading to a parental off limits placed on the creek for Gerald.

Accustomed in Goshen to a dozen close-in neighbors, Gerald and I were disappointed that we were really without a neighborhood–just the Beeshys with a college-age daughter and an older couple in the brick house. That which made up for neighborhood was our outlet to the world: the alley along which lived the Kohlis and D. C. Bixel, the jeweler-optometrist who had an office on the second floor of the Citizens National Bank. That alley led to the giant four-story red brick grade school building with a mansard roof of slate. Here I entered third grade with Beatrice Swank as teacher. Gerald entered first grade under Miss Cox (later the wife of School Superintendent A. J. B. Longsdorf).

A word about alleys. Many of my first memories of Bluffton are related to alleys–a favorite route of travel for us kids. Grownups, even girls, didn't walk down alleys, just boys. It gave us a different perspective on the town from our elders. We saw the other side: chicken coops, gardens, barns (a few who still kept a cow), privies, trash piles. And so I have always had a lingering sense of ownership in vacant lots and alleys.

That old grade school was imposing. On one of the first days we came to Bluffton Dana Whitmer, son of the Paul Whitmers, introduced us to the grade school building. He proudly demonstrated how he could edge his way all around the building on a narrow stone ledge, his back to the wall, never dropping to the ground. I viewed with awe Dana's prowess in what appeared to be a feat of mountain climbing. It was a wonderful old building that creaked when Mr. Potee, the janitor, rang the big bell.

At school I was introduced to worldly activities, like playing marbles "for keeps." My vocabulary in marbles was expanded to include the terms "commies" (five for-a-penny clay marbles), "glassies" and "steelies" (ball bearings). Our parents said "no" to us playing for keeps.

My most traumatic experience in third grade relates to going to the boy's toilet in the basement. I blurted out to anyone listening, "This smells like a cow shed." Classmate Quinton Diefendeifer rushed to Miss Beatrice Swank and announced loudly, "Robert said a bad word: "cows---" Miss Swank said, "Robert, that is not nice." Tearfully, I exclaimed, "I didn't say that. I said cow shed." But to no avail. Miss Swank repeated, "Robert, that was not a nice word." Quinton, wherever you are, may you be forgiven. An early experience in being misquoted.

In my grade were classmates with intriguing last names, names I had never heard before: Francis Badertscher, Marcella Niswander,

Jim Basinger, Edna Neuenschwander, plus Luginbuhls, Badertschers, Reichenbachs and more.

This was a cross cultural experience, getting acquainted with Swiss names and a Swiss culture and a dialect still to be heard on the streets of Bluffton. Across the street from the grade school was the yellow brick First Mennonite Church where we began attending Sunday School and church. Our family was then Old Mennonite and not accustomed to musical instruments in the worship service or stained glass windows in the sanctuary. At this big church I saw my first pipe organ, played by white haired and nearsighted Professor Otto Holtkamp who made the church tremble with his fortissimo chords.

At the opening of Sunday School an orchestra played. On two sides of the sanctuary were two huge stained glass windows, one of Jesus standing at the door and knocking and the other of Jesus cradling a lost sheep. Those two windows continue to carry for me captivating biblical memories–a sense of sacred space. Once a month, when Rev. S. M. Musselman preached in German, we were excused from attending the worship service. It was a congregation still close to its Swiss Germanic roots.

Our favorite place on Main Street was Hankishes where the folks bought oysters in winter (ladled into ice cream cartons from a cooler set outside on the street), bananas and dipping chocolate for making Christmas candies. At Reichenbach's grocery store I stood at the counter beside my mother as she went down her list item by item, Ed Reichenbach making a trip to the shelves and barrels for each piece of merchandise. On the Church Street side of Gratz's dry goods store I remember horses and buggies tied to an iron rail. And several times a day down Main Street lumbered the interurban connecting Bluffton to Toledo and Lima.

A vivid memory of that year on Spring Street was the report that a mother had died in Bluffton Community Hospital, leaving a newborn baby daughter. I heard Dad and Mother discussing whether they should offer a home for the baby. I remember Dad going to the hospital to inquire and returning to report that relatives were providing a home for the orphan child. Gerald and I, who wanted a sister, were very disappointed.

Living on Spring Street was like being caught in a magnetic field between the energizing, liberating force of school, church and Main Street in one direction and in the other direction, across Little Riley Creek, the powerful tug of Bluffton College and its beautiful wooded campus. Still one of the fairest campuses I know.

In the hip-roofed barn-like gym I heard for the first time Handel's "Messiah." The great chorus with orchestra was awesome. At the door of the same gym at the end of a commencement I had the temerity to secure the autograph of then Governor Cooper.

To our house came college students, giants on the earth. One was Rhoda Bender from Springs, Pennsylvania, a "baby sitter" before the term was coined. Most impressive to us were the visits of the Conrad brothers, Vernon and Irvin, star football players. Their father had sent from Sterling, Illinois, a barrel of apples for them, which we stored in our basement.

Dad took us to our first football game, played at the corner of College Road and Elm Street. Another player who attracted our attention was a family friend, Ike Geiger, who, playing end, wore no helmet. We had not yet heard of Gerald Ford of University of Michigan football fame.

In 1926 the city of Lima broke into my consciousness. Every Saturday morning we needed to drive in our Model T the 16 miles to Lima to see an orthodontist. Once a week in a task of straightening my teeth he would tighten the wires.

I remember the zig-zag route to Lima via Gratz Crossing and Beaverdam on Route 25, which everyone called "the Dixie." Four things impressed me: (1) the big, black brick or tile yard on the edge of Beaverdam, (2) between Beaverdam and Lima, the sprawling field of oil wells with rods extending from each pump to engines and the smell of crude oil in the air, (3) the enticing attraction of the roller-coaster and amusement park on the edge of Lima, (4) the maze of railroad tracks with roundhouse of two intersecting rail lines–the Pennsylvania and the Detroit, Toledo and Iron-town (DTI). Big bustling Lima offered a touch of modernity to us in a rural small town.

Seventy years (1926 to 1996) is a long time, but not so long in my memory. And yet I realize that 70 years subtracted from 1926 would have taken us from the time of President Coolidge back to 1856, the year James Buchanan was elected president and four years before the outbreak of the Civil War. That is a very long time ago.

In retrospect, the Bluffton of 1926 must have been a stimulating town for a seven-year-old youngster–about as many stimuli as he then could handle.

# 1997: Letter to Grandson James

*Letter written to Grandson James Eash on his graduation from Northwest High School, Wichita, Kansas, May 1997.*

Commencement Day, Thursday, May 29, 1997

Dear James:

Congratulations on your graduation from high school! You are the second of our eleven (soon to be twelve) grandchildren to achieve this distinction. We shall have to wait another ten years before the third grandchild qualifies for the honor. At one time, high school graduation was a rarity. For example, as far as we know, none of your great-great-grandparents graduated from high school—most of these no more than six years of elementary school. On the Kreider-Shoemaker side of your ancestry, only three of fifteen of your great grandparents' generation attended or even completed high school—two of those, your Great-Grandparents Amos and Stella.

As we reflect on your eighteen years, a series of images flash across our minds: Oma's trip to Ft. Madison, Iowa, by train to be picked up there by your Dad, who brought her to Kalona for her first sight of you.... The Amish family in the country where your parents took you and Rachel for day care.... The cabin at Estes Park, Colorado, where you entertained us by jumping endlessly from sofa to chair to hassock—island to island hopping.... At your new house in Kalona the birthday you shared with your Great-Grandfather Harley Nafziger—you, Heidi and Grandfather Nafziger all born on October 9.... You and Rachel engaging in your own voluntary service project of picking up trash in the vacant field behind your house at Kalona.... You standing on the bank of a tiny stream at the Berry Patch debating a long time whether you dared jump across. When finally you took courage to jump, you continued to jump again and again.... Making placemats with intricate designs for us: one with an airplane for Opa and one with an Et cetera shop scene for Oma.... Hearing you play your violin with other students on a Saturday afternoon in a house and garden store in Evansville.... After a horse race at the Evansville park, you and Rachel racing up and down the stands picking up beer and soft drink aluminum cans that you took to the recycling plant for money.... You, age six or seven, and Rachel flying unaccompanied from Chicago to Tokyo carrying with you suitcases full of paper cranes for Hiroshima.... On our European trip your comment at midnight on Red Square in front of the well-lit Kremlin and St. Basil Cathedral: "awesome." And then you and your Dad taking off to run around the Kremlin–you, then training for cross country running.... Your delight in finding a stave church in Legoland in Denmark.... You and Rachel chipping away at the Berlin Wall to salvage some artifacts from a piece of twentieth century history.... Your feat with your Dad and Opa of seeing three high school football games on one night: Marion (where Collegiate star, D'Angelo Evans, played a dazzling first half), Hillsboro and Goessel.... and lots more.

We are filled with quiet pride that you are our grandson. You are endowed with a diversity of gifts of body, mind and spirit. We observe your good mind and your wide-ranging interests. We see your affection and respect for your mother and father and your sister, Rachel. We watch your athletic talents–going deep, fielding a hard hit ball and throwing the runner out at first. We sensed this particularly in your baptism this spring at Hope Mennonite Church when you shared with casual eloquence your faith journey. We are pleased that you are committed to living a life rooted in the base of a faith community. On that occasion we heard from others how you have modeled the role of a good son and peer. We have felt satisfaction when you and your team received national recognition for your research paper on the stock market. We shared in your classmates' pride that you received from the Northwest principal the Leadership Award. And with all of this, we are amused and indulgent of your imperfections: your inability to come to terms with the joys of salads and particularly fresh tomatoes.

We shall watch with love and encouragement as you continue to grow in body, mind and soul, as your talents unfold and are tested, as you meet disappointments and crises, as you develop clarity in your life purpose.

All this we express with gratitude and love, Oma and Opa

# 1998: Charting the Next Generation

*Reflections presented at the end of a conference, "One People, Many Voices: Charting the Next Generation of Mennonite Historical Writing in the U. S. and Canada," May 9, 1998, Abbotsford, British Colombia.*

I must acknowledge that 15 of the more than 30 scholars presenting papers at this conference I had not heard speak before. On the stage have arrived a new cast of scholar characters. The ranks have been invigorated with new blood. This is exhilarating news.

One senses a substantial number and a growing community of scholars who are finding each other and are now in frequent dialogue. Observe the animated conversations in the corridors and in the coffee hours. This presence of such a network, aided by E-mail communications, was not in place 30 or even 20 years ago. For this we can be grateful.

Anabaptist / Mennonite scholarship has a personal, existential grip on each of us. Here we are studying issues that impact our lives. In contrast to sessions of the American Historical Association, here we are free to disclose our connectedness to subject matter:

"My two sons who like to play with guns."

"My mother, who was present in 1927 when they established the Menno Colony in the Chaco wilderness."

"Here is a 14-year old girl's essay–the girl, my mother."

In these settings we have no restraint in expressing feeling, even gentle bursts of passion. We are working with material that is *my* story, *your* story–thus, *our* story. And then there is *the* story.

It is, of course, presumptuous of me to chart the course for this new, this next generation of scholars. I can only say, "Play to your strengths and gifts, take counsel, and follow your curiosity." The field of Anabaptist and Mennonite studies will then be on a good course.

That said, I shall be so presumptuous as to give counsel:

1. I am intrigued by a unique challenge to you Canadians. You live in this slender 3,000 mile population strip that stretches from ocean to ocean and there immediately to the north all this wilderness that extends thousands of miles to the arctic north. I wonder how does this shape the Canadian Mennonite psyche? Set it in biblical terms. Walk east from Jerusalem past Gethsemane up to Bethany on the ridge. With one's back to the populous city one faces east into the Judean wilderness–the land of the prophets. Think of it, Canadian scholars on the edge of the wilderness. The fragility of God's creation, a creation that can be loved or that can be ravaged.

2. Thursday of this week I attended the memorial service for John Oyer, Mennonite historian, editor of the *Mennonite Quarterly Review*, Director of the Mennonite Historical Library, writer of books and articles. What struck me in attending this service was that despite all the significant contributions John has made as a scholar, all this recedes in significance as one contemplates the life of one who was a husband, a father, a grandfather, a friend, a member of the congregation–one who passes on the faith. This leads me to emphasize how we must give high priority to studies of child nurture, parenting, and the congregation as a nurturing community.

3. As Dow-Jones averages zoom and as Mennonite millionaires multiply, we must focus more attention on Mennonites and their relation to class and status, wealth and power, rich and poor, lay and professional, meetinghouse and counting house, marrying up and marrying down. In our community is a metaphor for this class/status issue in the peoplehood. On Newton's First Street is the mansion of Bernhard Warkentin–wealthy miller and entrepreneur, one of the founders of Bethel College. At the Kauffman Museum is the simple frame Voth-Unruh-Fast house, home to generations of rural, relatively poor Mennonite families. None of the progeny of Bernard Warkentin remain in the Mennonite Church; all around us and among us in our congregations are the descendants of the Voths, Unruhs, and Fasts.

4. Having been engaged recently in projects of family history, I urge that Mennonite scholars establish an alliance with Mennonite genealogists–genealogy sometimes viewed as one of the lesser of the scholarly crafts. Among family historians are a host of eager amateurs full of energy. They need help in raising genealogical studies to a higher level or to a broader agenda. For example, they have an entree to the study of the Mennonite diaspora, that is, the names and addresses of Mennonite drop-outs. Also they offer a door of access to data less likely to be found in archives: letters and family records of ordinary Mennonites. Family groups offer opportunities for the gathering of oral history that touches elusive data related to child nurture, class and status, wealth and land, the cultural and theological perceptions of ordinary people. These are the ones who do not leave a paper trail of articles in church papers and minutes in the archives.

5. With the solid scholarly base of five volumes of the *Mennonite Encyclopedia*, four volumes of the *Mennonite Experience in America*, and three volumes of the *History of Mennonites in Canada*, the story of the Dutch and Swiss streams of Mennonitism has been well told. We must now reach out to encourage and to empower the telling

of stories from new streams in the Mennonite experience: the Hispanic, African-American, Laotian, Chinese, and many more. This is preeminently a task of oral history gathering.

6. I confess to an uneasiness when we link the Anabaptist-Mennonite story too closely with the nation-state. In the long reaches of Christian history, the nation-state is a comparatively recent political phenomena. In the 470 years of Anabaptist-Mennonite history, it is essentially a post-Frederick the Great, post-French Revolution phenomena. In the emerging global world of Euro currency, Internet, Daimler-Chrysler mergers, satellite communications, the nation-state may be displaced by new political-economic-informational entities. Hence, it may be wise for us to shy away from bonding too closely the Mennonite story to nation-state categories.

7. The time is ripe for Anabaptist / Mennonite scholars to seek dialogue with scholars of other religious traditions that have lived on the edge of dominant cultures and those that have had strong ethnic components. One thinks of religious groups with a diaspora motif. Such groups on the margins are many: Armenians, Missouri Synod Lutherans, Coptic Orthodox, pre-Israel Judaism, Swedish Covenant, and more.

Savoring the experiences of this conference, I sense that this is the best of times to be engaged in Anabaptist / Mennonite studies.